1-07

OVERDOSE

Richard A. Epstein

OVERDOSE

HOW EXCESSIVE GOVERNMENT REGULATION STIFLES PHARMACEUTICAL INNOVATION

AN INSTITUTE FOR POLICY INNOVATION BOOK

Yale University Press

New Haven and London

Published with assistance from the Mary Cady Tew Memorial
Fund.
An Institute for Policy Innovation Book

Set in Galliard Old Style by SPI Publisher Services.

Printed in the United States of America.

Library of Congress Cataloging-in-Publication Data

Epstein, Richard Allen, 1943–
    Overdose : how government regulation stifles pharmaceu-
tical innovation / Richard A. Epstein.
        p.   cm.
    "An Institute for Policy Innovation Book."
    Includes bibliographical references and index.
    ISBN-13: 978-0-300-11664-9 (cloth : alk. paper)
    ISBN-10: 0-300-11664-0 (cloth : alk. paper)
    1. Pharmaceutical industry—Government policy—United
States.   2. United States. Food and Drug Administration.
    I. Yale University. Institute for Policy Innovation.   II. Title.
        [DNLM: 1. United States. Food and Drug Administra-
tion.   2. Drug Industry—United States.   3. Public Policy—
United States.   4. Government Regulation—United States.
    QV 736 E640 2006]
    HD9666.6.E68 2006
    338.4'761510973—dc22   2006006514

A catalogue record for this book is available from the British
Library.

The paper in this book meets the guidelines for permanence and
durability of the Committee on Production Guidelines for Book
Longevity of the Council on Library Resources.

10   9   8   7   6   5   4   3   2   1

TO EILEEN, IN GOOD HEALTH

CONTENTS

PREFACE

The past several years have seen the publication of a large number
of books that have been sharply critical of the pharmaceutical industry.
The complaints that have been lodged against the industry deal with all
aspects of its operations: research and development, intellectual property,
pricing and marketing, Food and Drug Administration (FDA) review,
and general liability issues. Most of the critics have written from a perspective that is deeply suspicious of private enterprise and voluntary markets,
and their books have uniformly called for greater levels of regulation of
all aspects of the pharmaceutical industry. The proposals for reform are
often inconsistent with each other, and together they pose a serious
threat to the overall long-term viability of the industry—an industry that
is already reeling under the powerful forces arrayed against it. Something
always has to give under any legal regime that simultaneously increases
the costs of doing business and reduces the revenues needed to meet
these obligations. And here it seems that something has indeed given: a
recent lead headline in the *New York Times* under Alex Berenson's byline
reads: "Big Drug Makers See Sales Decline with Their Image: F.D.A.
Grows More Strict, Pfizer, Merck and Eli Lilly Laying Off Employees—
Research Is Cut."

I have become aware of many of the deep tensions involved in these
reform efforts in the course of my academic and consulting work. Over the
past several years, I have worked on a number of issues relating to liability,
patents, and antitrust for Pfizer, along with a wide range of regulatory

issues on behalf of Pharmaceutical Research and Manufacturers of America (PhRMA). My academic work has increasingly involved issues of pharmaceutical policy as well. The entire matter came to something of a head two years ago when I was approached by Tom Giovanetti, president of the Institute for Policy Innovation, who had agreed to underwrite a medium-length study for IPI that outlined my views of the various difficulties facing the pharmaceutical industry. The original plan called for me to piece together the threads of my work in a short monograph that would trace the origins of the current squeeze on the industry and give my prescriptions for what should be done to cure that ailment. With time that project snowballed far beyond the scope of the plan, and with Tom's blessing and approval I expanded the study into this book-length treatment of the industry. It should be evident that I think that many of the recommendations for legal reform of the industry move in precisely the wrong direction. They call for increased controls at every level, while I believe in general that a more consistent policy of market liberalization is needed to bring the industry back onto an even keel.

In making these recommendations, however, it is vital to note that a criticism of the various regulatory initiatives in this area should not be taken as an implicit endorsement of every business decision made within the pharmaceutical industry. Quite the opposite; individuals more knowledgeable than I have much to say in criticism of the business and management strategies of many pharmaceutical companies. Yet those criticisms come at right angles to the central theme of this book. When firms make mistakes in their long-term plans, they should be punished both by their prospective customers and by the capital markets. It is only through those business decisions that markets are able to sort out successful from disastrous innovations, by rewarding the former and punishing the latter. Yet systematic changes in the legal environment hit all firms, smart and foolish, in exactly the same way, and if these are ill conceived, they can have adverse effects on the very firms whose innovations are so key to sustained levels of pharmaceutical progress.

This book, then, should be understood as one effort to respond to the systematic criticisms of the legal and regulatory framework of the pharmaceutical industry. In writing it, I have had the benefit of many opportunities to speak about the wide range of topics on which the pharmaceutical industry has found itself vulnerable, including workshops and discussions at the American Enterprise Institute, Case-Western University Law School, the Federalist Society, Stanford University Law School, the University of Chicago Law School, and the MacLean Center of Clinical Medical Ethics, also at the University of Chicago. In addition, I have had the benefit of helpful comments on various portions of the manuscript not only from Tom Giovanetti but also from Merrill Matthews, head policy guru at IPI, and Patrick Chisholm, an independent editor. I have also received detailed criticisms of this book from Henry Miller of the Hoover Institution, who brings vast expertise to understanding the policies of the FDA; from Katherine Mullinex, a consultant with many years of experience in the pharmaceutical industry; and from Mel Sokotch, who shared with me his broad knowledge of advertising and marketing pharmaceuticals. I would also like to thank Michael O'Malley of Yale University Press, who peppered me with questions, and the referees whom he asked to review the manuscript, whose queries forced me to rewrite more than one section of the book. A special word to my redoubtable and fearless agent, Lynn Chu, for spurring me along the way, on this as on so many other projects. Finally, I should like to thank my research assistants, Eric Murphy and Gus Hurwitz of the University of Chicago Law School and David Strandness of the Stanford Law School, for their steadfast support, critical intelligence, and sharp pens. Needless to say, any errors in argument or conclusion are mine alone.

PROPERTY AND PROGRESS

1

RISING EXPECTATIONS—AND DIMINISHING
RETURNS

In July 1945, Vannevar Bush, the director of the Office of Scientific Research and Development, submitted a report to President Truman entitled "Science: The Endless Frontier."[1] The report, which Bush delivered to the White House after the Allied victory over Germany, devoted much attention to the transition from a military economy to a peacetime one. Its main goal was to recommend establishing the United States Office of Research and Development, which in time morphed into the National Science Foundation (NSF) and the National Institutes of Health (NIH), chiefly to fund the basic research needed to undergird the full range of applied sciences.[2] Most conspicuously, the report brimmed with the optimism and confidence of that age.

The United States, indeed, had much to crow about regarding its scientific advancement during World War II, and the statistics that Bush cited seemed to justify his evident exuberance. In World War I the death rate from disease of army troops, both at home and overseas, was 14.1 per thousand. By World War II that number had been cut to 0.6 per thousand, a reduction of nearly 96 percent. At home, life expectancy had jumped over the past forty years from forty-nine to sixty-five years, chiefly because of major advances in combating infant mortality. Those astounding advances rested on relatively low-level technical advances, at least when judged in the hindsight of the following sixty years. The major wonder drug of the era was penicillin, whose synthesis in quantity protected millions against the ravages of disease. Similarly, much of the improvement on the home front took place from understanding how to deal with the major infectious diseases that had been such a scourge two generations before—dysentery, typhoid, cholera, diphtheria, typhus, tuberculosis, measles, and German measles. Penicillin, the great savior, did not stand alone. Surgical improvements, insecticides (particularly DDT), antimalarial drugs, and the extensive use of blood plasma played roles, along with thousands of other advances, both large and small.[3] Nor did anyone overlook the importance of rudimentary public health measures, such as the provision of clean water for drinking and other personal use.

These major advances are all the more astounding in light of the puny investments that brought them about. On the benefit side, the value of longer life and greater comfort is hard to estimate. But it is not, for that reason, small. Two University of Chicago professors, Kevin Murphy and Robert Topel, in a recent study that focuses on the second half of the twentieth century, estimate that increases in longevity and health produced aggregate gains of $2.6 trillion per year since 1970, with men at age fifty gaining $350,000 per year in additional satisfaction and women of that age about $180,000.[4] Don't sweat the details: the clear implication from these data is that the improvements in lifestyle in real terms of the earlier 1900–1950 period had to be far more dramatic. If people attach high value to extra years of life after age fifty, they certainly attach at least equal weight to extra years that are gained at the ages of twenty-five or thirty. Combine the modern valuation of additional life-years with the massive advances achieved between 1900 and 1950, and it is easy to understand the buoyant tone of the Bush Report: advances in medical research and public health had transformed the welfare of a nation.

So much for the wind-up; now for the bad news. The party's over. In part the road to progress has gotten steeper now that our easy successes are behind us. For that bittersweet truth we can only be grateful. In part, however, our collective uneasiness about the future is a problem of our own making, because on too many occasions, especially as of late, we as a nation have adopted a set of policies that treat drug companies as though their every advance comes at the expense of innocent consumers whom they are said to deceive at every turn.[5] The bulk of this book is devoted to critiquing the misguided set of regulatory judicial initiatives that have been proposed or adopted. These include various efforts to tighten up on conflict of interest regulation in ways that could weaken cooperation between government and industry, to weaken the scope of patent protection, to impose various forms of price controls on pharmaceutical products, to lengthen the FDA approval process for new drugs, and to aggressively pursue the various tort and consumer protection remedies against the manufacturers of drugs that have been alleged (but not necessarily demonstrated) to have caused harm to the people who have taken them. These issues will occupy the bulk of this book. But in order to keep the problem in perspective, let's look at the first question first: where has all the low-hanging fruit gone?

Start with life expectancy, which on average goes up with improved quality of life. Between 1900 and 1950, life expectancy increased about twenty-one years, from forty-seven to sixty-eight. During the next fifty years, it increased an impressive nine or so more years to seventy-seven.[6] But before we congratulate ourselves a second time, note the bottom line. We have obtained a lower percentage rate in life-expectancy growth from a far more extensive investment of resources than the puny sums to which the Bush Report referred, even when adjusted for inflation. In 1940 the total level of expenditure for all scientific research by industry and government totaled $309 million, probably twentyfold that figure in current dollars. The additional sums the report urgently requested were around $5 million for the initial year, followed by a steady stream of $25 million per year.[7] In contrast, the budgets for scientific research in the 2005 fiscal year were $5.47 billion for the National Science Foundation and $28.8 billion for the National Institutes of Health.[8] Likewise, in 2004 the budget for the pharmaceutical industry alone for research and development was $38.8 billion.[9] Additional research dollars are available from countless other sources. Nonetheless, no one can plausibly claim the material improvement in human life and enjoyment from these post-1950 changes matches in its impact the aggregate improvements made with much less investment in the period between 1900 and 1950. The second half of the twentieth century had no health miracle to match the computer or the Internet. The first half of the twenty-first century promises to be no different.

Nor should these somber truths come as a surprise. Medical science is not immune from the iron economic law of diminishing marginal returns. Sooner or later we reach the point where an additional dollar of investment generates a lower return than the previous dollar. More colloquially, it is always easiest to grab the low-hanging fruit than to reach the higher branches. Today's advances in basic science and instrumentation dwarf in technical sophistication those improvements made in that halcyon 1900 to 1950 period. Yet the social gains that the more recent advances generated are far lower. If you doubt the conclusion, ask the following question: do all the stunning advances since 1950 in the treatment of diabetes yield aggregate human welfare improvements greater than those initial improvements from Frederick Banting and Charles Best's initial haphazard discovery of how to isolate insulin, made in a cold and primitive laboratory at the University of Toronto in 1922? In 1923 Banting (but not Best) was duly awarded the Nobel Prize for Medicine.[10] A clear no-brainer. It doesn't take a Nobel laureate to figure out the impact of their work when the previous state-of-the-art for "treatment" of diabetes was slow starvation. Or try this comparison: could any combination of drugs to control pain, cholesterol, or hypertension match in human payoffs the gains from the control of infectious diseases celebrated in the Bush Report, or the development of anesthesia a century before? Yet there is more. Think back to the great advances in the first part of the twentieth century or even before, when the cause and cure were found for such time-honored scourges as pellagra, rickets, scurvy, and beriberi. All of these diseases were deadly, but all came from a single cause. A vitamin deficiency was the root problem; dietary supplements, with little fanfare and no pesky side effects, were the definitive cure.

In a sense, our fate has been sealed. The reward-risk ratio has rapidly changed. The ability of science and medical research to eke out an extra year of life expectancy is still worth trillions of dollars in the United States alone. The possibilities for gains overseas are surely greater, given the larger number of people who could profit mightily from elementary health expenditures, like basic sanitation and the use of DDT. But trillions in hedonic returns will require the expenditure of trillions in hard cash—with serious risks that newfound treatments will go awry. Our greater sophistication means that we shall suffer more reversals and disappointment no matter what institutional arrangements we devise. Quite simply, medical research no longer occupies that enviable "takeoff" position of one hundred years ago.

The Clear and Present Dangers to Pharmaceutical Progress

In one powerful sense, the pharmaceutical industry, like the medical profession generally, has suffered from the curse of rising expectations. In earlier times, when failure was the norm, success was greeted with adulation and cheer. But now that success in the norm, it is the failures that are singled out, not for praise but for rebuke. This basic insight frames our understanding of the many travails now facing the pharmaceutical industry, which has generated some, but by no means all, of the wonder cures we take for granted today. The industry is without question larger and better funded now than at any earlier point in its history. Its research sophistication far exceeds anything imaginable even a decade ago. The huge scientific effort will doubtless generate major advances in the understanding of the chemistry of life, aging, and disease. That research, however, will never be able in human terms to duplicate the heroic advances that started one hundred years ago. This point is not a secret but is reflected in the constant litany of stories illustrating the inherent limitations on pharmaceutical work. Pfizer has proved itself a veritable juggernaut in the pharmaceutical world, with thirty-eight thousand sales representatives, more than $16 billion in profits on $52 billion in sales, and research laboratories that spend upward of $8 billion per year. Yet the *Business Week* article that duly recites these statistics carries the title "Pfizer's Funk," in recognition that the firm may have difficulty in replacing the blockbusters Lipitor, Viagra, and Zoloft, not to mention Celebrex and Bextra.[11] These drugs have limited patent lives; overall sales are expected to decline by $14 billion as they go generic. The bottom line has been a 45 percent decline in the company's share price between 2000 and 2005. Unfortunately, many of the likely replacements are targeted for niche markets that cannot possibly generate the sales of the huge products that preceded them.

Today, therefore, we have this oxymoronic contrast: a professional sense of gloom about the prospects of pharmaceutical companies at the same time they are subject to attack for their excessive market power. The mixed signals and ambiguous social response to this clouded picture reflect the frustration of the age. Why, if medical science is so sophisticated, do we have to suffer so many disappointments and bad outcomes? Rather than note the basic trends, it is much easier to personify the targets of blame in order to vent the frustrations that surround the modern practice of pharmaceutical (and more generally biomedical) research. The rising expectations change the frame of reference. At one time, progress was the exception and lavishly praised. Now it is the norm; any slowdown in the rate of medical advances is greeted with sullen suspicion, while any conspicuous adverse event in new drugs or experimental treatments will trigger a quick investigation.[12] Yet the decision to lash out against major reversals and to institute ever greater precautions—more tests, tougher fines, quicker recalls—against their recurrence will only make progress harder to obtain. No one should issue a disguised plea for fatalism or passivity in research. Even if we cannot repeat the triumphs of an earlier age, we can still make substantial progress. Take some slowdown in overall progress as a given, and it is all the more important to avoid any additional mistakes of policy that needlessly retard the level of innovation. Just those mistakes, however, have crept (and are creeping) into virtually every aspect of pharmaceutical research and marketing. Current efforts will be stymied unless everyone accepts that each new regime for the diagnosis and treatment of disease and disability is fraught with risk.

An Agenda for the Future?

Our new environment raises new challenges, which can be conveniently clustered as follows: disputes over the mix of public and private arrangements to spur the new science and technology that make possible the discovery of new treatments and therapies; disputes over the scope of intellectual property protection, chiefly of patents and trade secrets; disputes over the approval and regulatory process of new drugs, under the supervision of the Food and Drug Administration (FDA); disputes over the pricing and distribution of drugs that survive the patent and approval process; and disputes over the liability issues associated with the use, withdrawal, and recall of various drugs. This study's purpose is to examine in some detail the major issues that arise over the life cycle of pharmaceutical innovation. I hope to determine where the current legal and regulatory framework makes sense, and where it has gone awry.

Today's overall picture evokes a mixed assessment. The current combination of basic research, done both privately and publicly, and typical privately funded commercialization is about right, or at least cannot be dramatically improved. Although there are many mischievous proposals on the horizon, to date, the government has run the patent system, by and large, in a sensible way. Nonetheless, those who think they can find a clever way to eliminate or circumvent some of the distortions of the patent monopoly now subject the system to substantial, if misguided, criticism. These reformers fail to fully appreciate the greater dangers posed by their untested schemes, which contemplate government regulation of patent prices, government acquisition of patented pharmaceuticals, or, most improbably, government entrance into the pharmaceutical business on its own.

The situation is still graver with respect to proposals that seek to impose limitations on the prices that patentees can charge for their wares. On this score the traditional legal view treats patents as forms of property that are subject to the usual incidents of possession, use, and disposition, where that last element, disposition, covers sales, leases, licenses, loans, and gifts. These multiple forms of transactions all allow an owner to select the persons to whom he shall make offers, the form of the transaction, and what prices, if any, to charge. As Justice Peckham wrote in 1902 in *E. Bement & Sons v. National Harrow Co.*, "An owner of a patent has the right to sell it or to keep it; to manufacture the article himself or to license others to manufacture it; to sell such article himself or to authorize others to sell it."[13]

Justice Peckham continued:

> The general rule is absolute freedom in the use or sale of rights under the patent laws of the United States. The very object of these laws is monopoly, and the rule is, with few exceptions, that any conditions which are not in their very nature illegal with regard to this kind of property, imposed by the patentee and agreed to by the licensee for the right to manufacture or use or sell the article, will be upheld by the courts. The fact that the conditions in the contracts keep up the monopoly or fix prices does not render them illegal.[14]

Today, unfortunately, it is easy to find a wide range of misguided proposals to limit pricing freedom, which *Bement* treated as an unquestioned
incident of patent ownership. These pricing proposals only compound
the problems with regulation and liability. The most notable proposal
requires firms to sell overseas at state-required prices unlimited quantities
of drugs, which are then eligible for reimportation back home. The full
picture bodes ill for the entire process of drug discovery and promotion
in the United States. Every initiative now on the table is intended to
increase the costs or reduce the returns of marketing new pharmaceutical
products. The overall social report card does not yield high grades for the
current crop of initiatives. The first half of this book deals with the property and pricing issues that form an inseparable part of the pharmaceutical
business.

Pharmaceutical policy is concerned not only with innovation and pricing.
It is concerned also with safety and effectiveness and the set of sanctions
that are brought to bear to prevent the occurrence of everything from
adverse side effects to major public health disasters. At present we have
two sets of institutions to respond to these issues. The first is the regulatory
apparatus of the FDA, whose oversight of the pharmaceutical industry
has been the source of renewed tension in light of the harmful side effects
of Celebrex and Vioxx. The FDA got into this business by degrees.[15] Its
original mission was to ensure that only pure drugs (foods and cosmetics)
reached the market. In 1938 it entered the rough waters of trying to
determine which drugs were safe enough for sale. By 1962 its responsibility
expanded to analyze whether new drugs were effective enough to receive
permission for general distribution. In the new high-risk environment,
some, perhaps many, drugs are likely to have potent and adverse side
effects that place harried FDA officials in the public crosshairs. The
agency's mission responds to these political pressures by encouraging key
public officials to give greater weight to the risk of allowing bad drugs on
the market than to the risk of keeping good ones off of it.

A relentless expansion of administrative responsibility is not the same,
however, as an improvement in social policy. A sound social welfare function, which weighs these two kinds of errors equally, has slowly been
displaced by one that both attaches inordinate weight to the visible
adverse consequences of bad drugs and puts aside the less visible costs

that result when sick people suffer and die because they are denied access to the desperate measures that might save them. This modern crusade for cutting down on only one kind of risk has drawn out clinical trials, which in turn has retarded the flow of innovation, and eroded the life of drug patents. At the other end, the FDA hair-trigger demands withdrawal and recall of drugs with adverse effects without a full appreciation of their relative risks.

These delays and uncertainties are accentuated by a second institution, tort liability. An aggressive system of personal-injury liability is instituted for known adverse consequences of useful drugs. In addition, a rash of consumer fraud suits demands full cash refunds for drugs that were successfully used before they were withdrawn from the market. A common maxim holds it wise to make errant firms internalize the costs of their own misconduct, especially when the harm in question is inflicted on strangers who have no ability to protect themselves. But the correlative of this principle is often forgotten: it is a gross mistake to impose costs on firms that have not misbehaved, especially when their patients are more than willing to assume the risk of an adverse drug reaction in order, rationally, to forestall the greater risks posed by the underlying disease. In situations where people harm strangers, the imposition of liability aligns private with social costs by rightly reducing the production of unwanted goods and services. In the consensual situation involving pharmaceutical products (and medical services), the imposition of liability enlarges the gap between private and social costs and thus reduces the production of needed social goods and services.[16] The major goal of policy should be to prevent the second initiative, while facilitating the first.

All of these issues constantly bump into one another, which hampers a linear exposition of the sensible social system needed for the creation, protection, and distribution of pharmaceutical products. But it makes sense to step back from current controversies to summarize the basic system by which these processes take place today, in light of the criticisms that are frequently advanced. After I illustrate the basic system, I shall discuss the individual issues.

The overall conclusions that I reach are not distinctive to the pharmaceutical industry but are consistent with the recipes for good government that have a long and distinguished pedigree dating back to Adam Smith and *The Wealth of Nations:* a system of strong property rights and clearly enforceable contracts, with minimal regulatory and judicial interference, offers the best hope for the revitalization of the pharmaceutical industry. No way exists for government, try as it may, to take the lead in developing new commercial processes. Likewise, no way exists for government to take over the task of ensuring that all individuals receive the safest and most effective care, or even to set by edict some minimum threshold with which all private firms must comply. The implicit paternalism of the FDA and the tort system hurts the very people it is intended to help.

2

PROPERTY GENERALLY: EXTERNALITIES, COORDINATION, AND THE PUBLIC DOMAIN

There is no question that the development of new pharmaceutical products (and, I will include routinely, medical devices) is a complex process that relies on the coordination of public and private efforts. The current system of scientific research begins by drawing a strong distinction between basic scientific research on the one hand and its commercialization by various forms of private businesses on the other, in line with the vision of the 1945 Bush Report. The impulse behind this system runs as follows: key information about natural processes must remain in the public domain; all must have access to it in the pursuit of their own work done with an eye toward commercial profit.

A moment's reflection makes clear why any successful system of scientific research requires a robust intellectual public domain. The insight does not depend solely, or even largely, on the observation that there has been more knowledge generated in the past fifty years than in all previous recorded history—if that can in some sense be said to be true. Rather, the coexistence of public-domain (or common) property and private property can be traced to the earliest legal systems. The Roman law, for example, understood that air and water (and "consequently" the beach) had powerful elements of the commons; that is, they were forms of tangible property to which all had access, and from which no one had the right to exclude others.[1]

The intuition behind the primitive division of basic property regimes retains its force to the present day. Organizing any system of property rights, or for that matter, individual liberty, poses two obstacles that cannot be overcome simultaneously. First, any strong system of private property rights (or individual autonomy) runs the risk that people will take actions or use property in ways that have negative consequences on others. Literally no one thinks that my ownership of a knife allows me to insert it between your ribs.[2] Legitimating the direct infliction of harm on others would be a catastrophic byproduct of any system of private ownership. Therefore all systems of private ownership protect bodily integrity by setting boundary conditions to separate one person from the next. Similar separation rules apply to tangible forms of property. For example, the law of nuisance since ancient times has prohibited anyone from discharging waste, pollution, gasses, and odors from his property onto the property of another or public lands and waters.[3]

Why adopt a system of property rights that requires policing boundaries between persons? Usually, because the alternative is worse. Eliminating private ownership may avoid negative spillovers, but it raises in its stead the daunting challenge of coordinating the use of commonly held assets among unrelated individuals whose personal agendas come into sharp conflict with one another. Without boundaries, joint governance is needed to prevent rivalrous individuals and factions from using their common resources inconsistently. The coordination and decision-making problems in such a community grow exponentially as the number of members increases. In the extreme case, the entire world could be treated as owned by all mankind in common so that, to prevent harm to strangers, no one could eat or drink anything without the unanimous consent of all others. That system has one dramatic drawback: the mutual blockades would guarantee mass starvation even in the midst of plenty.[4] In contrast, a system of private property has the huge advantage of drastically reducing the number of persons who will decide on the consumption, upkeep, use, or distribution of the asset in question.

The dilemma, then, is complete. Adopt a system of private property, and the law must cope with serious externality problems. Adopt a system of common property, and the law must cope with serious coordination problems. To make matters worse, the two problems stand in an inverse relationship. The steps that help alleviate the externality issue will aggravate the coordination problem, and vice versa. Clearly, the most that an optimal system of property rights can do is minimize the sum of these two difficulties. It cannot create a bullet-proof system that simultaneously provides perfect incentives for productive behavior and perfect deterrence against antisocial behavior. The study of human institutions is always a search for the most tolerable imperfections. The best system is the one that hurts us the least. What makes matters worse, the choice of the best legal regime is likely to be heavily resource dependent. That much was realized by the basic Roman decision to treat water as largely held in common and land as largely exclusive and individual. Worse still, any old synthesis may be disrupted by the rise of new technologies. What works for land may not work for oil and gas; what works for oil and gas may not work for the spectrum; and what works for the spectrum may not work for cyberspace. New forms of property have a way of destabilizing established patterns of use with familiar resources.

Even so, all of these difficulties taken together do *not* lead to the facile conclusion that for any given resource one property regime is just as good as another. We can dismiss that claim quickly by asking whether it would be a social improvement to adopt the common ownership of land while allowing individual riparians to blockade the use of rivers and seas for transportation.[5] Coordination problems loom larger for complex transportation *networks* than for agriculture, manufacture, commerce, or residential living. The initial choice of a system of common ownership for water reflects the high measure of interdependence between the actions of one person on the network and the welfare of a person located somewhere else. The initial choice of a system of private ownership of land (typically for indefinite duration) reflects the old agricultural metaphor that only those who sow shall reap. Creating temporal interests in property that lasted longer than immediate physical possession was *the* central conceptual shift that made possible investment in private resources.

The overall position can now be stated. In essence, the law has always gravitated to private solutions if the coordination difficulties are greater than the externality difficulties, and to common ownership if the reverse is true. The legal systems for tangible resources, moreover, are far more sophisticated than this strong dichotomy suggests. Rather, the choice between common and private ownership is by no means black and white. The law begins with "pure" types of property systems for both land and water, but through customary evolution and judicial decision, it sensibly blurs both systems at the edges. Thus, many systems of water rights allow riparians to take limited amounts of water for personal use on their adjacent plots. The first units of water turned to these private uses will have large benefits, while imposing relatively small costs on the commons. The extent of these private rights are often sensitive to local variation: limited rights to withdraw water for riparian use make more sense on a small English river than on the raging Colorado bordered on both sides by high cliffs. This same system of incremental correction also applies to property rights in land. For example, the elaborate set of "live and let live" rules allows landowners to inflict trifling invasions of sound, smell, and dust on the land of their neighbors in exchange for the neighbors' reciprocal right to do the same.[6] The basic insight is that the first unit of additional freedom of action grants more benefits to landowners than the first unit of invasive material costs.

Clearly, these property rules cannot achieve perfect precision, but their operation is universally guided by an implicit understanding that carries over to the intellectual property regime governing modern pharmaceutical products. Individuals should organize both private and common property rights functionally, to wring the most out of available resources, natural and human. Accordingly, any delineation of property rights requires some fine-tuning at the margin to generate workable trade-offs between liberty of action on the one hand and exclusive rights of use on the other. But throughout it all, the goal is instrumental: to improve the long-term satisfaction of all individuals.

Important limits, however, confine the tinkering with the customary margins between private and public properties. In some cases, the only way to acquire land to build a transportation infrastructure is to take it by state force. In principle, that coercive act could be accomplished without paying compensation on the ground that everyone "knows" that the value of land for a highway is greater than its value in private hands. In some cases, that intuition will be true, but it hardly follows that political institutions should be allowed to act on it. The power of condemnation without compensation can never be limited to "easy" cases; rather, it applies to all cases for a class of purposes. In many situations, where the highway should be located or how much land should be taken will be uncertain. The compensation limitation directs public officials to seek low-cost solutions, which (all other things being equal) improve overall social welfare by committing the fewest private resources to the achievement of a given task. The issue is, of course, more complicated because different highway routes will in all likelihood have different social values. The just-compensation requirement rationalizes the cost side of the equation; other political institutions have to pick up the slack as well.

The use of public force to rearrange property rights is not confined to situations in which private property is turned to public use.[7] The condemnation power also allows state power to alter the distribution of rights held in common. Again, water rights in the nineteenth century highlight the transitional issues emerging today with intellectual property. The customary system of common ownership, with open access, tends to work well when there is no need to invest resources to maintain or expand the river. But once dredging, widening, or damming the river is required, someone has to raise capital to implement improvements that can easily alter the river's course. Since privatization may cause serious harm to transportation, government programs take up the slack and fund improvements with tax revenues, user fees, or both. The problems in working these transitions are legion, and the case law, without doubt, has allowed the government's use of a national system of waterways to run roughshod over the customary holdings of adjacent landowners. For example, many cases have denied landowners their traditional rights of access without compensation.[8] The result is an excessive number of dams and a bloated public sector.[9]

3

INTELLECTUAL PROPERTY: THE PUBLIC DOMAIN AND PRIVATE RIGHTS

The same trade-offs that abound in the legal regimes for tangible property carry over to intellectual property as well. Once again, systems of common and private property both have advantages and disadvantages. Hence it is imperative to understand which regime, or which mixture of regimes, is appropriate for dealing with the array of inventions, writings, trade secrets, trade names, and trademarks that constitute the chief areas of intellectual property.[1] Just those considerations lend support to the present policy in this country to treat the fruits of basic research as property held in common, and to treat particular inventions or processes as property an individual can, with limited exceptions, hold or dispose of, to the exclusion of others.

The Public Domain

As is the case with tangible property, the story begins with common, not private, property. The history of intellectual property spans a much shorter period than that of private property in land or personal possessions. The Roman law, for example, had no system of patents, copyrights, or trade secrets, though its sophisticated systems for land and personal property shape every modern regime. The omission of intellectual property from these early legal systems reflects, first, sound intellectual judgments about the importance of a common intellectual heritage. Second, it reflects a keen awareness that institutional limitations made it wholly impractical to develop any system of property rights in intangibles.

The second principle is easy to illustrate. Intellectual property cannot be defined by metes and bounds; rather, it depends on complex descriptions of the protected interests, often deposited in some public registry. Those institutions were not robust in early legal systems, which had a difficult enough time organizing a system of transfers of land. Those technical limitations have been largely overcome, first with detailed registries, then, in recent years, with online recording of the relevant information. The ability to implement any protective scheme imaginable, however, only puts greater stress on the initial question: is privatizing various intellectual resources desirable in the first place, or should they be left to thrive—or languish—in the public domain? The proper answer to this question is the same split verdict reached with different forms of tangible resources. No one response best covers all outgrowths of intellectual labor. It is best to start with those interests that ought to remain in the commons and then move forward to the cases in which privatization proves appropriate. As with so many resources, in practice this simple dichotomy has to be refined (as, for example, with the copyright doctrine of fair use) to take into account important variations on the basic theme. The design of a sound—we will never quite get to optimal—system of property rights does not proceed by dogmatic deduction. It follows a principle of successive approximation, whereby propositions that seem to have general attractiveness are revised, but not rejected, in the light of powerful counterexamples.[2]

Let us start with those items that are regarded as indubitably, or inherently, a form of common property. From the earliest times to the present, it is commonplace to insist that no system of intellectual property should offer protection to ordinary ideas, to the common words used to express them, to the natural laws used to describe their behavior, and to those substances naturally occurring in nature.[3] The law of copyright may allow an author to protect a particular writing, but the author has no protection for the underlying ideas expressed in those words.[4] Just because Gibbon wrote a copyrighted book about the fall of Rome or Shirer about the rise of the Third Reich, that does not confer a monopoly on either to deal with his chosen topic. These topical monopolies would pose an intolerable threat to the free dissemination of information, and to the nature and quality of education and political discourse. Even if we could think of a sensible way to implement a system of exclusive rights to narratives of public events, the system would be wildly destructive of social welfare.

What is true about historical events is equally true about the discovery of scientific laws or mathematical proofs. No imagination is needed to ask what the world would be like if Newton—he had more than one very good year—had received intellectual property protection for his discovery of calculus, on the one hand, or principles of universal gravitation, on the other. Virtually all scientific work depends heavily on what has preceded it. If Newton (who, of all people, well knew that he himself stood on the shoulders of giants) had been in a position to copyright (or patent) his insights, every mathematician and physicist before or after could do the same, creating a transactional nightmare. The fear of informational blockages strongly favors an open-access regime similar to that developed for water rights, only more so, given that no congestion develops no matter how many scientists apply Newton's laws of motion simultaneously. Newton could garner a copyright on *Principia Mathematica,* but he should not have been, and was not, able to prevent any of his readers from producing a simpler and more compelling explanation of celestial mechanics that could lure away his entire readership.

The strong insistence that general laws of mathematics and nature remain in the public domain carries with it the urgent question of what to do to stimulate the research producing these beneficial discoveries without conferring private property rights to the discoverers. One should not dismiss with a wave of the hand the answer "nothing at all," if "something" means government action to stimulate ideas. Thus the clear want of incentive is apparent not only to academics and government officials but to ordinary individuals who have profited from scientific advances fueled by academic research. Private institutions can step—and more important, have stepped—forward to help fill the incentive gap when seminal ideas are kept in the public domain. No one could claim that the responses that have emerged have worked at just the right level. But at the same time, no one should disparage the effort to enhance public-domain work. One possibility, of course, is a set of prizes and honors for the best and brightest in a given field, of which the Nobel Prizes are the most famous. No system of prizes and awards need be state-created or state-funded to confer recognition on individuals whose rare talents have increased human understanding of natural and social phenomena. The Nobel Prize illustrates how that private operation works, and countless other organizations have offered prizes of their own to acknowledge the leadership of individuals in music, theater, art, architecture, and so on. Private individuals and organizations also finance the Oscars, Tonys, Edgars, and Emmys because they see gains from this recognition, even for endeavors that are fully protected by intellectual property rights. The use of these devices, moreover, should give rise to no misgivings whatsoever on any side of the political spectrum. The positive incentives do not generate any exclusionary practices that could produce welfare losses. Rather, everyone should be in a position to celebrate the farsighted vision of individuals who for a mixture of social and selfish motives—remember, it's the Oscars, stupid—take effective steps to solve the incentives problem that is the bane of systems of common ownership everywhere.

Nor are these prizes the only way available to spur development of valuable ideas without the creation of regimes of exclusive property rights. This book is written in part from offices in the University of Chicago, founded by John D. Rockefeller, and in the Hoover Institution of Stanford University, founded by Herbert Hoover (before he became president of the United States, no less) and Leland Stanford, after the death of his son.[5] Captains of industry have joined over the years with successful individuals in all walks of life to fund universities, institutes, and think tanks that are able to hire individuals to engage in the research that produces these external benefits. (John) Harvard, (Elihu) Yale, (John) Brown, and (Matthew) Vassar are all institutions of higher education founded by private individuals who helped fill the gap in incentives left by the refusal to create property rights in ideas or research.

The class of private incentive schemes may be still broader. Those individuals who, for fame, glory, or compassion, push the envelope further in the creation of common property may frequently have an additional private motivation. The first to develop some new concept or idea is likely to have a finer appreciation of its uses and limits than anyone else. The follow-on work that can come in his or her direction will also provide advancement opportunities that increase the willingness to participate. To give one example, the complex system of open-source software relies heavily on unpaid voluntary contributions of ordinary individuals—some of whom work with near-mystical devotion—to help build up its common core. The traditional skeptic would say that all individuals will choose to free-ride on the efforts of others, reserving their own talents to develop commercial offshoots they could then use for ordinary profit-making activities. Nonetheless, many individuals choose to contribute to the common core, not just because they are hobbyists who receive recognition for their contribution, but because in so doing they master a system of value to them in their professional work. The expansion of this system through voluntary interaction driven by mixed motives is perfectly consistent with classical liberal ideas stressing the importance not only of the commons but also of private property, voluntary exchange, and consensual organizations. The same set of mixed motives probably drives, at a guess, 90 percent of the gifts to various medical institutions. People don't just contribute to the curing of any old disease. Typically, they support work on the diseases that wreaked havoc in their own lives and those of their families. These resources help fill the incentive gap when ideas are left in the public domain.

Public Support and Patent Protection for Inventions

A quick review of the landscape, then, confirms the important role that prizes and honors play in stimulating advances in human knowledge. Granted, as the Bush Report recognizes, this approach supplies only one piece in a complex mosaic. Yet by the same token that report also rejects any view that this strategy is sufficient in and of itself to meet the challenges of modern science. The National Institutes of Health and the National Science Foundation today account for more than $30 billion in public resources; this money is spent in various ways in order to enrich the scope of the public domain. The basic theory of these organizations is that private subsidies for the creation and dissemination of knowledge will not produce the optimal level of research in basic science. Putting aside the objection that *no* regime will produce *the* optimal result, only a tiny fraction of innovation is touched by any feasible system of prizes, honors and awards. A more constant mechanism that hits the full range of research activities, not just the peak, is needed. Government funding of medical research—much of which leads to an understanding of basic biological mechanisms that pave the way for new pharmaceutical treatments—is needed because individuals who are able to internalize only a fraction of their gain from such research will underproduce, even with other private props in place. The public subsidy is thus justified on the ground that new information, when made accessible to all, is worth the additional costs and distortions of any system of tax-financed resources. The trade-off is just that, because no one doubts that taxation necessarily places a crimp on otherwise beneficial private action. The government is gambling that the free dissemination of information is worth what it costs to create. In general, we can assume that the political judgment is correct. The $30 billion of basic research generates much more bang for the buck than agricultural subsidies or other government giveaways. Perhaps we should cut back on public-funded research, but if so, that claim is no part of this examination of the pharmaceutical industry.

The key question is just what portion of scientific activities the public sector should support. The traditional line is that it supports research up to the point of "proof of principle." The illumination of basic processes of nature is left to the public sector. By contrast, the development of particular inventions is left to private firms, ranging from new start-ups to Fortune 500 firms. The life of these firms is made easier by virtue of the ability to start from a higher scientific base, given the extensive information lodged in the public domain. It was just this handoff arrangement the Bush Report contemplated; indeed, it governs myriad scientific endeavors today. This arrangement, moreover, is commendable for a number of reasons, even if it gives rise to some particular problems.

The first point of the analysis is that many of the inventions routinely subject to patent protection do not depend upon the vast efforts of basic research funded by the NIH and NSF. We had backroom inventors before the public sponsorship of research programs, just as we continue to have them afterward. The handoff problems that one finds in dealing with public-sponsored research, moreover, are not different in kind from those which involve handoffs from privately sponsored research. For example, university output also goes into the public domain. It makes little sense to remove from the equation the enormous spur toward invention from the patent system simply because we could expand the efforts of state-sponsored research and the tax burden it entails.

Indeed, one can go further and be wary of any effort by public figures to push various lines of invention through a centralized government system. One strength of the current system of grants administered by both the NIH and the NSF is that it relies heavily on a decentralized system of rotating peer review panels that are relatively insulated from political pressure. If the research ground rules are changed so that public actors choose the direction of inventive activity through their grants, the current wall of separation of the political from the professional side of governance probably could not remain intact. Too much money would be at stake for politicians to stand aside, whether we had a system of patents or not.

There is another way to make the same point. One unappreciated virtue of the patent system is that in dealing with covered inventions, the state acts only in a reactive, constrained fashion to examine whether the formal requirements of patentability have been met in an individual case. This restraint comports with general models of limited government in which the state defines and protects property rights initially. It then stands aside while ordinary individuals figure out the particular lines of research and development to pursue once they meet the relatively minimal requirements of the patent law. That law covers "any new and useful process, machine, manufacturer, or composition of matter."[6] Even so, it does not reach any idea or natural law. Furthermore, individual cases require proof of the novelty and nonobviousness of the invention, as well as technical conditions that specify the information that the applicant must include in a valid filing, which are traditionally listed as written description, enablement, best mode, and definiteness.[7]

The trillion-dollar empirical hunch that makes inventions and discoveries "patent eligible" (falling, that is, into one of the four legally specified categories) is that the grit and hard work needed to develop them cannot be supported in the broad run solely by a system of prizes and honors. The need for financial incentives is greater with these patent-eligible inventions. At the same time, the preclusive effect of any particular invention on the inventive activities of others is far less than the effect that would emerge if one person could claim the exclusive right to use or license the Pythagorean theorem or its modern equivalent. Accordingly, a central tenet of the patent system is to disregard evidence of potential profitability in making judgments about patentability. Any public effort to consider profitability would convert the Patent Office from a body concerned with the definition of property rights, in which state action is indispensable, into a state czar for industrial planning, charged with making futile guesses on the future direction of technology and consumer demand. To be sure, the patent system has major difficulties. As a result, critics have long held doubts as to whether we should adopt a patent system at all, given the preclusive effects of monopoly.[8] Nonetheless, as will become clear, monopoly is only one obstacle among many in dealing with a sensible institutional structure for pharmaceuticals.

PART

MAINTAINING THE PUBLIC/PRIVATE INTERFACE

4

TAMING CONFLICT OF INTERESTS

Before turning to the challenges to the current distribution of activity between principle and invention, it is useful to confront a key difficulty that may block a smooth transition from the public-domain world of principle to the private-property world of invention. This difficulty is of major importance with respect to universities and public laboratories because the question always arises whether a researcher who has engaged in the explication of a fundamental principle should be allowed, while wearing a different hat, to pursue the commercialization of that principle. The obvious objection to this practice is that once a researcher wears two hats, research endeavors in the public sphere will be tilted in ways that allow the researcher to gain a leg up in the patent wars that follow. Such conflicts of interest are indeed legion, for the greater the exclusivity of basic research, no matter how funded, the more difficult it becomes to rapidly disseminate basic scientific advances into the general research community. It is futile to deny this effect; the only real question involves a fair estimation of the social costs associated with its occurrence.

One way to beat back this conflict is to insist on a strict separation of effort. Individuals who work in basic research could be systematically debarred from engaging in the commercialization of new ideas. Employers could require that separation as a condition for work, and such a rule might make sense for government employees who have regulatory or adjudicatory functions. Indeed, in January 2005 the National Institutes of Health, reeling from scandals about alleged individual misbehavior,

implemented a total ban on any consulting or stock ownership arrangements between NIH scientists and key players in the pharmaceutical or
biotech world.[1] The new policy, which was greeted with much anguish
within the NIH, marked a strong retreat from earlier policies dating from
the mid-1990s that permitted more extensive conduct with full disclosure.[2]
At one level, the previous rules—adopted by Harold Varmus, the former
NIH head—seemed adequate because the high-profile cases involved
nondisclosure that violated the set of rules already in place. The reversal in
position was said to be needed in order to restore "confidence" in a flag-
ship public institution. But the new policy was regarded as an overreaction,
especially by those who noted the enormous gains that have come from
transfer of information from the public domain into individual private
firms.[3] At one time it appeared that the new rules were so restrictive that
serious conflict of interest issues were perceived by individuals who
coached Little League and similar activities. The guffaws were loud
enough to be heard within and outside the agency, and in August 2005 the
restrictions were cut back in important respects.[4] The new regulations no
longer required NIH employees to disclose and seek approval from the
NIH ethics committee to engage in unrelated activities from which they
received compensation, such as selling jewelry or singing.[5] But many of the
other restrictions still remained in full force, including the prohibition on
all consulting for the pharmaceutical and biotech industries. In addition,
the top two hundred or so officials in NIH were prohibited from owning
more than $15,000 in stock in a single company, including that which
might have been acquired as deferred compensation for services before
joining NIH. The rules also require that individual stock holding at lower
levels be examined on a case-by-case basis to see whether sale may be
required in some particular circumstances that are not, unfortunately, fully
set out in the basic ruling. Work in medical societies was generally allowed,
thereby reversing a prohibition that was placed in the earlier rules.

The implicit subtext of these rules is that lesser techniques of management—disclosure of conflicts, inability to participate in certain decision-
making roles, exclusion from key positions of authority, such as principle
investigator, on given projects—are all deemed to be insufficient on a categorical basis. The price paid for this enforced separation is the lack of
cooperation between the two sides. And we have some general evidence

that the total ban is too costly. Major private research institutions—unless subject to heavy pressures from the National Institutes of Health—in general do not insist on the complete ban on commercial work by their faculty members and graduate students. Rather, they regulate it to deal with both conflicts of commitment, which concern the amount of time that can be devoted to commercial ventures (and which are of little relevance here), and conflicts of interest, which raise concerns more germane to the general discussion.

Why should we tolerate, indeed encourage, the movement to the messy middle ground? In scientific research, as in so many other areas of life, a demand for a total prohibition against conflicts of interest comes at too high a price for the academic or nonprofit institutions that seek to recruit top-rate research scientists. A huge percentage of distinguished bench scientists wear two hats today. Under one hat they deal with endeavors in basic research, under the other with efforts—through small private start-ups or consultancies with large pharmaceutical companies—to convert the basic information into concrete commercial applications, with cash, stock, and options as the coin of the realm. As Thomas Stossel observes, much good has come from these arrangements. "Academic researchers joined venture capitalists in founding the biotechnology industry, leading to immense benefits—for example, the hepatitis B vaccine."[6] And he is equally right in his prescription. The total ban on collaboration is inappropriate. The more sensible approach is to deal with various kinds of restrictions on research that are inconsistent with the academic mission. Thus the NIH (like private universities) should not allow their employees to enter into arrangements that forbid, without sponsor approval, the publication of results of their sponsored research.

None of this is meant to turn a blind eye to the need to counteract the real possibility of abuse. But any decision to completely stop all transfers necessarily blocks *all* potential gains from trade that depend on smoothing the movement of information from research to commercial labs. The point is especially relevant because the bans themselves create a penumbra that goes beyond their actual terms. Thus, when I lectured on this topic at Stanford University in the winter of 2005, shortly after the NIH announced their rules, one entrepreneur in the audience reported that the NIH rules had created such a chill within the agency that individual

researchers were unwilling to answer emails about their research, to provide advance papers for publication, or to work *without compensation* on
any joint project—even on projects for which the entrepreneur had
received NIH development licenses.

As an empirical matter, that price is just too high. Even if one hundred
researchers work in any particular field, it is often the case that only a
handful are at world-class speed on specific sets of problems. Under the
strong ban, two consequences follow. First, the number of eligible players at the industry level is limited, with the unfortunate consequence of
reducing the number of independent players who can compete in the
patent and business markets. Second, the number of individuals prepared
to go into basic research also shrinks, because they are unwilling to give
up the potential large payoffs that come from working in a new venture
or large pharmaceutical operation. These scientists will take industry jobs
with the understanding that some of their work can be introduced into
the public domain. Yet cutting down the level of basic research makes the
private follow-on activities more expensive than would otherwise be the
case. An effective private sector cannot be built without keeping a vibrant
public sector. The problem at root is really no different from trying to
build elegant mansions in a community that lacks public roads. Therefore
a balanced approach is needed such that, ideally, the last dollar invested in
private research has the same social rate of return as the last dollar put
into public domain research—a goal only approachable, never attainable.

The blunt truth is that we have to learn to deal with conflicts, not to
banish them. The two watchwords in this venture are disclosure and
management. I have spent several years now as a member of the Conflict
of Interest Committee of the Immune Tolerance Network, a large set of
clinical investigations funded by a multimillion-dollar NIH grant.[7] The
conflicts model the committee follows, which is common in activities
of this sort, works far better than total separation of basic research and
commercial activity.

The first component of the system is that the members of the conflicts
of interest committee have no projects under the basic research program.
This condition is in general easy to satisfy, for the ability to work through
the web of financial and consulting arrangements does not depend on the
science that leads experts in various technical areas to double-up in their

roles. It is important to have basic scientists, physicians, and, yes, lawyers on a committee of this sort. Its membership should be large enough that nobody can dominate the committee but small enough to allow it to consistently handle the extensive number of cases that come before it. After all, all new program participants have to be constantly vetted, and the position of existing participants has to be reviewed on an annual basis to deal with frequent changes in status.

The second component of the program is to obtain from participants full information about their connections and activities to set the stage for the management decisions that follow. If the initial disclosures are not complete, or seem ambiguous, further clarification should be requested before making a final decision. Once the full information is acquired, the committee can determine whether the proposal can be included in the program. The basic reason conflicts of interest prove so intractable is the high correlation between conflicts and expertise. The number of close substitutes diminishes as the subfields grow ever smaller and more complicated.

Given the lay of the land, strong guidelines are preferable to the presumption embraced by the NIH. In general, for clinical trials, it is unwise to allow the individual who proposes new treatment to supervise the studies, for the dangers of bias are too great. But some participation in that work might be necessary, perhaps as a principal coinvestigator or as an altogether independent investigator. Some of these conflicts are sufficiently small that the committee needs only to take note of them. Others, however, are sufficiently grave that it is best to ensure the interested party has no role whatsoever in the clinical investigation in which he has a financial interest. Difficulties arise when a committee member is in a position to evaluate the proposal of a potential competitor. In these cases, it might be desirable to exclude anyone from passing on clinical trials if he has an arguable interest in their failure. But that approach cuts too deeply in many cases. The boundaries of potential competition are far from transparent at the early stages of research. Often it is hard to know whether a given treatment is a complement or a substitute, so the direction of the scientist's financial interest is hard to determine. In addition, since so many experts could count as real or potential competitors, an outright ban would lead to wholesale disqualifications that could doom the overall review process. In general, therefore, reviewers may sensibly disclose their interests to others, but they should not be, en masse, barred from participation, especially if one of them has the best information about a given proposal. However, at least one person who is disinterested should always be on the review committee, generally an easy requirement to satisfy.

This entire process is part art and part science, but in general it seems to work more smoothly in practice than one might suppose. The communities are close knit, and reputation counts for a great deal. Some individual case may make its unwelcome way into the newspapers even when all these procedures are followed. In general, however, it is far more likely that the troublesome cases will be those that fail for more mundane reasons, chiefly incomplete disclosure. Incomplete disclosure frustrates the operation of the program at its inception, which is just what happened with the NIH. In thinking of the thousands of physicians who are working in these parallel universes, the rare shipwreck seems far preferable to the risk of terminal stasis from an absolute government ban of any conflicts over the transition from public to private research. Indeed, one telling measure of the soundness of this general cautious position on conflicts comes from the current legal framework for government-sponsored research. As a business matter, the NIH insists that all its grantee institutions supply rigorous supervision over conflicts of interest. But even with its exposed political position on explosive conflicts issues, it currently imposes no total prohibition against researchers playing key roles in both basic science and applied research. That judgment represents a considered evaluation from the NIH, as a research sponsor, that any regime of strict separation would needlessly hobble scientific research. Scientific research would be crippled in practice if the NIH chose to reverse field and expand the total ban it now imposes on employees to its grantees and their employees. Of course, it is easy to trumpet a ban because of its strong protection against abuse. But in practice a ban should be avoided because it is both costly and disruptive. Strict separation should be a last resort, not a first option—even, as it turns out, for the FDA.

5

FEDERALLY SPONSORED RESEARCH UNDER BAYH-DOLE

Unpacking the proper interaction between federal sponsorship and private research has a second dimension: who, if anyone, should own any patentable inventions that this research produces? This topic is important because tech-transfer operations are big business today on many campuses, especially those with extensive engineer and biotech operations. A recent *Wall Street Journal* story notes, "In 2003, 195 universities and other research institutions received 3,933 U.S. patents, up 12% from the previous year, and generated $1.3 billion in licensing income from patents, according to the Association of Universities." Much of the income comes from single patents that possess remarkable utility: Columbia University has obtained from $116 million to $175 million in annual revenues from its tech-transfer operation. One blockbuster patent—which allows for complex DNA transfers of specific genes into cells that can reproduce specific proteins—by Dr. Richard Axel and his colleagues has been the source of most of this revenue.[1] Once universities and other nonprofits enter the world of commercial business, they quickly learn to act, for better or worse, as other commercial parties. They zealously protect their patents, and engage in the same dubious practices that have been used by ordinary business. For example, they attempt to engage in "double-patenting"—the effort to extend patent life by repatenting the original invention with minor variations after the original expiration. Federal courts rebuffed Columbia's efforts to repatent Axel's invention.

A somewhat different effort by the University of Rochester to assert a broad patent over the general processes of Cox-2 inhibitors similarly failed because it sought to control an entire technology and not a particular invention.[2] Even with these abuses, the issue of interface between public and private research does not depend on the wisdom of questionable decisions to push the patent law beyond its proper limits. Rather, the same standards that apply to everyone else who seeks patent protection should simply apply to universities as well.

The next issue to consider is what patent policy the United States should follow when it funds grant research. Three possibilities exist, with intermediate permutations. First, the invention could by agreement fall into the public domain. Second, the United States could retain the patent, which it could use either defensively or offensively. The defensive use blocks others from claiming the invention, while allowing all comers to use it royalty free. Alternatively, offensive use licenses the patent to particular parties while preventing others from using it. Third, the patent could become the property of the private grantee. Once again, two variations are possible. In the first, the patentee becomes an outright owner whose rights run against the world, including the United States. In the second, the United States retains a paid-up license that allows it, or certain designated parties, to practice the patented invention for free. The issue here is an old one. The Bush Report supported the last alternative of private ownership subject to government license. It has proven remarkably prescient:

> V. *Patent Policy.* The success of the National Research Foundation in promoting scientific research in this country will depend to a very large degree upon the cooperation of organizations outside the Government. In making contracts with or grants to such organizations the Foundation should protect the public interest adequately and at the same time leave the cooperating organizations with adequate freedom and incentive to conduct scientific research. The public interest will normally be adequately protected if the Government receives a royalty-free license for governmental purposes under any patents resulting from work financed by the Foundation. There should be no obligation on the research

institution to patent discoveries made as a result of support from the Foundation. There should certainly *not* be any absolute requirement that all rights in such discoveries be assigned to the Government, but it should be left to the discretion of the Director and the interested Division whether in special cases the public interest requires such an assignment. Legislation on this point should leave to the Members of the Foundation discretion as to its patent policy in order that patent arrangements may be adjusted as circumstances and the public interest require.[3]

The Bush Report offers no particular justification for its conclusion. In particular, it does not raise, let alone evaluate, the wisdom of keeping inventions resulting from government-sponsored research in the public domain for everyone—and not just the government—to use as they please. The question of patent policy was discussed elsewhere in the years following the war and led to the passage of the Bayh-Dole Act.[4] A Report of the National Patent Planning Commission took a more cautious line that was intended to assure, first and foremost, government access to its intellectual property. It ensured this access usually through disclosure (which would undermine anyone else's claim of novelty) or through patenting when necessary, especially for defensive purposes. The commission equivocated on whether private grantees could routinely patent their inventions, contenting itself with the observation that exclusive licenses should be granted when needed to stimulate work that might not otherwise be done.[5] A 1947 attorney general's report inclined toward keeping all inventions in the public domain, and viewed government patents as one way to achieve that result, even when disclosure was available.[6] Exclusive rights in private parties were thought to increase the risk of favoritism in the competition over these valuable rights. As Professor Rebecca Eisenberg notes, "these two positions framed the debate in the decades that followed between advocates of a 'license' policy, who urged the government to limit itself to retaining a license to use the inventions resulting from government-sponsored research, while leaving title in the contractor, and advocates of a 'title' policy, who urged the government to acquire full title to the inventions."[7] The years between these early reports and the adoption of Bayh-Dole gave rise to repeated examinations of the matter. But the uniform response across government agencies awaited the 1980 passage of Bayh-Dole.[8]

In the lead-up to Bayh-Dole, the older public domain approach was criticized on the grounds that too many useful inventions languished in both government and private laboratories because no one would undertake risky commercialization without patent protection. In an effort to stimulate the level of overall inventive activity, postdiscovery, the statute pointedly seeks "to promote collaboration between commercial concerns and nonprofit organizations, including universities," with an eye to promoting marketplace competition.[9] The statute as drafted applies only to nonprofit organizations like universities and "small businesses firms," but a 1983 Reagan executive order still in effect extended Bayh-Dole to large government contractors.[10] On a more chauvinistic note, the act is intended "to promote the commercialization and public availability of inventions made in the United States by United States industry and labor."[11]

To jump-start the patent process, Bayh-Dole stipulates that each grantee of federally sponsored research, including research universities, elect whether to file a patent application for inventions that emerge in the course of the funded work. This statutory obligation could not require the covered parties to patent all inventions, given the costs of filing patents for inventions that are likely to be of dubious value. In line with the recommendations of the original Bush Report, once the grantee institution elects to file for a patent, the relevant federal agency has "a nonexclusive, nontransferable, irrevocable, paid-up license to practice or have practiced for on behalf of the United States any subject invention throughout the world." The act also imposes an obligation on the granting institution to share royalties with the inventor and to plow back its share of the profits into its own research ventures, which it is likely to do in any event. If any eligible institution chooses not to assert patent rights for the invention, the federal agency, after consultation with interested parties, can allow the inventor to file the patent in his own name, subject to the usual barrage of regulations. The one distinctive condition imposed on the Bayh-Dole patentee pertains to the creation of so-called "march-in" rights. Under narrow circumstances, never invoked, these rights allow the federal government to take for itself or some responsible party a nonexclusive license if the original patentee has let its invention languish, or if urgent matters of health and safety are not addressed by the licensee in its use of the patent.[12]

The most important contribution of Bayh-Dole lies not in its administrative details but in its fundamental policy choice. In principle, the United States could, without constitutional complication, condition all grants to research institutions on their willingness to place patentable inventions or discoveries in the public domain, as frequently happened before Bayh-Dole.[13] The policy question for Bayh-Dole is whether it is worth incurring additional costs to create patent rights in inventions, given this public-domain alternative. At first blush, it seems odd to regard privatization of inventions as a goal of public research, given that any system of exclusive use normally leads to less intensive utilization of the invention. One possible explanation for this result ties in nicely with the so-called "prospect theory" of patents. This theory, most notably developed by Professor Edmund Kitch, postulates that patenting is justified because owners are likely to increase investment in particular inventions *only after* the inventions have been patented.[14]

Apart from its generality, the central difficulty with Kitch's claim is that it takes into account only the greater efforts by the inventor, but does not explicitly set off the reduced efforts from outsiders who would otherwise be able to utilize the invention. In most industries, we do not generally create exclusive rights to manage inventions or writings that for some other reason fall into the public domain. Furthermore, the allegedly improved manageability of the invention in the hands of a single owner also does not justify the extension of existing copyrights or patents.[15]

In general, patent protection should be regarded as a (most) necessary evil, but one that should *not* be endured unless it provides an incentive to create in the first instance. If the prospect theory does not work, however, perhaps the right to patent the inventions from grant research should be respected under the traditional rationale for patent protection. Namely, the patent provides positive incentives on production stemming from the exclusive right to produce the protected invention. In this context, it might be argued that this extra boost is not needed for grantees who have already received public money for research, so that the patent protection requires the public to pay twice for the same invention.[16] That analysis presupposes that the same inventions will hit the marketplace whether or not patent advantages are supplied to the grantee, which, however, need not be the case. Recall that the patent incentive operates cumulatively with grant payments, so that two carrots work better in combination than either carrot works in isolation.

Viewed in this light, the Bayh-Dole patent policy may supply three useful benefits. First, it may induce institutions and individuals who envision patentable inventions at the end of their quest to apply for grants in the first place. If all inventions went into the public domain, the most promising research ventures would shun public funding of research. The problem becomes more acute for grantees who raise supplemental funds from multiple private sources, since these sources could easily demand that grantees patent the inventions and give them a piece of the action. Why force a range of attractive grantees outside the public grant system if these individuals are most likely to produce the best inventions and provide the most significant contribution to basic research? And why risk arguments that invite difficult guesses as to whether the government has contributed a sufficient fraction of the total funding to insist on the public-domain status of certain inventions that have also received private support? As long as the government receives its own paid-up license and the grantee freely disseminates the basic research results, the private ownership of patents is probably better over the life cycle of government research than public-domain status—although the point is hard to prove in theory or by empirical evidence.

Suppose that we reject the public-domain approach (which for these purposes includes government patents that are not enforced against any practitioner of the invention). The next question is who should be the proprietor: the individual inventor, his home institution, or the government. On that issue, the better solution seems to gravitate to the private side. The government is not some monolithic entity but contains a myriad of departments and agencies, which may well vary among themselves in terms of overall competence. The same can be said of the full array of universities and private businesses. It is foolish, therefore, to posit any uniform level of competence that cuts across the public-private divide at any given time, let alone over time.

Given the level of internal variation on both sides, the arguments in favor of private ownership under Bayh-Dole reduce to three. Although none is dispositive, taken in the aggregate they seem persuasive. First, diversification is generally a sensible strategy. The dangers of recentralization of policy seem greater with government agencies than with private firms because the agencies fall in a direct line of control to the president and are subject to government-wide directives from Congress. Discontinuous shifts in policy are therefore more likely to occur, and on balance, are more dangerous with government ownership. Private owners will probably try a wide range of strategies and learn from each other's mistakes. Second, on balance the private grantee has more information about the patentable invention than the government agency funding it. Likewise, the grantee knows better how the invention fits into the full array of other patents, trade secrets, and know-how which might be needed for its successful commercialization. In particular cases where a government laboratory works with a private party, some sharing arrangements might be appropriate, but if so, it should be by special arrangement and not general policy. To the extent one cares about the transfer of *bundles* of patents and other intellectual-property rights, the private system of control reduces the frictions and transaction costs relative to government control, even if it increases these costs relative to a pure public-domain solution. Third, we generally presume that the internal incentive structures within private firms and universities are more flexible, and hence more congenial to risk-taking activities, than ossified government bureaucracies severely constrained in compensating their successful and energetic employees. Privatization is in general a good, and no strong reason exists to deviate from that basic presumption for intellectual property once we have passed the stage of basic research.

In the end, alas, this issue, like so many others, eventually devolves to a question of transaction costs. If these costs are kept low enough—to the limit of zero—the initial allocation of rights would not matter.[17] The single inventor could costlessly contract with outsiders in ways that allowed their efforts to improve his invention. Alternatively, if the rights were widely diffused, all the separate inventors in a zero-transaction-cost world could form an alliance to achieve the same end, with a somewhat different split in the proceeds. But since transaction costs are positive, the best we can do is make intelligent guesses as to which system yields the largest net product. Of the three possible regimes—public domain, public ownership, and private ownership (subject to the paid-up government license)—the last seems the best, just as the Bush Report urged long ago. The division control and royalty between inventor and firm are best resolved by contract.

Thus far I have considered Bayh-Dole insofar as it covers the full range of patentable inventions. However strong the case for public-domain status or government ownership in other areas, that case falls especially short with pharmaceutical patents (which do not include the biotech patents needed for their fabrication) because of the critical second tier of regulation from the need to obtain FDA approval before marketing patented or unpatented drugs. The great fear with public-domain drugs is that no one will take the initiative to seek FDA approval for them. Once a new drug receives generic status, a second firm can sell the identical product for less because it did not bear as much, if any, of the initial approval costs. No one will take on the role of a first mover if patent protection is not given, unless some other form of exclusive right is adopted, perhaps depending on the data the initial licensee submits on questions of effectiveness and safety—a troubled topic which I examine later. Thus the Bayh-Dole regime has a special cogency for pharmaceuticals, making it more justified in this context. The creation of private patents does not preclude others who are not in a position to market the drug in any event. But it gives the initial holder the incentive to run the patent through the FDA gantlet. The success of this scheme depends critically on how the FDA operates. We shall turn to that topic after we investigate some fundamental objections to the patent system in all cases, not limited to those funded with government research.

INTELLECTUAL PROPERTY AND ITS REGULATION

The next topic in the life cycle of pharmaceuticals concerns the proper mode for organizing an industry that depends heavily on intellectual property. The exercise is in a deep sense one of rival imperfections. The current system relies on patents to stimulate investment and thus embeds some measure of monopoly power into the heart of the system. That result has its well-known shortcomings. The challenge for the lone monopolist that produces single products for sale is less a problem of bargaining strategies and coordination than a simple exercise of pricing. Under classical economic theory, the single monopolist raises price and cuts output in order to maximize his private gains; in so doing he reduces overall social welfare. To be sure, if the exercise of monopoly power only transferred wealth from potential consumers to potential producers, we would be forced to make an esthetic argument over whether one distribution of wealth is preferable to another. That judgment is especially problematic in this context because there is no simple comparison between rich and poor. Both the patentee and its customers are likely to be complex entities owned by broad groups of shareholders or other types of members. Fortunately, however, the argument against the monopoly does not rest ultimately on its muddy distributional consequences. Rather, the use of monopoly power creates an unambiguous social loss because the higher monopoly price excludes from the market individuals who can meet the competitive, but not the monopoly, price.[1] The effect of the monopolist is not only to secure a wealth transfer, but also to secure a wealth loss.

The critics of the patent regime take this analysis a step further to argue that any patent monopoly necessarily creates that loss in social wealth. The ostensible gains from the strong incentives to produce are offset, at least in part, by the reduced dissemination of the finished invention. The holy grail of patent policy is to obtain the ideal incentives for *both* initial innovation and postinnovation distribution. But that happy ending is always unattainable because the two requirements work at cross purposes. The strong exclusive rights that encourage innovation defeat efficient dissemination of the product so created. Any "solution" to this dilemma is strictly second-best.

The policy debate involves which of the myriad second-best solutions is preferable. We can identify five broad answers. The first view is that no patents should issue for inventions. I have already considered and rejected that argument and will not return to it now. The four choices left on the table are the following:

- The traditional limitations and rights granted under the current system of patent law.
- Direct systems of controls over the price of new pharmaceutical drugs.
- Some more intrusive programs of patent purchases or prizes by government that seek to marry strong incentives for production with broad dissemination spurred by timely government intervention.
- Socializing research and development to co-opt much of the private patent process.

In the next several chapters, I consider each in turn.

6

THE ANTICOMMONS

Perhaps the central dispute in the law of patents (and copyrights) concerns the vexed relationship between property rights and monopoly power. Stated in a sentence the source of the difficulty is as follows: while private property is a good, a state-created monopoly is a bad. The problem with the sentence's application lies in the inescapable point that in the context of patents, state monopolies and private property are not simply just opposite sides of the same coin. They are, as one anonymous wag put it, the same side of the same coin. Quite simply, the argument starts with the observation that there is in theory no way in which the state can create an exclusive right to an invention under a patent without creating at the same time a patent monopoly.[1] However great our affection for private property, it is matched by our equal distaste for state monopolies.

Why? Although commentators often give multiple explanations for this distaste, these explanations boil down to two answers. The first deals with a case in which multiple patent monopolies might stand in the path of intellectual advancement; the second deals with a situation in which a single monopolist is present. The first allocative imbalance arises because the *multiple* monopolies of separate patent holders prevent the coordination of research efforts needed for the further development of pharmaceutical products. The second imbalance arises because the *single* monopolist charges too high a price and thus sells too few units of the relevant good. Both of these issues have generated an immense literature in recent years.

In this chapter I deal with multiple monopolists, each with blocking power, often described as the anticommons.

Biomedical research, like all sophisticated human activities, is complex and requires the coordination of multiple actors for its success. Voluntary agreement is the ordinary device for achieving cooperation among individuals, whereby each person contributes either labor or property to the common venture in exchange for a share of the total output. In general, the structure of the deals the interested parties can strike to advance their goals is subject to few, if any, regulatory limits. Some individuals supply needed standardized inputs under ordinary contracts of sale or hire. The landlord may only receive a fixed rent for his efforts, and the same may be true of the supplier of stationery, accounting services or electricity. Yet other inputs are uniquely tied to the venture; the firm may cut more complex deals for these inputs to give them some stake in the overall success of the venture. Many of these unique inputs, including the research tools or compounds needed to make them go, are subject to patent protection.[2] These patent holders might position themselves to set up blockades that will prevent the easy assembly of research projects. This holdout potential can offset the gains patents supply by giving incentives for new invention.

In a now classic article, Michael Heller and Rebecca Eisenberg speculated that the rich profusion of patents has created an "anticommons," which will retard the pace of biomedical innovation.[3] Heller first coined the term *anticommons* in 1998, to bring to this context an analogous concern to "the tragedy of the commons," a concept that Garrett Hardin had popularized some thirty years before.[4] Hardin observed that natural resources could not be preserved in a sustainable fashion when situated in an unregulated commons to which all individuals had unlimited access. In this setting, the forces of individual self-interest lead to collective results no one desires. Each individual takes into account the gains he receives from removing something of value from the commons, but ignores the losses his actions impose on the multitude of unrelated individuals who share the commons with him. The greater the number of uncoordinated individuals, the more rapid the dissipation of the underlying resource. The anticommons suggests the converse image of the "blockade," whereby a single owner vetoes the effective use of some common resource subject to divided control. The case that most readily comes to mind is that of a river along which there are multiple toll stations, each manned by a separate owner. Although commerce could thrive if a single owner charged one toll, the balkanization of separate tolls makes the river wholly worthless. Overfishing and blockades may look to be disparate problems, but analytically they reflect the same principle: multiple control over a single unified resource leads to parallel risk of overconsumption or blockade.[5]

Heller and Eisenberg express the fear that the extensive use of patents creates a blockade situation similar to that of multiple toll owners. As evidence of the basic problem, Heller discusses the vivid contrast in Russia, where shuttered stores stood side by side the informal stands thriving along the sidewalks. The breakdown in the formal Russian economy could be traced to the proliferation of separate permits that any individual store-owner had to receive in order to set up shop. Rather than running this hopeless gantlet, ordinary merchants simply moved over to the informal economy, where, in practice, no permits were needed. Better some business gets done than all business be strangled under red tape.

In response to the problem of the anticommons, some commentators propose the creation of a compulsory license system, which could extend to such critical elements as DNA sequences or the full range of research tools.[6] The effort is twofold. First, the mandated royalty is designed to protect the investment that each individual owner has placed in his patent. Second, the forced exchange is introduced to deny him the hold-out power over the patent in question. The situation, so the argument goes, is little different from eminent domain in real estate, in which the government acquires land from numerous private individuals to build a highway. This guarded and structured use of coercion will therefore lead to an overall improvement in social welfare.

The state invocation of some form of the takings power may have the desired effect in some cases, but before committing to this alternative, we must address the major dangers of these forced exchanges.[7] In order for this system to work, the compulsory licenses must provide gains to both the licensor and the licensee. At a minimum, the regulator needs knowledge of how to set the compensation term of the transaction. The voluntary licenses that are frequently negotiated for biomedical research provide an obvious place to look for this knowledge, and these licenses are complex instruments in which a compensation schedule is only one of many negotiated items. In addition, any compulsory license must contain provisions dealing with the following items: the materials covered by the license, the sharing of research results, the assignment of rights, the delegation of duties, the sharing of trade secrets, the definition of net sales, and a host of other record-keeping and administrative matters that often vary by case. The compulsory licenses by definition must be much cruder, and may often misfire if their terms are not correctly calibrated. In addition, the system of voluntary licenses has the clear advantage that individual firms get to choose their trading partners. That selection is critical for at least two reasons. First, any sharing arrangement requires trust, which only voluntary arrangements can inspire. Second, voluntary licenses avoid the major span of control problems that would otherwise arise if large numbers of firms or individuals demanded licenses of a single critical patent.

These compulsory transactions have serious drawbacks, and whether they are worth their cost depends on whether the holdout problem is as severe as Heller and Eisenberg intimate. Both theoretical reasons and empirical evidence suggest that they are not.[8] On the former, it is worth looking at the two examples that give rise to the initial concern. The first looks at the empty Russian stores; it has, alas, too many American parallels. One familiar feature of the modern regulatory state is its extensive reliance on the permit power. Real estate development projects often require dozens of permits, often from different agencies, operating in loose coordination at the federal, state, and local levels. The great advantage of a permit is that it stops activities in their tracks before they can cause harm. This loss prevention could easily be critical when the damage is irreparable (as with serious injury or death) or where the losses (such as those from the disclosure of a trade secret) cannot be accurately quantified but nonetheless are certain to be substantial. The permit system has two great vices, however. First, the individual activity is stalled on the mere possibility that some untoward harm may take place. In this regard, it differs from the standard private injunction, which is typically used only to stop harm that has already begun or is imminent.[9] Second, the proliferation of permits could turn any real estate project or new drug application into an endurance contest.

Whether one deals with Russia or America, the incentives that govern the behavior of government officials are quite different from those that motivate the executives who run biotech firms. Government officials are not eager to complete deals. Quite the opposite, their power often comes from holding back approval to satisfy some other interest, such as those of a politically well-connected competitor who does not want a new business to enter the field. The entrepreneur may choose to bask in his holdout power. However, that strategy makes no sense. He cares about revenue generation, which critically depends on the pace at which deals are concluded. It is likely, therefore, that businesses will make strenuous efforts to overcome these transactional barriers when faced with looming holdout problems; we expect no such behavior from government officials, who operate under a very different reward structure.

The toll-booth example used above raises different issues. We do have individuals who have proprietary position; the blunt truth is that if the cooperation of all is required to complete a single journey, the tragedy of the anticommons is likely to occur. But note that the geographical construction of the river lends itself to the conclusion that every riparian landowner occupies a monopoly position from which he cannot be dislodged. When there are more than five or six, it becomes impossible for them to negotiate a single toll that would increase the flow of traffic and their overall revenues simultaneously. But the standard description of the patent business is not that of a river but that of a thicket.[10] Once we think of the issues in this way, the capacities for blockade do not increase automatically with the number of patents in place.

The thicket metaphor is not entirely apt because it suggests that additional patents, like additional bramble bushes, only make things worse. Yet why is that necessarily so? The simplest way to see the point is to question the use of the thicket metaphor in the first place, and resort to the more structured situation of multiple toll booths along the river. Now the key question is what happens when one additional patent is added to the patents that are already in place. If it occupies a distinctive place so that no research of a particular kind can go forward without its use, the patent has the potential to create a holdout problem. At the same time, without the distinctive patent, the entire line of research might not be possible; it is hard to treat this new addition as blocking off the research that would not develop without it. At any rate, in many cases the new patents may create *substitutes* for some existing technology already under patent. At this point, we have not added another toll booth downstream but rather have created a "side-stream" that provides an alternative pathway for development. As the number of patents increases, the entire network might become more complicated; inventors can play off one patent holder against the other, just as they can entertain multiple bids from landlords or accountants. Therefore, one cannot tell in the abstract whether the increase in the number of patents is likely to add to or detract from the holdout power of any given patent.

The empirical evidence points in the same direction. First, it seems clear that the number of new patents in the pharmaceutical industry continues to increase.[11] Yet if true systematic obstacles were present, this trend would reverse itself. The patterns of high activity suggest that people can overcome the blockade through a variety of cooperative arrangements. Of these arrangements, cross-licensing and patent pooling are among the most important because they allow individuals to share information without having to put a dollar value on each patent subject to these reciprocal licenses. In addition, in at least one case, Merck took the lead to place certain genetic fragments, known as express sequence tags, or ESTs, into the public domain precisely to make sure it (and, necessarily, other companies) would have access to them in its own research.[12]

Of equal importance, the one empirical survey on this question suggests that the key players in the industry are cognizant of the problem but not overwhelmed by it. In the study, reported in *Science,* John P. Walsh, Ashish Arora, and Wesley M. Cohen surveyed seventy attorneys, scientists, and managers in the pharmaceutical and biotech industries to detect evidence of the patent blockade. Almost none of the respondents thought that their research agendas had been blocked because of the patent protection for research tools. Rather, in industry and academia alike, researchers adopted strategies of "licensing, inventing around patents, going offshore, the development and use of public databases and research tools, court challenges and simply using the technology without a license (i.e. infringement)" to achieve their particular goals.[13] All of these devices carry some cost. Thus the case against compulsory licensing cannot rest on the easy assumption that these coordination problems do not matter in the conduct of social science research. But in dealing with some of the unhappy consequences of the patent system, one must remember that the supposed cures also have their imperfections, whose magnitude in many cases exceeds the problems they are trying to solve. Indeed, the cure seems to be more harmful than the disease in dealing with the patent protection concerning the inputs for scientific research. As I note in the next section, this fact is also true of efforts to displace the patent power with respect to the outputs of the research—namely, the pharmaceutical products and medical devices that are subject to patent protection.

7

THE SINGLE MONOPOLY: CURRENT PATENT
LIMITATIONS

Before considering alternative patent models that have been proposed, we need to understand the limits of the current system. No one
doubts that current patent law is sensitive to the dangers of monopoly
power. But how best to respond? The first approach is in many ways the
most effective. The system adopts legal rules that limit the scope of
patent protection to particular inventions. Therefore no one person can
preempt an entire field of development with a single patent. The most
famous illustration of this position is *O'Reilly v. Morse,* which rebuffed
the effort of Samuel Morse to obtain a patent that gave him the exclusive
right to use the entire electromagnetic spectrum for communications at a
distance. More specifically, the claim covered the exclusive use of "elec-
tro-magnetism, however developed for marking or printing intelligible
characters, signs, or letters, at any distances," which would for the patent
period have given him the exclusive right, for example, to develop the
telephone or radio.[1] The phrase that signals doom for this claim is "however developed," which would give Morse a veto over inventions not yet
made. A sensible claim properly covers a particular *device* that exploits the
understanding of basic scientific laws, but that leaves open the development of rival technologies utilizing the same laws.

More recently, the same principle applied to the University of
Rochester patent application that sought to block the development of
different families of Cox-2 inhibitors by claiming a patent over the natural discovery of how these compounds worked—that is, by "selectively

inhibiting PGHS-2 [prostaglandins] activity in a human host."[2] The conflict arose between a research institution and a pharmaceutical company, G. D. Searle, which had patented a particular molecule (Celebrex) that achieved the desired effect. The company was rightly able to knock out the Rochester patent under the general rule in *O'Reilly*.[3] The point is instructive because it reminds us not only that old principles carry over well to new inventions but also that drug companies do not have a reflexive interest in broad patents in all cases. On many occasions, the large companies know that their own projects' success could depend on a narrow reading of some other patent claim. Ex post—that is, after the applications have been filed—various members of the industry can dispute with each other over various matters of patent scope and validity. Yet ex ante—that is, before any applications have been filed—those disputes illustrate that industrial firms often find themselves on both sides of the coverage question. As a result, the overall industry is not likely to stray too far from the social optimum.

The basic position has powerful implications for the pharmaceutical field. It may be that someone can obtain a patent for one Cox-2 (cyclooxygenase) inhibitor—for example, Celebrex—and even for the family of compounds of which it is a part. But as is the case with the telegraph, this patent cannot, any more than the invalid Rochester patent, cover all potential compounds that might utilize the same mechanism. It can cover only drugs whose configuration builds from the same underlying chemical structure of the patented drug (for example, benzene rings in certain configurations with each other), where different elements are placed at different points on the lattice. Suits for these similar drugs are called Markush claims.[4] Change the lattice, however, and a second patent is needed, unless the change is only a trivial extension from the first.

This detour into the legitimate scope of patent claims might appear as an exercise that seeks to count the number of angels standing on the head of a pin, but it is a deadly serious business with critical implications for evaluating a charge that the exclusive rights under any particular patent create an (unwanted) state monopoly. Stress the mechanism, and all Cox-2 inhibitors are covered by the first patent. The result is a huge monopoly whose only competition comes from other products (for example, general Cox inhibitors, like ibuprofen) that operate in a fundamentally different fashion.

Take the narrower definition stressing molecular structure, and Vioxx is not covered by the Celebrex patent. The new entrants can then compete for the same therapeutic market niche occupied by the first product. The same concerns are present with statins (for example, Lipitor), which are used to control cholesterol level. The six or so drugs on the market all depend on the same basic mechanism, but they differ in molecular structure and operational details.

The sensible feature of Hatch-Waxman is that it seeks to coordinate the activities between the patent system and the FDA, each of which operates a system of exclusive rights. The implicit assumption of both systems today is that the introduction of new drugs into a given class works to the general benefit of the public at large by limiting the dangers of monopoly associated with both systems of regulation. This whole synthesis is, unfortunately, placed at risk today by the constant drumbeat about the scope and direction of medical research, as well as the attacks directed against the pharmaceutical industry because it has spent too much time in developing me-too drugs instead of genuine pioneer breakthroughs.[5] But here there is little reason for any concern. Cases of pure duplication are covered by the current patent law, with its nonobviousness criterion. And there is no reason for the patent law, or for that matter the FDA, to get itself involved in business and commercial judgments as to which of these new products is worth having, and which is not.[6] Certainly no one thinks that the state should restrict entry into crowded markets in areas that involve neither patents nor state regulatory approval, and that same approach should apply here. On average, it seems that new entrants put greater pressures on established firms and should be welcomed for that reason. "Me-too products reflect and create competition among drug and device manufacturers, and that competition is also a powerful driver of better quality and lower cost."[7]

Behind this debate over me-too drugs lies the crucial question of whether some product differentiation among patents creates a competitive market. The answer might be thought to be no, but only if we adopt an unduly restrictive definition of competition that is satisfied only when there are multiple sellers of fungible products. These products are identical in all relevant dimensions so that potential buyers regard them as perfect substitutes for each other, much like bushels of number 2 wheat sold by different farmers, or gold bullion. By that definition, the only possible competitive market is one with generic drugs once patent protection has expired. Nonetheless, this definition of competition is too narrow for its own good: it excludes cases in which substantial but imperfect competition is present across broad product classes. The wine business is intensely competitive. Competition remains though each of countless vineyards produces somewhat different varieties of grapes and uses different processes—which could themselves be protected by patents or trade secrets—to turn the grapes into wine. Modest heterogeneity does not undermine the competition in the wine business; it gives greater variety to consumers at the small cost of creating some modest monopoly niche that each seller may hold for some fraction of loyal consumers.

Drugs operate in more or less the same fashion. The small patentable differences in composition may not matter much to many consumers, but particular individuals will do better on drug A than on drug B, with the reverse true for others. Any effort to raise prices solely for individuals who "absolutely, positively" have to have the particular product is difficult to achieve. These people do not self-identify, and other users with weaker preferences will migrate to a substitute if the price is raised too much. That shift is perhaps even more pronounced today when insurers and hospitals make large purchases for individual users. The threat of the large buyer's taking the business elsewhere is often a powerful source of secret rebates that tends to lower overall price levels. The level of interaction and interdependence makes this market competitive under a more sensible definition, which values increased consumer opportunity from product variation. If so, we can identify one critical qualification to the claim that exclusive patent rights are tantamount to monopoly positions. Sensible limitations on patent scope allow for the creation of competitive brands.

The market in patented goods need be no more monopolistic than the ordinary residential resale market in which no two houses are quite alike. To the outer gaze, the housing market appears intensely competitive, as buyers constantly trade off location with size, with room configuration, and with a thousand other variables that make one house different from another. Once the contract of purchase is signed, however, the buyer is entitled to the deed to his "unique" property; he should not have to settle for damages, often large but difficult to measure, should the seller decide to breach. For the particular individual, that one plot of land does have distinctive features that cannot be duplicated in the market. But these vital variations do not lead us to think of the real-estate market as monopolistic, and the same sensibility should be brought to our understanding of patents. The claim that any patent creates an economic monopoly must be carefully confined to those cases in which one patented invention is not in price competition with a second.

The second point is as important as the initial point on competition. The legal system does not grant a patent, even for a term of years, simply because someone asks for it. The second-tier requirements of nonobviousness and novelty for patent-eligible inventions ensure that no one obtains a patent for devices and compounds that persons skilled in the trade with knowledge of the prior art already know or could discover with minimum effort. The patent requires some degree of differentiation from all that has preceded it. In addition, the patent holder must in a sense plant the seeds of the patent's destruction by disclosing the information that allows others to imitate it after its expiration and that may contain clues on how to invent around it during the patent period—placing a downward pressure on price. Of course, some bad patents sneak through, but these are vulnerable to judicial challenge after the fact. And while that level of correction is not perfect, the overall system tends to be reliable, especially for pharmaceutical patents, which tend to receive extra scrutiny because of their huge potential value.

The third offset to monopoly power comes, oddly enough, from the traditional right of a patent holder, as owner, to price discriminate among its various purchasers. Price discrimination follows from the traditional view that ownership gives absolute control over the right of disposition. Since a patent holder is not a public utility, it can charge each user whatever fee it sees fit. This power of price discrimination allows the patent holder to lower the price toward the competitive level for those individuals who cannot pay the monopoly price, while increasing an already stiff price for those who can pay something extra. The combination of price increases and decreases will surely influence the distribution of wealth among producers and consumers. More important, however, it allows, in a halting way, the seller to undo the allocative inefficiency from monopoly power by bringing low demanders back into the market. At the extreme, a seller that engages in perfect price discrimination will serve the identical set of consumers that are served in the competitive market. The only differences will be distributional: the seller will capture much (and in principle all) of the consumer surplus, the difference between one's reservation price and the price paid.

As mentioned earlier, distributional issues have relatively little bite in the patent context: complex organizations hold patents, and products covered by these patents are sold or licensed to other organizations or to individuals with various forms of insurance coverage. It is therefore difficult to identify a discrete class of persons who win and lose under various schemes of regulation. The key questions are allocative. How do we get the greatest use of patented inventions? With perfect discrimination, allocative concerns would be answered entirely. In practice, of course, it is hard to discriminate between high and low demanders, and price discrimination is not a sustainable strategy if one class of buyers can resell to another. Consequently, the most that can be claimed for the capacity to price discriminate is that it moderates the effect of monopoly power. Further, in those cases in which two patents are imperfect substitutes for each other, price competition gives some large buyers wiggle room to play off one seller against the other.

The fourth device to deal with monopoly is a product-specific one that relates to the Hatch-Waxman Act, which attempts to smooth the transition from the patented to the generic drug market.[8] To back up for a moment, the standard length of a pharmaceutical patent is twenty years, after which it goes into the public domain. In practice the holder of a perfected patent does not have twenty full years in which to exercise that exclusive right because a healthy portion of the patent life is exhausted while the patentee seeks to obtain FDA approval to market the drug. A patent may give the *exclusive* right to sell, but it does not guarantee a *right* to sell. The combined interaction of the patent law and the FDA truncates the effective return from the invention. The Hatch-Waxman Act, at one end, extends the length of a patent to partially offset the reduction in useful patent life for the preapproval clinical trials the FDA requires. One day is restored to a patent for each two days consumed in the clinical study process and for each day consumed by FDA review of the new drug application. The act sets a maximum restoration of five years so long as the total useful patent life does not exceed fourteen years. Even with this restoration period, effective patent lives in the pharmaceutical industry typically run only nine to thirteen years, compared with more than eighteen years in other industries.[9]

Hatch-Waxman also simplifies and expedites the process for developing and approving generic copies of innovator drugs. This simplification works to cut down the power of the incumbent monopoly toward the end of its life. In particular, the act takes away innovator patent rights by creating a special exemption under the patent law, which permits the generic firm to manufacture and test its drug during the incumbent's patent period. The generic manufacturer will thus be ready with a commercial launch the moment the prior patent expires. According to the operative statutory provision, "It shall not be an act of infringement to make, use, offer to sell, or sell within the United States or import into the United States a patented invention solely for uses reasonably related to the development and submission of information under a Federal law which regulates the manufacture, use, or sale of drugs."[10] The statute obviously contemplates that this protection from infringement should be available for drugs that require FDA approval. *Merck KgaA v. Integra Life Sciences I, Ltd.* gave this provision a broader reading that protected the developer of a new product, here Merck, that conducted preclinical research on the patented product, which produced data that the firm ultimately decided not to include in its FDA application.[11] A unanimous Court, speaking through Justice Scalia, found that the plain meaning of the exemption was broad enough to encompass basic research with an eye to finding patentable compounds, so that exemption held. In so doing it reversed the federal circuit, a full-time patent court, which had insisted that the exemption covered only those cases in which there was some direct connection between the research development and some planned FDA submission. Justice Scalia downplayed this connection, holding that "*any*" information that was collected sufficed. His nontextual reason was that the trial-and-error nature of drug research makes it unlikely that the exemption should be so narrowly construed as to block any of the preparatory work needed to identify those drugs worthy of further clinical evaluation.

As is common in these patent cases, Justice Scalia did not address the broader question of how the exemption should be framed. And in a sense that is just as well, because that question is more difficult to answer. The petitioner in *Merck* was an established company that tested compounds—new peptides that affected cell adhesion—that were a large part of the intellectual property of a smaller start-up firm that had obtained patents on these substances. Had the legal rule been set in the opposite direction, it should not have been too difficult for Merck to acquire, as is commonly the case, a research license from Integra to market the product in question. The hard question of social policy is whether the exemption should extend this far or be read in the more limited fashion of the federal circuit. The instinctive answer to that question is that the broader the exemption, the more rapidly goods will reach the market.

The fuller answer, however, is much more complex because of the implicit trade-off that this one-dimensional argument overlooks. Research progress will in fact take place more rapidly, *given* that the first product has already reached market. But small start-up firms in the position of Integra may well cut back their research efforts precisely because the broad exemption dilutes the value of the original patent. The two effects therefore tend to cancel each other out, so that ultimately the choice is a matter of relative magnitudes, which are notoriously hard to assess. Nor is it clear in the long run who benefits from the new rule; in this patentee-versus-patentee world, the players operate behind a de facto veil of ignorance, because it is not clear which side they will take in the next case. The difficult economic choices help explain why Integra could not inject a takings claim into the overall mix. But a better appreciation of the fine-tuning aspects of the problem *might* lead to the conclusion that the exemption should be narrowed by statute to the reading preferred by the federal circuit, that some licensing fee be required for the exercise of the privilege—which raises other thorny questions. For these purposes, this entire episode points out just how treacherous is the path to an optimal patent policy when all variables are taken into account.

Hatch-Waxman has other important features. For one, it strips innovators of the exclusive and perpetual rights to their data on safety and effectiveness; without this information generic applicants would have difficulty in working their own products through the FDA. In return for giving up this information, the innovators receive only limited exclusivity periods of five years for new chemical entities and three years for other approvals. Furthermore, Hatch-Waxman greatly simplifies the data requirements for generic drug applicants, substituting a simple bioequivalence test for the exhaustive safety and effectiveness testing required of the innovator. That rule in effect says that the new entrant does not have to start from ground zero, as did the first applicant, but need only show that its produces are the bioequivalent of those which have already been tested. These provisions speed the entry of generic drugs at the back end of the patent period. For the most part, this system has proceeded smoothly, with generic drug market share rising from less than 20 percent of prescriptions before Hatch-Waxman to almost 50 percent today.[12]

Widespread reports, however, have illustrated dubious strategies to protect against generic drugs by expanding the scope of patent protection— late registrations, registration of patents of dubious validity, and the like. I have no desire to defend these strategies, but note only a couple of points. First, these devices can be tried by anyone; they are not distinct to pharmaceutical firms. Second, they are usually rebuffed when attempted, which suggests the current prohibitions have held the line against abuse. Third, these strategies, even when proper and successful, provide patent protection for the *improvement* covered by the new patent, not for the original product, whose patent has expired. Remember, the basic patent system already denies any patent for new inventions that do not constitute a nonobvious advance over the prior art.[13] Moreover, even if such small advances did run the patent gantlet, they would by definition provide only limited protection for any patent holder. On expiration of the original patent, the generic need only market the older product at a small price discount to offset the trivial improvements from the new patent. Alternatively, if a single valuable product is protected by multiple patents, that combination should not obtain generic status when the first of its ingredients does. To hold this position is to truncate the term of the later patents. The correct strategy, therefore, is to allow the patented inventions to slip into the public domain one at a time. If the original holder found market value in a subset of the final patent, so should its generic competitors.

In many cases, the holder of the new patent will aggressively market it in order to win away customers from its previous near-expired patent. For example, Astra-Zenica famously pushed its new Nexium product after the expiration of its Prilosec patent.[14] If the new patent was not sufficiently different from the older one, it could be invalidated on the grounds that it failed to meet the standards of nonobviousness or novelty. But if it differed sufficiently, it would be perfectly appropriate for a firm in the pharmaceutical industry, as in any other, to seek to expand its market through aggressive but truthful advertisements. The marketing expenditures can easily reduce the price per pill by expanding the underlying demand. Nor is there any serious risk of imposition of unfair practices. This market has serious players on both sides; if the various physicians, insurers, and pharmaceutical-benefit managers choose the new product over the old one, it is hard to attack this decision on the ground that they are ill-informed or have no bargaining power.[15] In any event, whatever the dramatic tales in individual cases, litigation is the exception and not the norm. In the vast majority of cases—approximately 95 percent of the time, according to Pharmaceutical Research and Manufacturers of America (PhRMA)—generics are content to wait until patent expiration to begin commercial sales.[16]

The Hatch-Waxman Act also contains provisions that give the first generic manufacturer to enter the system a protected period of 180 days during which only it is allowed to compete with the incumbent party. The exclusive right is given to encourage challenges to the existing patent and could generate substantial sums for some blockbuster drugs that generate billions per year while under patent protection. In effect, during that period the two parties operate in a duopoly, such that each can charge a price somewhere between the competitive and monopoly levels. This provision has generated, unavoidably, some difficult litigation, especially in cases where it is unclear that the first generic entrant is entitled to enter the market. The patent dispute will turn, in connection with the so-called paragraph IV certification, on the question of whether the new drug infringes on the old patent, or, if not, whether the old patent is for some reason invalid. In these cases, the controversy is brought to a head when the new entrant files an abbreviated new drug application (ANDA) that refers to its paragraph IV claim under the act, after which the new entrant must immediately notify the patentee of its claims.[17] Thereafter the patentee has to bring suit within forty-five days, and failure to bring suit can result in the FDA's granting immediate approval of the drug.[18] The situation is still more complex because once the original patentee files its suit, it is in general entitled to receive an automatic injunction for thirty months or the duration of the patent, whichever is shorter.[19] The theory here is that if the new entry takes place, it can cause irreparable harm to the patentee, which is especially vivid in cases in which the new entrant seeks to invalidate a patent long before it is due to expire.

The settlement of these patent disputes is a necessary part of any comprehensive litigation scheme under Hatch-Waxman. Yet at the same time serious antitrust claims can arise if the original patentee and the first generic agree in some fashion to limit production and to raise prices. Any evaluation of the legality of these various agreements is hard to come by, and the case law itself is divided on the proper standard, which will probably take a Supreme Court decision to resolve. In the easy case, the patentee makes a payment to the new entrant in exchange for its decision not to market its product under the ANDA license, an arrangement that some courts have treated as evidence of cartel behavior.[20] That result seems correct in those cases in which there is no doubt that the generic firm has the right to enter the market, but the analysis is considerably more complex when there is some uncertainty about the ultimate success of the infringement claim. In ordinary settlements it is quite permissible for the incumbent to maintain that it retains its original patent unimpaired, but to pay the generic a sum nonetheless to abandon its otherwise plausible claim. In these cases a rule-of-reason analysis may well be more appropriate.[21] There is a full range of intermediate cases, and one plausible solution requires some degree of judicial supervision, which will support the settlement if the underlying claim has some strong probability of success.[22]

Taken as a whole, the patent system takes modest, important steps to counter monopoly power. First, competition, via new entry, is made possible through the narrow patent scope. Second, one can obtain a patent only if it is nonobvious, novel, and registered. This full disclosure of information allows competitors to study the patent to create competitive products. Third, the patent holder can engage in price discrimination to serve those who cannot afford the monopolistic price. Fourth, the Hatch-Waxman Act has allowed for greater generic competition. What Senator Orrin Hatch (R-Utah) said about the act in 1984 remains true today: "The public receives the best of both worlds—cheaper drugs today and better drugs tomorrow."[23] All these efforts to tweak the patent law have produced what looks like a workable response to the monopoly problem. Can we do better?

8

—

RATE REGULATION: AN UNNEEDED SWAMP

A second common social response to monopoly power is a system of rate regulation, which limits the prices that a monopoly firm can charge its customers. Rate regulation began with the rise of *network* industries in the period between the end of the Civil War and the First World War. The emergence of large firms with monopoly power in the telephone, railroad, electric, and power industries drove the new movement. The basic feature of these industries is that, considering all relevant outputs, a single firm can produce the desired quantity of goods or services more cheaply than any set of two or more competitive firms. Speaking generally, "these [network] markets cannot function as competitive markets," unlike, for example, the markets for grain or automobiles.[1] The reason for this so-called natural monopoly, then, is the declining marginal cost of production over the relevant range of output.[2] Stated otherwise, natural monopolies have high initial costs to create the physical infrastructure but low costs for adding additional customers once the infrastructure has been established. To insist on competition in these markets is to require the costly duplication of basic facilities.

One possible cure for this problem is to allow the monopolist to price as it pleases, on the theory that the high prices it charges will induce new entry into the market. This view suggests that the *static* inefficiencies of the monopoly are more than offset by the *dynamic* efficiencies in the absence of regulation. The theory certainly has its strengths. For example, no one doubts that the baroque system of pricing of wire line

services under the 1996 Telecommunications Act created massive dislocations. In the absence of regulation, the entire problem would have
quickly solved itself, as cell phones, Internet telephony, cable, and even
electrical connections have become viable alternatives to the wire line
service. Indeed, since the passage of the act the total number of land lines
has dropped while the number of cell phone lines has increased.[3] Carried
over to the patent field, this approach is consistent with the limits on
patent power discussed above. The approach relies on both the new entry
from other patented molecules and the steady rise of generics to counter
monopolistic pricing, at low cost and with little risk of political capture or
misbehavior.

In general, neither Congress nor the states have been content with network industries to allow monopoly power to wither away over time.
Rather, state actors have proposed different schemes of rate regulation in
an effort to force the public utility to supply its goods at figures
approaching competitive prices. Broadly speaking, states have used
two approaches. The first determines the amount of investment that the
regulated utility has made in its equipment, and excludes from that base
all those expenditures not used and useful in the business.[4] Since the firm
bears the risk that some of its initial investment will be disallowed, it must
receive an upward boost in its rate of return. The alternative system
allows the rate base to include all the expenditures made on the business
without disallowance.[5] The upshot is that the firm receives a lower rate of
return because it takes fewer risks.

Both these systems of rate regulation were subjected to constitutional
review for one simple reason.[6] The public utilities all had high initial
investment levels followed by relatively low marginal costs for additional
units of service. In the absence of some form of protection, the aggressive
regulator could provide compensation that covered the marginal costs of
production without allowing the firm to recover the initial cost of its
investment. With only its variable costs met, the firm would have an
incentive to stay in business rather than to shut down in the short run,
even if it could never cover its fixed costs over the useful asset life. While
such an artful scheme of confiscation might work once, it would effectively chill investment in all cases thereafter. The entire enterprise of rate
regulation at its best represented an attempt to steer a narrow path

between the risks of monopoly expropriation, on the one hand, and state confiscation, on the other. On balance, the experience with this system has been tolerable, but not truly distinguished.

Pharmaceutical Price Controls

The key inquiry for these purposes is the way this system of rate regulation carries over to the pharmaceutical industry. Here, as a general matter, the price controls in question are imposed on a range of pharmaceutical products that are typically in competition with each other. In addition, the basic industry is highly competitive in the initial effort to acquire patents. The firm that gets a lucrative patent has not, on average, made a supercompetitive rate of return, adjusted for risk. After all, it makes its initial investments without any guarantee that it will win the patent race. Nor does victory in a patent race guarantee a successful market reception for the patented product. Owing to the inherent legal and business risks, we should expect that price controls in the pharmaceutical industry will have the same baleful consequences that they have elsewhere. They will lead to a constriction in investment that anticipates the sharp reduction in the rate of return. The problem is of especial danger with pharmaceuticals where even the *threat* of price controls tomorrow could easily deter long-term investment today. Indeed, a recent study commissioned by the Manhattan Institute took a stab at estimating the effect that price controls might have on future investment, taking as its benchmark the types of controls in place in Europe and under Veterans Administration rules. One does not have to swear by the results to be troubled by the ballpark estimate: "The researchers found that R&D spending will drop by nearly 40% over the next two decades, resulting in a loss of nearly $300 billion in R&D and 277 million life years."[7]

Here are some of the reasons why that venture is likely to be fraught with risk. As with public utility natural monopolies, pharmaceutical products are characterized by an extremely high fixed cost to get a given product to market, coupled with a relatively low marginal cost for the production of additional units of the product. The exact costs for the development of new drugs are subject to dispute, but the best estimates, which take into account the long lag between the time of initial investment and the realization of a return, have put the number at somewhere around $802 million, and more recently at an eye-popping $1.7 billion.[8] A far lower estimate, at around $240 million, has been offered by Public Citizen, but its estimate is fatally flawed because it refuses to take into account the time value of money, though a substantial fraction of the expenditures in new drugs are made years before any revenue is returned.[9]

Other laments about the high price of pharmaceutical drugs often conflate two different issues: total amount of money spent on drugs versus the cost per unit of a drug. We should welcome increases in the first of these costs in any event, because they often imply that ordinary individuals can avoid more costly and risky surgery or alternative treatment. The second point is exceedingly difficult to deal with because the price increases may be influenced by increases in the cost of the product or the risk of liability, or by a host of other factors.[10] In addition, professional buyers and the increased presence of generics in the marketplace—where the United States is generally more efficient (because less regulated) than its overseas rivals—exert real pressures to constrain prices.[11]

Most importantly, no system of pricing in an unregulated market can deal with the strong tendency toward price discrimination resulting from the vast disparity between the cost of the first pill and the cost of all subsequent pills. Once the initial user cannot be asked (surprise!) to pay more than $100 million (to take the lowest estimate) or more than $800 million (to take a more credible estimate) for the first pill, the manufacturer has to recover the cost of making that pill by boosting the price of subsequent units. Consequently, neither the first nor the subsequent users pay for the marginal cost of the pill they consume. Yet no simple algorithm announces how much each will pay. Instead, all users have a strong incentive to shift as much of the cost of their pills as possible onto other users. In the end, price discrimination and secret deals form an indispensable feature of the pricing landscape, so much so that it is not possible to infer collusion among several firms by virtue of the odd swings in prices. Bulk purchasers—for example, health plans—which have the capacity to play off one product against a rival, will receive far lower prices than others, such as retail pharmacies, that are obliged to carry a full product line.[12]

The question then arises whether any system of price controls can work in so complex a market. The usual effort to find a rate base for a single product will not work in this particular case. The research effort inevitably pursues many leads at once; therefore it becomes quite impossible to disentangle the particular expenditures that count as costs of a particular drug. In addition, dry holes are a normal part of pharmaceutical life. Today these losses are made up by the revenues from the successes, and any system of price controls will have to increase the rate base to take into account these expenses of unrelated projects. Yet no one who has thought of this has any idea of how it should be done. And even if this technical feat were accomplished, some explanation would be needed as to why a second restraint (beyond its duration) is placed on the patent. The practical difficulties cannot be solved in any fashion, especially if any of the constitutional constraints on rate regulation are respected.

Some Misguided Proposals

The First Generation

In practice, the proposals for price controls have followed a completely different path, chiefly by targeting the element of price discrimination. The first of these proposals, the Greater Access to Affordable Pharmaceuticals Act of 2001, which passed the Senate but died in the House, had two key features.[13] First, the Greater Access bill proposed to make it unlawful for any manufacturer to discriminate against a pharmacist in the sale of prescription drugs.[14] That provision, in and of itself, is welfare reducing because it would have forced the manufacturer to charge the single price that maximizes revenue. It would have excluded from the market all those consumers who were willing to pay more than the competitive but less than the single monopoly price. It would also reduce the profits to the patent holder by denying it the option of charging still higher prices to the most intensive demanders. That restriction on pricing freedom is socially undesirable because any smaller yield from the patented product reduces the incentive to innovate, and thus delays the likely time that particular products reach the market. It is ironic that everyone seems to be in favor of price discrimination when it allows the supply of needed drugs to reach poor countries. Yet the identical logic calls for the differentiation of prices in the United States as well.

The Greater Access bill was still more mischievous because it explicitly denied the manufacturer the right to set the single nondiscriminatory price for its products. Instead, it stipulated that the only nondiscriminatory price that could be charged had to equal the *lowest* price charged to any nonhumanitarian or noncharitable organization, either domestic or foreign.[15] The bill was also unclear whether this measuring rod included sales made before its passage. Nonetheless, a single sale at marginal cost for the benefit of a rural clinic could deprive a manufacturer of billions in potential revenues. Thus the consequence of this illogical scheme would have been to *deprive* these rural clinics access to the drugs.

Matters are even worse because national governments, which set their prices unilaterally to suit their internal convenience, dominate foreign markets. If those sales could not be resisted—and often they cannot—this bill would have placed all domestic sales at the mercy of a single foreign government. In addition, it would make it nearly impossible to offer any compassionate rate for foreign governments. Price discrimination for so many reasons is a necessary tool in any modern market: let anyone who thinks that we can live in a world of single prices check hotel or airline reservations online. The economics of this bill were, and are, ruinous. Its constitutional ramifications were not examined by its sponsors, but it is hard to see how an industry can survive if the entire revenue stream from an existing patent is at risk of regulation. Recall that the dominant rule from *Bement* gave absolute pricing choice to patent holders.[16] The Greater Access bill did not come close to protecting those preexisting rights. Indeed, by its terms it did not even offer firms a chance to recover their costs and a reasonable profit thereon. Hence it should be regarded as flatly unconstitutional as a matter of theory. Whether that conclusion would have resulted in practice is, in such uncharted territory, regrettably, anyone's guess.

A Second Generation

The second generation of proposed legislation took a different form. It is common knowledge that many Americans have purchased their medicines abroad, especially in Canada, to take advantage of the lower rates available in that marketplace. So long as the number of transactions was small relative to the overall size of the market, this effort to avoid paying American prices did not have serious consequences for drug prices—or, as it turns out, for drug safety. In principle, the ideal private strategy to counteract this difficulty is to attach conditions of sale forbidding any drug sold overseas to be resold for consumption in the United States. A breach of that covenant by the seller should render it liable in damages for the amount the American firm lost on account of the resale, which in turn would induce the foreign distributor not to authorize resale of the product in the United States. In addition, good reasons suggest that any person who purchased these drugs with knowledge that they were sold in breach of contract could be treated as a purchaser in bad faith. Therefore the purchaser could be subject to a remedy that at least required it to cough up the difference between foreign and domestic prices, taking the incentive out of this dangerous form of arbitrage.[17]

Contract remedies, however, are difficult to come by in this international setting; the same is true with respect to remedies against persons who purchase from those who sell in breach of contract. At this point, the dominant strategy for drug companies is to restrict the supplies sold in foreign markets to the estimated level of their domestic consumption to minimize the surplus available for reimportation by foreigners. In order to forestall this opportunity, the Senate introduced the Pharmaceutical Market Access and Drug Safety Act of 2004.[18] The Market Access bill, under the name of "free trade," would have required American firms to sell to those distributors in certain designated foreign nations whatever quantities of particular drugs they desired at a price equal to that at which that same drug was sold (often under government order) in the local market. The drugs in question could then be acquired by any firm and sold anywhere in the world; thus these new buyers could compete with the original seller because of the arbitrarily low price. That competition, moreover, would have occurred not only in the United States but also in other countries, where we have no interest in trashing the market position of companies, domestic or foreign, that supply the American market. In addition, the manufacturer of the drug for the American market had to seek, at its own expense, FDA approval of the imported drugs, some of which were sold in dosages and preparations not normally used in the American market. As a capstone, the 2004 bill would have required the patent holders to abandon all rights to bring suits for patent infringement, whether the drugs were manufactured domestically or abroad.

One strong objection to this legislation is that it lengthens the chain of custody, which increases the risk of adulteration and impurities. For that reason, the FDA has under Presidents Clinton and Bush refused to certify those drugs as safe for importation. The common response to the FDA's position on this score is that since the local governments certify these drugs for their own populations, no added health risk exists in the United States. In fact, that argument fails for two distinct reasons. First, once it is known that these drugs are destined for export, foreign governments will probably not incur the costs of inspection for drugs not consumed by their own citizens. Instead, they will develop some system to segregate the products for domestic use from those for export, which seems to be the position in Canada today.[19] Second, even if foreign governments did not follow this strategy, nothing that is done in any designated company blocks the risk of contamination or adulteration thereafter. The longer the chain of custody, the greater the health risks—period.

For this purpose, however, I shall put the dominant health risks to one side and note that the pricing issues raise the identical concerns that the earlier legislation contained. In effect, the United States has engaged in a complex price control regime that allows *foreign nations* to set the prices for domestic (and foreign) sales of American drugs without any attention to whether drug companies receive a permissible rate of return once those restrictions are put into place. It is difficult to see how any system of even minimal protection could find that system constitutional. As with general ratemaking exercises, the focal point is again the takings clause, only here the matter is sufficiently straightforward that there is little reason to tarry over the difficulties associated with determining rate base and permissible rate of return. Forget for a moment the complexities of the pharmaceutical business, and just envision a situation that involves a plot of land, owned by X, that is worth $1,000. The government does not decide to take it for $200, which would result in a constitutional deficit of $800. Instead it orders the individual to sell that land to a third person for $200, and then allows the buyer to do with the land what he pleases. Surely there can be no difference between an order for mandatory sale at below-market price and a taking for the same sum of money. To be sure, the pharmaceutical case is a bit more complicated because patented drugs carry with them different prices depending on the path by which they are sold. But all those fine points go to the amount of the unpaid government bill, not to the obligation to compensate in the first place. Pure and simple compulsory orders for sale should generate an order for compensation that covers the lost revenues from sale, ideally at a point that leaves the profit position of the regulated firm just where it was before the regulation was put into place. There is not a pretense that the revenue-savings features of the proposed legislation will come from cost-savings in the marketing or distribution of drugs that leave the basic profit position unimpaired, as the standard constitutional analysis requires.

The Third Generation

The force of this argument, it now seems clear, has persuaded even its supporters that mandated sales for importation at bargain rates cannot survive the takings objection. Accordingly, its 2005 reincarnation, now in the form of the Pharmaceutical Market Access and Drug Safety Act of 2005, seeks to finesse this difficulty by offering a new option to a drug manufacturer. The obligation to sell in the foreign market—and therefore to reimport into the American market—at the local overseas price "applies only to the sale or distribution of a prescription drug in a country if the manufacturer of the drug chooses to sell or distribute the drug in the country."[20] Once a company decides to take that course, however, the obligation to sell at bargain rates would attach. To make that system work, U.S. patent law would be relaxed so that it would not count as "an act of infringement to use, offer to sell, or sell within the United States or to import into the United States any [FDA approved] patented invention that was first sold abroad by or under authority of the owner or licensee of such patent."[21]

This newly crafted provision is an instructive example of the homage paid by vice to virtue. A statute that is profoundly antithetical to the protection of intellectual property rights and freedom of contract seeks a measure of self-validation by making it appear that acceptance of the statutory obligations are voluntary to the pharmaceutical company. In doing so it taps into the general constitutional-law theme that no property owner can demand compensation for risks that it assumed in the ordinary course of its business. The subtext is that notice of the regulatory scheme counts as a full acceptance of its consequences.

Unfortunately, this voluntarist account fails to achieve its objectives. To be sure, the argument works in those cases where a party receives a grant from the state that allows the property to be reclaimed by the government at any time, either at will or subject to some stated condition.[22] At that point the risk is assumed because the loss of property, no matter how great, takes place in accordance with the initial terms of the state grant. But the United States does not act pursuant to a grant under the Pharmaceutical Market Access and Drug Safety Act. The simple fact that pharmaceutical companies are left some residual choice under regulation does not make their decisions voluntary. The simplest counterexample is the robber who quite happily gives his victim a choice between her money and her life. He would prefer to get the money, and she would prefer to keep her life, so the bargain is struck that leaves each with his or her preferred asset. But the key inquiry here is not whether the victim made a rational choice under duress but whether the robber was entitled to put her to that choice in the first place. Since his victim was initially entitled to *both* her money *and* her life, this choice just represents an option to surrender the asset you value less. Treat it as legitimate for the robber to impose that choice, and civilization will fall in ruins by the repeated use of this simple tactic.

The options given pharmaceutical firms under the act are scarcely better. Start with the point that once the patents are issued, and the drugs approved for sale, any patent holder, in the pharmaceutical industry or beyond, enjoys the exclusive right to sell in all markets where that patent is lawful. The act says that the only way for the patentee to preserve that exclusive right in the United States is to forsake sales under patent in foreign markets. Nor, moreover, can any company avoid the sting of the act just by steering clear of the Canadian market. There is no real protection of prices on the home front so long as importation can take place from Australia, New Zealand, or the entire European Union. So at a minimum, the patentee has to ditch all of its foreign sales to keep the American market safe from infringing goods. Yet even that step turns out to be an illusory prophylactic, for other nations would quickly require the patent holders to sell in their markets at some administered price or face the risk of having the drug go generic, which only increases the risk of its low-cost importation.

In one similar case, *Philip Morris v. Reilly*, Massachusetts's Disclosure Act required Philip Morris to reveal its trade secrets about its cigarette additives if it wanted to continue to sell its cigarettes in the state.[23] The three judges on the federal circuit differed as to why and how this action constituted a taking but were unanimous in treating this requirement, imposed without any serious health or safety justification, as a compensable taking. The linchpin of this analysis is the elusive (and all too restrictive) tripartite test for a regulatory taking set out by the United States Supreme Court in *Penn Central v. City of New York*, which asks "(1) whether the government action may be properly said to interfere with 'the reasonable investment-backed expectation' of the owner; (2) the economic impact that the regulation has on the owner; and (3) the character of the government action."[24] This test is all too favorable to the government in that no one quite knows what content to give to "investment-backed expectation" that makes that phrase a tolerable translation for the term "private property," which has the virtue of a stable historical meaning that stresses the exclusive right of possession, use, and disposition of a particular thing.[25] That fuzziness of thought has worked real dislocation in dealing with the conditions that the Environmental Protection Agency may place upon its licenses, since the Supreme Court has said, erroneously, that the uncertainties of the basic approval process mean that no firm can protest if it is forced to surrender its trade secrets as a condition for receiving a drug license. After the passage of the statutory scheme, "Monsanto could not have had a reasonable, investment-backed expectation that EPA would keep the data confidential beyond the limits prescribed in the amended statute itself. Monsanto was on notice of the manner in which EPA was authorized to use and disclose any data turned over to it by an applicant for registration."[26] The notice provision is thought to count for assumption of risk within the regulatory framework of EPA. The FDA would have to be treated in the same fashion.

This reasoning is wrong in its own terms, for it assumes that the state can use its licensing power as a bargaining chip which allows it to exact whatever condition that it wishes to impose as a matter of right. But the license does not make the state a co-owner with the private owner, or give it any power to accept or reject transactions at will, which only owners have. Rather, it should be understood as a sensible public substitute for private injunctions against dangerous actions by other individuals. No individual could go to the state and ask for an injunction unless someone revealed its state secrets, and the EPA or FDA should not have that option when acting on behalf of those individuals whom the state seeks to protect, any more than they should be able to demand of potential licensees that they turn over the keys to factory A in order to gain permission to use factory B. The basic insight is that the only conditions on which it is proper to deny a permit are those which, if they came to pass, would in principle be actionable by the aggrieved parties—which is the case for pollution and similar woes.

This point has some real resonance in the case law, for the United States Supreme Court tiptoed around the *Monsanto* decision when it held that the state could not require a landowner to surrender a public walkway across the front of its house in order to gain a building permit for a large home, treating the connection as an "out-and-out" case of extortion.[27] And the same cautious attitude toward Monsanto was equally evident in *Reilly*, which struck down the Massachusetts Disclosure Act because it did not offer compensation for the lost value of the trade secret.

Yet even if *Monsanto* was correctly decided under the framework of the *Penn Central* case, it would not matter for these purposes. *Monsanto* dealt with the trade secrets of products that had yet to make it to market. S. 1392 deals with drugs that have already made it through both the Patent and Trade Office, and the FDA. If there is no investment backed expectation for those patents, then the phrase is entirely empty, for it will always be possible for the government to take any property for nothing by announcing early on its intention to do so. In this case therefore the investment-backed expectations are shattered. Yet the government interest in so doing does not advance any interest in health and safety—and in fact undermines those goals by exposing American consumers to higher risks of counterfeit products in exchange for the short term benefit of lower prices. The whole episode seems deeply ironic: the first business of government is to control risks to health and safety. Yet S. 1392 undercuts that end by using impermissible means.

Medicaid Restrictions

Fortunately, the constitutionality of these blunderbuss price-setting statutes has never been tested, because as of this writing they have never been passed. Yet the same issue arises in much more nuanced form in connection with more limited price controls. One notable instance comes from Maine—"An Act to Establish Fairer Pricing for Prescription Drugs."[28] This statute builds off Medicaid legislation that in general requires pharmaceutical firms to grant negotiated rebates for customers who acquire their medicines under Medicaid.[29] The basic logic behind the provision is that the federal subsidy was meant to ease the plight of poor patients, not to line the pockets of drug companies. Yet just that would happen if the companies could raise their prices at will to capture the full subsidy and more. The precise amount of the reductions in question is hard to decide in the abstract; the goal in principle should be to allow the firms to earn the same revenue they would obtain in the absence of the restriction. The Maine program added the peculiar requirement that the lower prices for the Medicaid recipients be extended to other individuals who were treated as needy, though they did not qualify for Medicaid. The stick for program compliance was that any firm that did not extend the rebate would find its drug no longer included in the Medicaid formulary, which meant it could only be ordered for patients upon special request. The effect of this provision is to slash the demand for the product.

The Supreme Court dealt with the Maine statute in *Pharmaceutical Research and Manufacturers of America v. Walsh*. The technical issue was whether the federal statute preempted the state program because Medicaid recipients would find it more difficult to obtain the drugs they needed if the state could impose this threat on suppliers. The Court punted on this issue, noting that the Health and Human Services Secretary had not declared an opinion on the state program.[30] But the lurking issue in this situation is whether any system of partial reduction in prices that is *not* used to offset a state subsidy should be regarded as a form of confiscation. It appears that such is the case.

Recall that initial patent right allowed for marketing as its owner saw fit. Now, however, a new set of regulations reduces the prices that can be charged without providing the kind of offset available in the Medicaid setting. The vested rights on *existing* patents should not be compromised in the end by restrictions on price not announced when the rights were first created. The restrictions have exactly the same effect as a government reduction in effective patent term without compensation. To do so is to remove, without compensation, part of the reward otherwise promised for the new invention. With respect to new innovations not yet patented, Congress should in principle be able to condition the patent on the patentee's willingness to accept price controls, just as it could shorten the patent term on a prospective basis. In sum, however, this analysis suggests price controls, for patents are often self-defeating or unconstitutional. The question is whether some policy can blunt the patent incentive to price above marginal cost without doing more mischief in hampering innovation than is alleviated in pricing competitively. On balance, it doesn't look like Congress can accomplish this feat.

One local form of price controls deserves some brief mention as well. In the past year the District of Columbia passed the Prescription Drug Excessive Pricing Act of 2005.[31] Its operative provision gave no definition of an excessive price but created a presumption that any price should count as excessive if it were "over 30% higher than the comparable price in any high income country in which the product is protected by patents or other exclusive marketing rights."[32] The high-income countries were the United Kingdom, Germany, Canada, and Australia. The statutory presumption could be rebutted only by an elaborate and costly showing that the drug prices were justified in light of the cost of its development, global sales, and profits, public funding for research, and impact on the citizens and government of the District of Columbia.[33] There was no glimmer of recognition that the revenues from successful products have to cover the costs of unsuccessful ventures.

The Excessive Pricing Act, moreover, carried with it an enormous threat to innovation, because outside buyers could flock to the District of Columbia to take advantage of these low prices. The act also improperly negated the pricing authority that federal patent law normally gives to patent holders, and offered no guarantee that its procedures would supply a reasonable rate of return on initial investment. Fortunately, the district court sidestepped these thorny issues in invalidating the act. Its key provision made it "unlawful for any drug manufacturer or licensee thereof, *excluding a point of sale retailer,* to sell or supply" that patented drug.[34] The italicized phrase sought to immunize local sellers from regulations aimed at out-of-state manufacturers and their licensees. Accordingly, the district court struck down the statute on two conventional grounds. First, the district court held that the statute was preempted by federal law because "the D.C. Act, as drafted, is a clear obstacle to the accomplishment and execution of the purpose and objectives set by Congress in passing federal patent laws relating to prescription drugs."[35] Second, the district court held that the D.C. act impermissibly sought to exercise its powers beyond its jurisdiction as applied to commerce that took place solely outside its borders.[36] In a real sense, the truly striking feature was the willingness of the District of Columbia to pass this statute, not of the district court to strike it down.

The isolated nature of the District's ill-fated initiative raises other troubling questions about its place in the federal system. If the District is able to impose these restrictions, then a parallel right inheres in every other state; yet there is no mechanism to coordinate these various proceedings, which only opens the door to further abuse. In addition, it is hard to see how the provision could be limited to the benefit of the citizens within the District, when resale to anywhere in the United States, or for that matter, the world seems hard to prevent. In addition, international obligations under the TRIPS agreement (Trade Related Aspects of Intellectual Property) echo the strong property rights perspective of American property law, which entertains only a narrow exception that allows "nations to exclude from patentability inventions, the prevention of which is necessary to protect *ordre public* or morality," which does not translate into allowing a disregard for patents because prices are thought too high.[37]

Viewed at a distance, the whole system seems to be so bizarre that it is scarcely worth further comment. It only shows the lengths to which some groups are prepared to go to undermine the system of property rights that have made innovation possible in the first place. It bears stating one more time that the adverse effects of any system of price controls are not only felt by the pharmaceutical houses, their shareholders, employees, and suppliers. It is borne in part by the public which will see the supply of new products dry up under the restrictions. The pharmaceutical business may feature patents that create monopoly, but so long as these are not acquired by a wave of the hand, everyone will cut back investment to reflect the low valuation that any system of price controls, however convoluted and indirect, imposes on the system. It is a mug's game that cannot be won here any more than with price controls on gasoline or rent controls on apartments.

9

PATENT PURCHASES: A SECOND SWAMP

Apart from the price-control schemes just considered, a common proposal for improving the patent system relies on government purchases of pharmaceutical patents, either by voluntary or by compulsory process, to overcome the monopoly problem. Many pharmaceutical patents have huge value—billions in sales for a single year—so we do not have to face the problem of purchasing literally thousands of minor patents, when the cost of implementing any voluntary- or compulsory-purchase regime is likely to swamp the value of the patents so acquired. With this advantage, the argument for some form of government buyout runs as follows. We need to keep the patent system to preserve the incentive to create; we then purchase, by condemnation if necessary, the patent, which is duly placed in the public domain for all to freely use. The upshot is that consumers can acquire patented products at marginal cost from a sufficient number of competitive suppliers. The deadweight losses associated with patent protection are therefore eliminated by the purchase. The implicit subtext of the claim is that the costs of running this acquisition system are smaller than these deadweight losses.

This scheme for patent purchase has clear historical antecedents. Commentators first developed the proposal to introduce marginal-cost pricing as a response to the monopoly problems associated with public utilities, such as power plants, waterworks, electrical utilities, and even railroads. In this context the government funded the fixed costs of public utility creation in order to bring the price down to marginal cost.[1]

These schemes have by and large been rejected for public utilities on the simple ground that any effort to eliminate the dislocations in one area only creates dislocations elsewhere. As John Duffy has aptly written: "In short, modern public utility theorists generally do not recommend using pervasive public subsidies to chase the Holy Grail of global marginal cost pricing."[2] That skepticism should carry over to drug pricing. Patent-purchase proposals suffer from an excess of ambition that, while identifying the obvious Achilles' heel of the patent system, overestimates benefits and underestimates the costs of the various alternatives. Part of the answer to this challenge is contained in the previous section, in which I identified the ways the current law mitigates the dislocations patents create. In turn, these limits reduce the need to wrest individual patents out of private hands. The rest of the answer lies in a fuller appreciation of the difficulties in running a system of either voluntary or forced purchases, each with its own obstacles. Let me deal with the voluntary system first and then turn to a compulsory system.

Voluntary Purchases

One way to move patents into the public domain is for the government to purchase them from any pharmaceutical house willing to sell at a mutually agreeable price.[3] Successful transactions of this sort should counter the deadweight-loss problem without creating new ones in its stead. Since the transaction is voluntary, the patentee cannot protest the transaction. Since the state knows what it is doing, the public is better off as well. The move looks to be win-win, but only if it can overcome— which it can't—some formidable obstacles, which I will discuss in turn.

First, an Excess Burden Either Way

The chief reason for adopting the marginal cost approach is to eliminate the loss of beneficial transactions arising whenever price is set above marginal cost. But welfare loss when price exceeds marginal cost applies regardless of the source of the gap. Thus a tax that raises price above marginal cost by X dollars has the same effect on the buyers of the goods as a monopolist who raises that cost by X dollars. The difference between the two regimes does not affect the willingness of buyers to enter the market. It only determines *who* receives the payments in question: the government in the case of taxation, the seller in the case of a public utility or patent monopoly. Once this point is recognized, in general equilibrium the only choice is whether to concentrate this excess burden (the lost transactions due to the rise in prices) on the patented product or to spread it out across the full range of goods and services that must be taxed to raise the money for the transfer payment.[4]

As a first approximation, relative size of welfare loss under these two scenarios looks to be about the same. But in this case, this optimistic assumption will probably not hold. As will become clear, a voluntary-purchase system for pharmaceutical patents is likely to be every bit as complex as the vast enterprise of public utility rate regulation, which generates numbing complexities of its own. Hence this heavy dose of administrative costs increases the total excess burden. Thus the ultimate choice is between a larger deadweight loss spread out over many goods and services or a smaller one concentrated on particular patents. If this were the only trade-off involved, the switch that brings patents into the public domain would be at best dubious from the point of view of overall social welfare. But, of course, other factors lurk in the background of this unknown venture.

Second, Which Patents Are Acquired?

Let us suppose that we wish to go forward with some program of voluntary acquisition. Which patents, if any, should be acquired under this process? In part this answer will depend on the budget Congress allocates to the process, which would be difficult to set for a patent acquisition process that has never been tried. But at a guess, it seems virtually certain that no sensible government would take title to all patented drugs. So which ones should the government acquire and why?

This situation is made more complicated because typically many drugs in the same class are patented at about the same time. The developer of a new drug (say, a statin) that knows it faces one patented market competitor can adjust its pricing estimations to take into account that single source of competition. It thinks of the market as an (imperfect) duopoly. But what should it do if the government enters into extensive negotiations with both firms, while planning to buy only one patent to place in the public domain? At this point, the firm that retains its patent has to compete from day one with a drug priced at or near generic levels. That creation of a generic substitute necessarily reduces the price the second firm can charge for its own patented product. The second company, of course, will be alert to this danger and should therefore now be willing to sell its patent for less than it could have fetched in a private marketplace that contained two patented drugs. After all, it does not want to be left behind with a near-valueless patent. If the government-purchase threat reduces the combined revenues from both sources—patent sales to the government and market sales—for both patented products, the incentive to innovate will dissipate more rapidly than it would if the public domain competition arose only after the expiration of the normal patent period. The incentives of the patent system may not, therefore, be successfully preserved with selective voluntary purchases. Patentees as a class no longer take the same income stream as before, but only in lump-sum form. Rather, the overall size of the revenue stream for patent owners diminishes, and the total amount of investment declines.

Third, When Is the Purchase Made?

Public utility regulation usually sets rates for a particular period, say a year, and then revises the rates over time as the relevant costs vary. This system is by no means easy to operate, but at least its outcome does not depend on a single roll of the dice. In addition, regulated industries tend to be relatively stable over time, so that the permissible rates of return often fall within a tolerably narrow band. The situation with patents, however, is far different. Patents are by definition wasting assets, so that the likely pattern of purchase will cover the patent for its entire useful life. How should this transfer be structured? Unlike public utility regulation, no one has any real experience in negotiating a transaction of this magnitude. Yet the range of issues on the table is legion.

Start with the question of timing: does the transaction take place before or after the drug has received its initial FDA approval? The advantage of going early is that it reduces the price paid for the patent product. But the disadvantages seem still more pronounced. Taking over a patent then leaves in limbo the question of who will shepherd the drug through the FDA approval process. To place that task in the hands of the government raises immense conflicts of interest. Does the government application get a preferred place in the queue relative to private parties? Does the government have to hire some kind of an expeditor to move the new drug application through the system? Are any downward adjustments made to the purchase price if the FDA approval is postponed or denied? Any upward adjustments if new clinical uses for the patented product are identified before, or after, it reaches the market? In general, a transaction of this complexity cannot take the form of a "clean deal," in which each party goes its separate way after the basic transfer has taken place.

So now the transaction has to be moved to the postapproval process. But that shift in time does not remove the potential conflicts of interest. The question of whether the United States chooses through one of its agencies to acquire a particular drug will still be a matter under extensive discussion before the patent process or FDA process is complete. How could anyone ignore the progress of so public a process? The issue of favoritism for government products does not evaporate because FDA approval has been obtained. The presence of a government interest in one of several new compounds will have a profound effect on the competitive balance among private parties; the scope of either the patent or the FDA approval necessarily influences the appropriate sales price. As before, it is asking for trouble to place the United States in the dual role of regulator and product owner.

Other conflicts remain because of the inherent risks of approved drugs. Just think of the difficulties that will arise if the drug patent is invalidated in whole or in part once the transaction is concluded, or if the patented drug is removed from the market for health and safety reasons after the purchase price is paid but before the patent life has expired. Indeed, no one would know whether the United States, if inundated with individual suits, could claim various forms of immunity from tort liability for its role in bringing the new drug to market. The blunt truth is that in a world of continuous regulatory oversight over both patent and safety issues, there is no good time to consummate the transaction. It seems much safer to keep the government out of any dual role. On this score, remember that the government has *no* dual role with respect to generic drugs once the patents have expired. The difference between public domain and state ownership matters.

Fourth, How Is Price Determined?

Any decision on which patent to purchase depends on whether both sides have sufficient information about the full transaction to be confident that it leaves them better off than before. Yet just how is any patent to be valued? Start with the negotiation over price. At this point, each side will have some information the other does not. The individual firm will know about its full portfolio of projects and can sense whether these projects will add to or detract from the value of the patent sold. In addition, the private value of the patent depends on such collateral matters as trade names, know-how, and marketing plans. The first is not likely to be included in the purchase (which generic manufacturer would use the name?) and the last may be obsolete if the patent is eliminated. In some cases, the second may be important to the patent-production process. However, the firm might be unwilling to reveal or sell know-how, which has to be separately valued, if that know-how is also used for other drugs or projects not put up for sale.

The purchase transaction, therefore, need not involve solely a patent. The parties must address lots of complementary assets, as is the case in normal voluntary transactions. The set of contingencies is vast, but the parties will indubitably seek to do something to reduce the uncertainty. The usual strategies are for the transaction to have a flotilla of warranties and recitals, some of which are conditions for the deal and others of which are not. The choice of price, which is hard enough to determine when terms are constant, becomes far more difficult in light of the variation in surrounding terms. Some drugs might have, as a first approximation, prices in excess of $25 billion, which propels the transaction into the same class as megamergers. There is no reason to believe that these large transactions could be (or should be) consummated, given the heavy tax burden in calculating gain and loss, and the uncertain rate of return.

If these transactions are as complicated as I have suggested—and they are probably more so—the use of auctions will provide no magic bullet. Nevertheless, one proposal, suggested by Michael Kremer, calls for a system whereby individual firms could be encouraged to put their patents up for bid, with private parties as the bidders.[5] In most cases the government would acquire the patent for the price of the winning bidder. But to ensure that the bidders have incentives for honest valuation, the government would require they take the patent for themselves in a fixed percentage of cases, say 15 percent. In essence, the monopoly problem would be eliminated only in those cases in which the government is able to free-ride on the privately generated information.

These concerns with implementation, however, remain truly insuperable because auctions can be held only after someone else settles all the collateral issues on terms mentioned above. Try as one may, the only auctions that work are those in which the bidding is over a single dimension—namely, the price. The result is achievable when a house is put up for sale, or even when a block of spectrum, which can be precisely described by the frequency equivalents of metes and bounds, is available. In these defined contexts, auctions neatly truncate the process of sale and usually allow an asset to move quickly to the user with the highest value. For that reason, using auctions in allocating spectrum or broadcast frequencies surely tops the current administrative system of public hearings and useless criteria to solve the allocation problem. To be sure, the willingness to pay in one transaction may be influenced by the prices that are paid for other lots that are for sale in the same auction. Furthermore, the entire question could become mired in complex bankruptcy proceedings if the successful bidder is unable to complete the purchase because the market has turned.

Yet all these problems are child's play compared to what is at stake with respect to a patent (and its associated intellectual property). The key warning sign is simple: private firms act with extreme caution when they engage in any sale or auction of patent rights, even though no legal auction stands in their way. Occasionally transactions do arise in which patent royalties are sold. Usually these involve intensive competitive bidding on products, after launch, that have a known financial track record. In one highly publicized transaction, for example, Emory University sold its royalty interest in Emtriva for $525 million. One distinctive feature of the transaction was that its lead buyer, Gilead Sciences, Inc., was the commercial developer of the product.[6] Major pharmaceutical patents, especially in the early stages of their development, are rarely sold individually. Typically, their transfer, to the extent that it takes place, is through mergers and acquisitions, in which shares—which reflect in part the value of a diversified patent portfolio—are acquired. What firm could take a valuable patent, subject it to an untested pricing system, and hope to resist the derivative suits disgruntled shareholders would bring as share price plunges?

The firm would face several pitfalls in its quest for sale. At a minimum, any prospective buyer has to be able to inspect the operations and records of the seller to understand how to make a bid. While a firm might use rigorous confidentiality contracts to share information with one potential purchaser, it would probably not place that information on a Web site for the world to see. And even if it did, the question remains of who would bid. In a full market, several dozen patents may be for sale (in some configuration) at any one time. The bids tendered on one patent will depend heavily on both the results in other auctions and the financial commitments, if any, a particular bidder undertakes by winning an auction. Furthermore, most individual firms probably could not afford to bid on patents. Pooling arrangements would create serious problems of antitrust liability. If that hurdle were surmounted, the few remaining bidders would create a thin market, in which the auction price could be as inaccurate as it sometimes is in the much simpler foreclosure market for ordinary single-family homes. Finally, who will spend millions in preparing a bid if most of the time, the victory produces no tangible result except a pat on the back by the United States?

Fifth, Subsequent Commercialization

The patent acquisition programs face yet another obstacle. Who promotes and pushes the generic product once it reaches the marketplace? The situation is quite different from that which arises after a patented product becomes generic. At that point, the previous owner has done a huge amount of work to promote the drug and to make it visible to the market. The generic manufacturers are not in the business of persuading potential customers to take drugs that they have never used before. Instead, they are in the business of persuading customers, often hospitals or health plans, that they should purchase the generic equivalent of a previously used patented drug at lower prices.

In the initial-sale market, in contrast, no one can piggyback on the original efforts of the patentee. None of these companies will seek to promote and advertise the drug when it knows that a large fraction of the sales will go to other firms that make the same product but do not incur the same expenses. Stated otherwise, it is difficult to know how competition will arise in a market in which no potential seller has any distinctive market component. It is, in a word, a rerun of the original Bayh-Dole debate over the question of whether to encourage patenting as a way of getting new products into the market. If Bayh-Dole is right, then this approach looks to be wrong. In this context, moreover, any uncertainty is fatal: if the government experts are not sure that a new drug launch is done better by a group of generic firms than by a single proprietor, then how could they recommend that the government incur the huge cost and uncertainty to switch from one form of production to the other? The entire grand enterprise seems to fall of its own weight.

Even if this experiment were undertaken, we would face the same problem that arose in the original marginal-cost controversy in connection with public utilities. Suppose you could build for $1 million a bridge that can be operated at zero cost. How should the owner charge for the property? One possibility is to pick some positive price X dollars, which allows the owner to recover the total costs of its initial investment. However reasonable that scheme looks, it is not perfect. There are individuals who value the use of the price at greater than zero dollars (its marginal cost) but less than its price, X dollars. They are excluded from this market even though ideally it would be better if they could use the bridge. In order to cure that problem, one possibility is to open the bridge for free. Only now we face the flip side of the original problem. If we take the total consumer surplus (that is, net satisfaction, since marginal cost in this hypothetical is zero dollars), we do not know whether it was worthwhile to build the bridge in the first place—or to purchase the patent. In both cases, it will be exceedingly difficult to know whether the government paid too much or too little, because the new channels of free distribution make it far harder to value the product after state acquisition than if it generated a revenue stream. With a zero price for the patented material, it is easy to assume that all users value it above marginal cost. It is impossible, however, to determine whether they value it at a sum that in aggregate covers its fixed cost, whatever that may be. At the level of theory and at the level of operations, the voluntary program is a nonstarter.

Compulsory Purchases

The condemnation power offers yet another way to acquire patents, either before or after FDA approval. After 9/11 the United States entered into extensive negotiations with Bayer, the holder of the patent on ciprofloxacin, for purchases of large quantities of the drug, useful in the treatment of anthrax. When the negotiations broke down, many commentators suggested that the government should adopt a system of compulsory purchase of the needed quantities, or just condemn outright the patent, which had about six months left to run.[7] This approach would have been terrible because the condemnation threat is a club that can be used to force firms to submit to losing market transactions. But ironically, that particular condemnation proposal would also have been a disaster for the United States, because the anthrax scare did not pan out: what if the patent had been condemned and generics had been rushed into production? Standard law requires that the government compensate for the taking with the value of the patent at the time of the taking. This compensation would have been a bonanza for Bayer; the large lump sum payment, however, would not have survived the political outrage that would have been triggered once the anthrax scare fizzled.

The difficulties from this simple case suggest the difficulties of any compulsory scheme. Even if we put the particular case aside, this system will still contain many of the problems that face the voluntary-purchase scheme outlined above: the excess-burden question still remains; it is still necessary to decide which patents should be acquired for public use, to recognize that the condemnation of any single drug or device reduces the commercial value of substitute products that remain under patent, to address the hard issues of commercialization once the licensing has occurred. But in principle, the compulsory approach would eliminate serious holdout problems of the sort that might have arisen with Cipro. In addition, the use of condemnation could avoid the risk of having the government overpay for patents in the voluntary market.

Yet the elimination of one risk only creates another. With both compulsory licenses and condemnation, the crux of the difficulty is public valuation. To put the problem into perspective, it is necessary to recap first the constitutional protection afforded to takings of private property. The applicable constitutional text reads: "nor shall private property be taken for public use, without just compensation."[8] The cleverest reform that fails to meet that constitutional standard will be dead on arrival. But the reason for dwelling on this text does not rest solely on some fastidious devotion to constitutional norms. Rather, it rests also on the broader claim that the constitutional mandate is powerfully congruent with a sound social program for the use of state compulsion. The basic economic logic proceeds as follows: Initially, patents, like other forms of intellectual property, count as private property protected under the Constitution.[9] Of course, Congress need not, in the first instance, exercise its power to create any regime for patents or copyrights; a power is not the same as a duty.[10] But once Congress puts some patent regime into place, the Takings Clause protects patents created under the regime as much as any other form of property, whether land, corporate stock, or trade secrets.

The prudential question, to which the Constitution does not speak, is *when* should the use of state power bring privately held property into public hands for public use? As a matter of social welfare, that transfer of rights should take place only if the value of the particular asset to the public exceeds its value in private hands. Otherwise, the state uses its power to transfer assets from higher- to lower-value uses, forcing all citizens to pick up the tab. The insistence that the United States pay just compensation for the property in question is an effective way to achieve (but not guarantee) the objective of using state coercion only when it moves the property taken to a more valuable use. If the property in public hands is not worth the price, proponents of the transfer will find it difficult (but not necessarily impossible) to organize a winning coalition to fund its acquisition. The prospect of a clear social gain, on the other hand, should make that coalition easier to organize. The shortfalls in the political process, moreover, should be laid not at the doorstep of the Takings Clause, but at the political ground rules governing taxation and expenditures, which today operate free of any effective constitutional limitation.[11] How then does the Takings Clause interact with existing patents?

First, the Constitution, as (mis)construed today, places no serious limitation on the state's ability to force the surrender of a patent in exchange for just compensation, so long as the program has some "conceivable" public benefit.[12] That test has become the focal point of public controversy in connection with the recent Supreme Court decision in *Kelo v. City of New London,* which by a 5–4 vote authorized the use of the power to take ordinary private homes for the possible future benefit of private developers.[13] But the controversy that swirls around that decision is of no moment here. The generic production of any drug surely counts as a taking for public use, even under standards that are both stricter and more sensible than those in place today. On any view, therefore, the nub of the inquiry is just compensation for the property so taken. The myriad proposals for forced purchases of patents are united in only one feature: they are blissfully unaware of the endless valuation questions raised even when it is conceded that the government has taken private property. Justice Holmes set the stage, correctly, by noting that the basic compensation standard measures "what has the owner lost, not what has the taker gained."[14] Only by following this rule is it likely that condemnation will take place in those cases, and only those cases, where it improves social welfare. On the one hand, if land is worth $20,000 in private hands but $100,000 when put to a distinctive public use, the state does not have to pay the full gain to the original owner of the property. Conversely, without this rule, the state could take a plot of land worth $100,000 to its owner for only $20,000 if that were its value in public hands.

Unfortunately, the true salience of this maxim in actual condemnation cases lies in the details of its application. The usual measure in these cases is the market value of the land, which is typically measured by the amount a willing buyer will pay a willing seller—assuming one can be found.[15] That figure, of course, always *under*estimates the loss to the owner, because in most well-organized markets, the property is typically owned by the person who values it most. The decision to compensate at some stated market value in effect allows the property to be taken for an amount that does not reflect its best and highest use. After all, no buyer in the voluntary market is prepared to pay what the current owner would ask. Under the current legal formulation, all distinctive and subjective elements of value are deemed beyond measurement, and thus treated as having zero value.

Nor does this formula compensate fully, even in the simplest cases of vacant but developable land. Investments in off-site infrastructure, design studies, and marketing plans are today not compensable because they don't count as part of "the property" taken.[16] Nor does one include in the property taken any site-specific goodwill, nontransferable licenses, or other similar assets.[17] The standard rules require that attorney and appraisal fees be borne by the condemnee as well.[18] The denial of recovery for the full range of "consequential" damages necessarily leaves an owner worse off than had he been allowed to retain the property. Other complications arise when the property taken is part of a larger constellation of assets, some of which lose their value by virtue of the loss of the complementary assets through condemnation. Today the law falls far short of Blackstone's dictum that condemnations should proceed "not by absolutely stripping the subject of his property in an arbitrary manner; but by giving him a full indemnification and *equivalent for the injury thereby sustained*."[19] Instead, undercompensation becomes the institutionalized norm. The fierce resistance of many landowners to condemnation is explained by the simple observation that they are left worse off by the government action.

All these issues will surface in one way or another in connection with the proposed condemnation of a complex pharmaceutical patent. We should start with the most elementary question of how these products should be valued. Robert C. Guell and Marvin Fischbaum propose "that the government buy prescription drug patents at a price equaling the net present value of the profit they would have generated and distribute the patents to U.S. drug manufacturers."[20] The proposal is, and always will be, unworkable. As noted earlier, the touchstone for usual condemnation cases is the amount at which the property would change hands in a voluntary transaction. But pharmaceutical patents are rarely sold back and forth between firms like buildings or plots of land. Thus they have no readily identifiable market price. Instead, at each stage, new players agree to commit some resources to a particular task under an agreement that calls for an appropriate share in the proceeds as they emerge later. To be sure, people have at least some sense of what the potential range of returns might be before entering these agreements. But they do not have to fix a once-and-for-all price on the patent in advance of how the valuation question plays out. Yet the condemnation system, which insists on a single valuation for an outright transfer, tries to do in an adversarial setting what business partners never attempt in a cooperative setting. The determination invites litigation that could easily consume much of the value of the patent.

One strategy used to value real property in condemnation hearings looks at the market value of properties comparable to that which is taken. Those comparisons are not available in the restricted universe of patent transfers. Hence the only way to value these patents is to roll out highly technical and hopelessly unreliable quantitative valuation techniques. This analysis cannot be content to estimate revenues from a stable business in setting value; instead, the judgments in question give rise to sharply discontinuous outcomes. Think of some of the possibilities. The drug in question may face unanticipated competitors in its own class; the drug may be topped by a new generation of competitors that rely on a superior mechanism for the same result; or the drug may prove to be effective in combination with other drugs or medical treatments not yet on the market, some of which may be in development by the patent holder and some not. Furthermore, the drug may be recalled because of serious dangers that would have exposed the current patentee to serious tort liability or loss of goodwill, not only for the drug itself, but for its entire product line. Running a condemnation case like this could consume an inordinate amount of expert time and resources, which are better devoted to product development.

The problems, of course, run deeper because the drug in question does not simply sell itself while in private hands. Extensive expenditures in marketing and brand management are part of the day. In principle, these costs are avoided if the federal government takes over the drug before the firm incurs them. But they, too, have to be discounted to current value when their scope is heavily dependent upon the initial reception the drug receives in the marketplace. We thus have to reduce an unknowable future revenue stream and an uncertain set of avoidable costs. Atop all these valuation questions remains the treatment of those business costs current law assiduously excludes from the compensation base: legal fees, appraisal fees, loss of goodwill, loss in the value of private proprietary information from the proprietary situation, to name a few. The errors will be huge.

Guell and Fischbaum are aware of these problems in fixing net profits, and they propose a mixed solution in which the drug is marketed on a limited basis in a test area in order to supply some data points on valuation.[21] But these data themselves would be hopelessly tainted because the pharmaceutical company will be tempted to overstate its profits by shifting revenues and cost, in order to maximize the value of any future award. Nor do sales data from a select, and perhaps nonrepresentative, market give any clue as to the contingencies that depend on future events, not current revenues. Other proposals, most notably one from Steven Shavell and Tanguy van Ypersele, seek to avoid this difficulty by finding the level of social surplus that one anticipates from a given invention.[22] This level becomes the measure of compensation for the patent. Good luck. It is easier to bottle quarks. Shavell and van Ypersele's model presupposes that firms have some knowledge of the overall demand for their products, which in the early stages of patent life is subject to all the uncertainties of fortune that block valuation under the more traditional formulas.[23] Condemnation hearings cannot work where the object of valuation falls in the class of elusive nonobservables.

10

SOCIALIZATION OF R&D: THE FINAL SWAMP

The difficulties with mandated devices have led to yet another approach to eliminating the deadweight losses of patent monopolies. This commendable, if unsuccessful, effort need not kick in only after new patentable chemical entities have been discovered. We could instead adopt a still more ambitious program that seeks to co-opt the patent process altogether. Thus Peter Stein and Ernst Valery recently proposed that instead of relying exclusively on private firms to produce patentable drugs, the government enter into this market by expanding the research activities of the National Institutes for Health. Stein and Valery take this middle position because they acknowledge that a variety of obstacles stand in the path of excluding private research firms from seeking patent protection for their own research invention.[1] Furthermore, the TRIPS agreement requires a steadfast preservation of a patent regime. At the same time, any public institution has to be funded and organized from scratch to undertake the search for patentable products to put into the public domain.

In an effort to skirt these difficulties, Stein and Valery propose that an expanded NIH compete directly with current private firms, with the understanding that its inventions would grant "royalty-free, nonexclusive manufacturing/marketing licenses for domestic sales to all qualified producers."[2] Sales to foreign operations (which contribute nothing to the domestic funding), on the other hand, could be done on a commercial basis. This foreign-domestic distinction, however, is a key reason for patenting the inventions instead of putting them into the public domain. In the authors' view, the NIH has already proved its mettle by organizing high-quality basic research, and this expertise could continue to work in the area of commercialization. The recent conflict-of-interest imbroglio suggests that this proposal has been overtaken by events, for the rigid rules against consulting agreements and stock positions would not be available to fuel initiative in the public sector. Putting these conflicts of interest aside, the problems are still multifaceted.

One obvious question the authors address is the public price tag required to keep the flow of new drugs at its present level. To make that estimate, they start with the estimated amounts of research expenditures incurred by private companies, which the industry reported at just under $20 billion in 2000. Stein and Valery reduce that amount to $15.1 billion based on the estimate of Uwe Reinhardt.[3] In the first instance, they claim independent evidence suggesting that the pharmaceutical houses have overestimated the amount of money they spend on research. They conclude that a smaller base is thus appropriate for figuring out the direct level of social support needed. The authors then take the position, which I have disputed above, that all me-too drugs are socially wasteful. Consequently, the government can avoid the huge private investment in these molecular entities in the search for pioneer therapeutics that yield (but only when they work well) much higher social rates of return. In their view, a heavy portion of firm research has been devoted to activities that are privately beneficial but socially wasteful. They envision a 60 percent savings in output, which further reduces the costs in question, realizing savings at a level for which we can only dream, but never count on.

I am not the first to think this proposal is, if anything, more risky than the purchase postinvention schemes criticized above. The initial point depends not on the particulars of this scheme but on a general view of the difficulties of radical transformations, especially those engineered by governments. They always sound easier in principle than they are in practice. The current scheme has defects evident from years of working in a system in which price is consistently above marginal cost. But any critique of the distribution of pharmaceutical products is heavily dependent on matters located *outside* the patent system, which could, and should, be addressed by other means. For example, third-party insurance (especially when supplied by government) certainly creates a risk of overconsumption that touches some prescription drugs. But don't lay that problem at the doorstep of the patent system. The same argument applies with respect to all medical treatments and to the purchase of generic goods. The solutions, if any, to these myriad problems rely on the reform of collateral institutions, and I shall not attempt to resolve them here. I will note, however, that the departure from market principles (for example, insurance mandates, price controls), not the strict adherence to them, creates most of the problems.[4] It never makes sense to cure the problems in one system (the public support for health care services generally) by attacking a second system (pharmaceutical patents).

The second point is that before one thinks about the introduction of a public corrective system, it is critical to have some sense of the social loss of the current system. Deadweight losses will always occur; as noted earlier, if scientific research is funded by taxation, the government has only transferred them to other regions. The matter is more urgent because of the need to have a good estimate of the amount of deadweight losses in the pharmaceutical industry. As a general economic proposition, any field that has four or more competitors does not face a serious monopoly problem. Entry has cured most of the problem; potential entry can cure the rest. In some pharmaceutical markets, we do not have that luxury; but in others, the presence of me-too drugs reduces the deadweight loss from monopoly. Any effort to steer research away from these products is not an unalloyed good because these expenditures should not be considered a social waste any more than the presence on the market of four kinds of automobiles or breakfast cereals. And even if we adopted such a misguided philosophy, we would be hard-pressed to implement it. The pharmaceutical market is far more variegated than the Stein and Valery proposal admits. Some product lines are competitive today; others may well be tomorrow. Any decision on funding particular lines of research could easily produce generic products in heavily competitive niches down the road.

Stein and Valery compound this problem by systematically underestimating the systematic gains from the patent system. In their view, all patent races are wasteful. As they analyze the situation, the social value obtained from granting the patent is never commensurate with the length of the patent term, but is reflected only with the difference between the time the first party made the invention and the time of its nearest competitor. That result is correct only if we assume that the measure of social benefit is the difference in filing times for the first and second competitors. But it is a grievous error to ignore the influence the patent system has on the time the race begins, or on the stock of other useful inventions that help to move matters along. If the whole development curve is advanced by several years, it is the earlier onset of the race to produce the new invention, not the gap between the first and second contestants, that gives some measure of the worth of the patent. That time differential could be huge even if any time differential between the first and second claimant is tiny.

The point is not confined to pharmaceutical patents, moreover, but applies across the board. If government-sponsored research were appropriate because of the demand for instant generic pharmaceuticals, that same argument would apply to all patentable inventions. But so long as universal public funding of inventive activity is a financial impossibility, the deadweight losses of the patent system have to be shown to be greater with pharmaceuticals than anywhere else. And on that key question, Stein and Valery do not present a shred of evidence. Indeed, most independent observers are much more conflicted about the use of small patents in the software business than they are about composition patents in pharmaceuticals. The useful life of these software patents is generally far shorter, and the risk that they will create blocking positions seems greater than it is with pharmaceuticals, where the market is characterized by a smaller number of highly valuable patents.

The problems with the Stein and Valery scheme are not confined to their misspecification of how the present system works. Rather, that shortfall in their analysis is compounded by the regrettable confusion over how any research system, including one with government sponsorship, works. The problems here are endemic both to all forms of government research, and to the pharmaceutical industry in particular.

More specifically, their proposal is ignorant of the public-choice problems that crop up whenever government agencies are given broad spending mandates. Large and powerful interest groups will often grow up in response to the newfound government target, and they will influence the way government revenues are spent. But who will make those decisions on the basis of nonmarket criteria which have yet to be developed? The history of the public distribution of either cash or in-kind resources is not encouraging.

The closest illustration relates to the 1946 decision of the Atomic Energy Commission to rely on a system of rewards to deal with patents relating to the use of atomic energy. As Joseph DiMasi and Henry Grabowski have recently pointed out, however, in their rebuttal of a similar proposal by Tim Hubbard and James Love (to which I shall turn presently), the history of weapons procurement under this system proved anything but impressive, with a government monopoly offering "miserly" rewards for patents of tremendous value.[5] This result should surprise nobody, given the incentives on government officers to avoid being labeled spendthrifts in the Congress and press.

With this track record of government performance in various direct industrial situations, one should not think the NIH, whose best work is carrying out and funding basic research, will have the ability to identify and hire the people skilled at sniffing out commercial opportunities that depend on the interaction of current scientific know-how and future market demands. The differences among the various missions (and the cultures needed to sustain them) are critical and manifest themselves in many ways. The usual commercial laboratories develop incentive programs to ensure that the scientists who engage in successful discovery gain a fraction of the future profits. If the government decides to issue royalty-free patents, it could not use this traditional form of commercial compensation. Since (as with the bridge that is built from public funds) no one can figure out the value of a patent when it is distributed at zero price, it becomes difficult, if not impossible, to construct a shadow pricing system on which to reward inventors.[6] If the entire system of compensation that private firms use cannot be used within the public sector, why should we think the discovery process that takes place there will do as well as on the private side, even if the distortions from political influence are put to one side?

The Stein and Valery proposal also assumes that the appropriate investment path concentrates on pioneer drugs only. But why does that make sense? Suppose one fruitful line of research indicates that patentable substances are close substitutes for each other. The well-managed private firm might pursue multiple paths. How could the public firm avoid doing the same? After all, it does not know at the outset which of the multiple compounds will work, and hence it would be foolish to put one aside before another is fully established. But if the multiple projects are on parallel paths, it makes sense to invest small sums of money, relatively speaking, for the second product once the first is developed, especially since both could founder in clinical trials that have yet to occur.

It is also critical to make some judgment on the effect of these public funds on activities elsewhere in the market. The argument parallels those that surround selective purchase or condemnation of one drug of a particular class. Target research to attack a market served today by a patented drug, and slow development means that the newer product could reach the market only when the first product has gone generic. Invest in a new line of research today, and there is the further question of whether any private firm will take up parallel research if it knows its proprietary drug will have to go into competition not with another patent product but with an instant generic that could undersell it, even if less effective clinically. Or perhaps the firm will gamble that it can get its patented drug out before the government. But there is no reason to think that adjustments made on the private side will be efficient so long as they have to respond to the fundamental difficulty of trying to run a commercial operation against a subsidized one. Yet nothing in the Stein and Valery proposal asks whether additional *subsidized* competition should be treated with the same enthusiasm as unsubsidized competition. Those who believe in a level playing field will have serious doubts.

Furthermore, the Stein and Valery proposal fails to appreciate that the requirements of successful scientific research differ sharply from those needed to run even a well-oiled NIH. The NIH does not have any of the expertise in house to deal with the relevant issues. It does not have the needed libraries of basic molecules that aid in the synthesis of new drugs. It has no expertise in the techniques needed to speed up the production of those molecules that are shown to have desired properties. It does not have experience in organizing a licensing system, or in preserving trade secrets. From a distance its skill set may look like that of the present companies, whose expertise differs substantially one from the other. But up close these differences loom so much larger to one who is faced with the challenge of running a successful business. The NIH would have to set up shop from scratch, without the slightest reason to think that it knows what it is doing.

Finally, there are serious questions as to how these patented drugs should work their way through the approval process with the heavy burden of clinical trials. The NIH might seek to run this task itself, notwithstanding its heavy cost. But if it does so, do government programs get equal or preferred treatment from the FDA? Intergovernmental pressures could easily complicate the approval process. The alternative allows a private firm to obtain the rights to push the drug through the FDA process. Presumably this could be done by putting the new compound up for bid in a complex auction. But now the game is over. We have introduced the identical monopoly at the FDA-approval stage that we thought we had avoided at the research stage. Anyone with the exclusive rights to an FDA license has the monopoly position that this whole proposal was designed to eliminate. It is easy to see how exclusive FDA approval works for patented substances. It is much more difficult to see how it could ever work with public domain products that no one wants to see through clinical trials. The greater ambition of the Stein and Valery proposal makes it more mischievous than the prior group that wished to buy the patent rights only after approval. This proposal should not get off the ground, and, mercifully, it won't.

The misguided proposals to favor government research for pharmaceutical products have also taken on an international coloration. Distressed by what they perceive as high prices and unequal access, Tim Hubbard and James Love have proposed to allow an individual nation to dispense with the intellectual property protections required internationally under the TRIPS agreement. In place of this protection, the nation must design an alternative institutional arrangement that basically allows for funding at levels equal to those which are currently involved in drug research. They hope to create "an efficient R&D virtual market" under which a set of government-licensed intermediaries would compete for funds from individuals (or employers). These funds would then be turned over to do research responding to the needs of the overall public. As might be expected, in their view the chief villains are the me-too drugs and the exclusion of research directed to the diseases of the poor. They assume further that marginal-cost pricing will eliminate some market distortions, without noting the others created in their place.[7]

This proposal, which has already been effectively rebutted by Joseph DiMasi and Henry Grabowski, is subject to all the dangers that afflict any effort to displace the patent system, either in whole or in part, within a particular country.[8] There is no reason to believe that state-funded research will be able to sniff out the targets of opportunity which they can then effectively exploit. Consequently, at the most basic level, the paper involves yet another stark illustration of the Nirvana fallacy, in which the known imperfections of established institutions are overrated relative to the as-yet undetected imperfections of some proposed system. But in this case, the difficulties go still deeper.

In the first place, Love and Hubbard misunderstand the current operation of the system. They write as though patent protection runs for twenty years, when in fact, as we have seen, much of that time is lost in the premarketing approval process, so that the effective period of patent life is often in the neighborhood of nine to thirteen years. It would be far better to streamline or eliminate the approval process, so that patented products could make it more quickly to markets, but that remove is left unmentioned. Love and Hubbard also note that pricing policies are intended to maximize firm welfare and not social welfare—a proposition that is true of all goods and services, including generic drugs.[9] But they miss that in a world of unregulated pricing, price discrimination will be able to bring price close to marginal cost in areas where demand is low, including third-world countries of limited wealth. In order to make this system work, however, the pharmaceutical manufacturer must be given freedom to price and to receive protection against cross-border arbitrage. Otherwise, the drugs it sells cheaply in one nation will be resold at higher prices in other locations. Allowing property protections to facilitate price discrimination is one way to increase access to drugs, but again it is ignored by Love and Hubbard.

The list of the objections against this program does not stop here. For starters, this proposal necessarily removes revenues that current companies are entitled to under their patents, which is in breach of TRIPS. One virtue of the patent system is that it necessarily directs revenues to firms that have demonstrated some prowess in the market. Under the Love and

Hubbard proposal, however, revenues are diverted so that this reward system is effectively undermined. Over time, state-operated programs of unproved worth will displace all proprietary research. Globally, this cavalier disregard of intellectual property rights also creates a pall of instability over international agreements. If arguments such as those Love and Hubbard advance are sufficient to upend TRIPS in this context, no set of intellectual property arrangements is secure against political intrigue.

At a more institutional level, there are real questions of how this new system will work. No enforcement mechanism ensures that the diverted revenues will go to their intended purposes, or that those purposes will be sensible and effective. The amount to be collected from each nation remains to be determined, without any obvious metric, given that the current set of prices often reflects the highly interventionist policies of local governments. Many governments find it easy to impose price controls precisely because they have no domestic firms that sell to the local market. The Love and Hubbard proposal may divert funds in undeveloped nations to local research facilities often in nations ill-equipped to deal with the challenges of modern pharmaceutical research. Yet at the same time, the rigid percentage set off could hamper efforts to increase the level of research expenditures in response to new research opportunities. And at every juncture the politicization of research will make it hard to prevent the pork-barrel politics that has created a complex web of state subsidies for many large government projects, such as supersonic transport.[10]

In the end, it is not possible to find a system of government intervention, whether by taxation, by regulation, or by purchase, that can eliminate the deadweight loss problem—the elimination of some sales that would take place in competitive markets—without creating worse problems in its stead. That somber but sensible conclusion does not presuppose that all private efforts to undermine the deadweight loss are doomed to fail. Even today there are notable instances of private firms assuring open access to various forms of intellectual property, either by allowing all to use protected material without royalties or by putting it straight into the public domain. The Wellcome Trust followed the latter strategy when it decided to place its detailed description of the human genome directly into the public domain.[11] That process avoids the genuine distortions of private property rights that the systems of state coercion create. Rather, this strategy depends only on the willingness of individuals to invest their own resources to create inventions that others may use free of charge. The key point to note about both these movements is that no one can challenge their legitimacy, at least within the framework of traditional conceptions of property and contract to achieve their particular ends. If some individuals wish to make their intellectual property freely available to others, it would be odd in the extreme to insist that they should be under a duty to charge the going rate in order to shelter their commercial competitors. The correct approach is to allow the development to happen, given that someone must always pick up the financial cost of the operation privately.

It is easy to raise legitimate questions as to how long these behaviors will last. We have already seen the extensive development of the open-source software movement and the rise of Creative Commons (which facilitates copyright licenses for credit only).[12] In some instances, as with the open-source software movement, the diffuse control of a commons may not in the end suffice to manage a far-flung enterprise. The management may, I believe, tend to coalesce; a loose agglomeration of individuals will become a joint venture of a number of firms that by an express (or implied) contract agree to contribute to a common platform which all are free to share. But it should be suggestive of the trend line of these cooperative ventures that the dominant players in the open-source software movement are not the lone individuals who program for the joy of it but the large groups of employees of major corporations whose assignment includes work on open-source software.[13] Nor, of course, are these the only potential players. The NIH and other government and university labs are still active in the general area of biotech research, so it is not as though commercial activities have, or ever could, crowd out other forms of development. The current mix seems to being work well. There is little need to rework the overall rules of the game. At this very moment, all sorts of entities are at work in pharmaceutical research, and any device that brings more players in should be welcomed by anyone who thinks that free entry, not state regulation, is the engine of economic and social success.

IV

THE FDA: PURITY, SAFETY, EFFECTIVENESS

11

THE STEADY EXPANSION OF FDA POWER

The patent system represents only the first hurdle that any new pharmaceutical product must overcome before it can reach the market. The next hurdle, which is every bit as large, is the premarket review that all new and generic drugs must receive from the FDA. By any standard, the FDA is a powerful regulatory body, but in recent years all sides have closely scrutinized and extensively attacked its performance. The FDA's perennial critics argue that it has inadequately protected the public against the dangers of pharmaceutical drugs, both before and after they reach the market.[1] A constant drumbeat has called for modifications in its internal operations; most recently, suggestions called for the government to establish a postmarketing review body *outside* the FDA to review those products that already have survived its formidable administrative gantlet. In truth, the most withering criticisms of the FDA should come, and sometimes do come, from the opposite direction.[2] As a matter of principle, the FDA has too much power and steps should be taken both to tamp down the scale of its functions and to expedite the work that remains. In order to illustrate the reasons for deregulation and the sensible theory of government intervention, I shall briefly trace the relentless expansion of government authority over drugs in the past one hundred years.

Before examining the processes by which new drug treatments are developed, we must answer the critical question of *who* should decide whether a particular patient should take a particular drug: the state, acting on behalf of individuals, or the individuals, acting on their own behalf or through agents? We cannot answer that question in the abstract; it depends on the nature of the risk to which individuals are exposed. On this question, one clue to the problem is that the first Food and Drug Act of 1906 dealt exclusively with questions of drug purity, broadly defined.[3] These matters of purity are of the utmost concern to all individuals, for there is no patient, no matter how sick, who wants to take contaminated, diluted, adulterated, mislabeled, or altered drugs. The mere presence of impurities—at least when they rise beyond a defined, acceptable level—is conclusive evidence that the product that has in fact been delivered was not the product that was first promised under contract. In the early development of product liability law, a large fraction of litigation concerned these so-called manufacturing defects, whereby tobacco was defective not because it could cause cancer but because it contained impurities that were unknown to the potential buyer.[4]

The same attitude clearly carries over to all forms of medication. But in light of the serious inability of individuals to detect these contaminated goods, the government undertakes a legitimate function to prevent the intentional or accidental sale of goods that do not measure up, on matters of purity and potency, to what has been promised. In general, there is no principled opposition to this function. Those companies that sell reputable products will benefit from a government seal of approval. Their dishonest rivals will be subject to a set of public sanctions that will kick in even if they are unable to pay the judgments entered against them when sued by injured parties. Most believe that the government has a role to play against the use of force, fraud, and breach of contract; the only question that remains is whether an FDA concentrated on this function contributes to the existing methods of private enforcement. One can safely assume that systematic oversight of the entire distribution network serves powerful social functions. Ironically, the only serious dispute here, to which we shall turn later, is whether the effort to use imported drugs from foreign sources undermines this function.

The FDA's second function is that of assuring product safety. To be sure, that function is necessarily served in the "purity" cases when the FDA guards against contamination, dilution, and other forms of product defect. But in the modern regulatory context, safety takes on a much broader meaning. Now the FDA is concerned not only with ensuring that a product meets its own description and warranties but also with determining whether the product, even if manufactured in accordance with specifications, should be allowed on the market at all—with or (almost never) without warnings as to its potential dangers. This expansion in its power came with the passage of the Federal Food, Drug, and Cosmetic Act of 1938 (FFDCA). The 1938 act responded to a dramatic incident in which diethlene glycol, well-known to be a potent poison, was used as an untested solvent in the marketing of a regular drug.[5] When more than one hundred people died before the compound was pulled off the market, Congress did not content itself with adopting an expanded definition of contamination; rather, the 1938 act vested the FDA with the broad power of premarket review.[6] Firms that wanted to market a new drug had to file an application that provided sufficient information about the compound in question and the uses to which it would be put for the FDA to determine whether the product should be licensed for sale. The application was deemed approved unless the FDA, within 60 days after the application was filed, requested further information, at which point a final decision had to be made within 180 days of filing.[7] The undefined statutory phrase "safe for use" makes it appear as though safe and dangerous are dichotomous categories that can be settled by scientific means. Nothing turns out to be further from the truth.

In practice, the FDA has no choice but to permit a product to be sold, coupled with warnings about its risks. These two approaches are fundamentally different. The former displaces private choice by creating a (benevolent) government monopoly. The latter approach denies the government the power to exclude, and does not give it a monopoly over the information that is supplied with its use. To be sure, information about drugs is freely available from nongovernmental sources, which reduces the power of FDA warnings. Yet by the same token, once a serious, or black-box warning is placed on a drug label, it will have powerful negative consequences on the level of sales. Patients, especially those who are not closely familiar with a given field, will shy away from these, and physicians will be reluctant to prescribe them if they know that injured parties will have a leg up in any malpractice action that could follow on the heels of some adverse event. In dealing with these twin weapons, the most vital question is not argued but assumed: why give the FDA a virtual stranglehold over safety matters?

The 1938 act did not complete the expansion of the FDA's power. In the wake of the thalidomide disaster of the early 1960s, the 1962 Kefauver amendments to the FFDCA gave the FDA authority to determine not only the safety of the drug in question but also the effectiveness of the drug in treating the condition for which it is needed.[8] In one sense, the double-barrel approach of the FDA makes sense because a rational consumer would make a choice of medications based both on safety and on effectiveness. At the extremes, nobody would ingest a drug that was perfectly safe but known to be completely ineffective, or one that was effective but virtually certain to be accompanied by life-threatening side effects. As before, however, the central choice on institutional design was elided. The question should have been, Who is in the best position to make decisions on safety, the individual or the state? Instead, the relevant inquiry became, How does the state make and implement its choices on effectiveness?

Yet what set of assumptions justifies this federal assumption of power? In practice this question divides itself into two closely related issues. The first concerns the key decision on when and how to let a new drug on the market. The second question concerns the conditions under which the FDA should be able to withdraw a drug from the market in light of new evidence that goes either to its safety or to its effectiveness.

12

FDA VERSUS THE INDIVIDUAL: UPSTREAM OR DOWNSTREAM DECISION MAKING

In order to answer the questions raised in the previous chapter, it is necessary to have some sense of how the decision-making process operates both at the FDA and at the individual level.[1] This issue, of course, has gained salience with the highly visible public debates over Merck's voluntary withdrawal of Vioxx from the marketplace on September 30, 2004 (and, as of May 2006, its unlikely reintroduction).[2] That decision was followed by Pfizer's decision to leave both Celebrex and Bextra on the marketplace, while discontinuing all direct-to-consumer advertising.[3] But clearly the issue transcends these two cases, important and visible as they are. The key question remains: where should these decisions be made, *upstream* by the FDA or *downstream* by the individual drug user, aided by professional assistance?

The problem is not trivial because there is no inherent reason to assume that any viable solution will lodge all decisions at either the individual level or the collective level. Thus the question is how to partition the tasks between the two. One obvious argument in favor of centralized control is that the FDA can possess a level of expertise not available to ordinary consumers. But clearly this argument is not sufficient to resolve the matter, for ordinary people are not unaided in making decisions about drug use. Even today, once the FDA allows a drug onto the market, it is not consumed like peppermint candy. Rather, people who don't have the foggiest idea of what drugs to take in what dosages and combinations often *do* know enough to rely on third persons, or have family and friends to help them get better information. For prescription drugs, they are obliged to rely on their own physicians, but they also increasingly join various patient groups and check information on the Web. The question, therefore, is whether the downstream protections negate any initial informational advantage the FDA might have.

On this critical point, a number of elements cut against ceding the FDA dominance over which products should be allowed to reach the marketplace and when. The first of these goes to the consequence of an FDA decision. If the FDA decides to let a drug onto the market, no one is obliged to use it. Any mistake to permit the sale of a drug is therefore subject to downstream correction by individual users. But a decision to keep the drug off the market is impervious to downstream correction by individual users. In the alternative, the FDA could issue warnings, perhaps very severe warnings, as to the risks associated with product use. These warnings could be so strong as to frighten off people who on balance might benefit from the drug. But while this issue points out one serious risk of a system of tort liability for inadequate warnings, it has much less salience here. The simple point is that despite their apparent affinity, warnings and bans start from different places within the legal firmament.

The critical reason for distinguishing between them is that in the population at large, individuals will have widely varying perceptions of risk and widely varying willingness to undertake it. In other words, some who have received the warnings may nonetheless decide to run the risk, while others may not. Of course, the warnings could well influence how that decision is made, but even the most imposing of warnings can be disregarded, especially by people who have already used a drug which they found helpful for their own condition. The recent decision by the FDA, for example, to require a specific black-box warning on various antidepressant drugs—including Zoloft and Prozac—that have been extensively used in the treatment of teenage depression shows how large the warning issue can loom.[4] Decisions of this sort can have a profound effect on the level of drug use. Thus there is widespread fear on the part of many psychiatrists that the warnings will unduly alarm parents and deter doctors from prescribing drugs that are vitally needed by depressed patients, while others think that these are long overdue.[5] Indeed, after the FDA imposed a black-box warning on the use of antidepressants in children, their usage plummeted, leading the American Medical Association, under pressure from its physicians, to ask the FDA to run a follow-up study to assess the consequences of its earlier action.[6] The point here is the same as before. If it is true that on balance the use of an antidepressant does more good than harm, then the black-box warning is socially destructive if it reduces use below the optimal level. The market in information can be as much distorted by overgloomy predictions that lead to excessive caution as it is by exuberant industry-wide promotion that leads to excessive use. Both kinds of errors have to be taken into account.

In addition, black-box warnings should not be thought of simply as information devices when they also trigger other mandatory measures. Advertisements of products with black-box warnings are more restricted than those without such warnings. Dispensation of these drugs is much more complex as well, for FDA rules prohibit pharmacists from dispensing pills from a common vat and require that they be sold in closed bottles with thirty pills, which makes it hard to write prescriptions for larger or smaller quantities.[7] On balance it seems that the extra warnings could easily be excessive, especially since it is so difficult to figure out, even with statistical techniques, whether in any individual case an antidepressant caused, averted, or delayed a suicide.

On balance, the use of black-box warnings should be carefully circumscribed precisely because their collateral consequences take on the appearance of a partial ban. Yet the use of ordinary warnings from the FDA will not carry with it those collateral consequences. In these cases, it is absolutely critical to understand that the FDA does *not* have any monopoly over warnings. Individual physicians and patients can consult other references that deal with drug interactions, read Web sites devoted to particular diseases or conditions, or throw darts at a target to make their decisions. Let the FDA warn away, and it will still be subject to competitive pressures from other individuals and groups that have their own testimonies and judgments to offer. The emergence of any such voluntary market in warnings is yet another reason to deny the FDA any comprehensive power to ban, or even to issue the black-box warnings that raise the costs of product distribution. The sources of information available—the FDA, drug companies, Public Citizen, and physician groups—should in the aggregate improve the overall level of decision making. Owing to the possibility of imperfect competition in the warning markets, the hard question is, Why believe that the FDA is so reliable in its judgments that it should be allowed to make decisions another individual cannot reverse? Here are some reasons why the current law vests too much power in the FDA.

Two Kinds of Error

One key question concerns the incentives that drive the FDA. On this point, it is critical to begin with the standard distinction between Type I and Type II error, which is rightly stressed in virtually all works critical of the FDA chokehold on drug release.[8] Type I error arises when a drug that should be kept off the market is allowed onto the market, where it causes *visible* harm to its users. Type II error arises when a valuable drug is kept off the market, thereby making it impossible for sick individuals to benefit from its use. As a matter of social welfare, the right decision should be to balance both types of errors, so as to minimize the total number of lives lost or seriously damaged. In making this decision, the mechanism of causation—whether harm inflicted or benefit denied—should be regarded as utterly immaterial to the ban decision, for that is the way in which rational patients would so regard it. In figuring out the expected utility of a given decision, the adverse consequences of deaths or serious injury are the same whether caused by a drug intended to cure a dangerous condition or by the underlying condition itself. Individuals seeking to maximize their expected utility will rightly be indifferent to the source of their loss. They will be willing (in the simplest case) to take a 90 percent risk of death from a given course of action if they believe (ignoring any increment in treatment cost) that the risk of death without that action is 91 percent. That is the decision that they would make with last-ditch surgery, when the FDA is nowhere to be found. It is the same decision people should be allowed to make with drug use, even after the FDA is involved.

The key question, then, is whether the FDA has incentives to make choices that capture in general the desire of any individual to maximize expected utility of alternative courses of treatment (or, as we laymen say, give us the best chance to get well). The answer has long been understood to be no. The key lies in the difference between visible and nonvisible harm.[9] When thalidomide leaves many children with deformed limbs, the harm is easy to see, and by virtue of its distinctive nature is easy to assign to a given therapeutic agent. Its virtues, which turn out to be real, are largely ignored until tempers cool, when, rechristened Thalomid, it is reintroduced into the market as an effective treatment for one of the after-effects of leprosy.[10] The FDA catches all sorts of grief for its decisions that let drugs on the market. In the first instance, it did not matter that the drug might have had valuable uses in other settings. The tendencies in all cases is to have a bureaucratic incentive to avoid the heat, which means that Type I errors are rated within the FDA at a substantial multiple of Type II errors. One possible justification for this stance is to apply the Hippocratic approach, "First, do no harm," to the FDA. But the injunction was meant as a guideline for physicians, and so long as they remain gatekeepers, there is no reason for the dual application of the maxim. Nor is it clear how the maxim plays out in a regulatory context, when "first, do no harm" could lead to a posture of nonintervention by a remote agency. Maxim or no, the difficulty with the FDA's position stems from the unequal weighting of the two types of error. By rating Type I error so highly, the FDA introduces a systematic deviation between the objectives of the agency and the social welfare of the individuals whom it is said to serve. The upshot is that too many products are kept from the market as the FDA attempts at all costs to avoid causing visible harm, without taking into account the losses that must be absorbed by delaying or removing products from the marketplace.

This first institutional disadvantage is then aggravated by a second one. Are more efficient decisions made upstream by the FDA, with its knowledge of generic risks, or downstream by individuals with knowledge of the particulars of their individual condition? In principle, there is no uniform answer to this question. Thus take an extreme case in which a proposed medication will kill every individual who takes it. When the FDA has reached this determination, it should pull the drug from the market. Since Type II error is zero, any decision to let the drug onto the market can do no better than the FDA decision to keep it off. But if even one person decides to use a product that is known to be fatal, then allowing the downstream decision will result in a Type II error that the unitary control over the FDA could avoid.

This example shows just how extreme the conditions have to be before the FDA dominance is an unambiguous social improvement. Yet if the case is this dramatic, the issue is, What drug company would choose to market this product, even on the assumption that it suffered no tort liability for the deaths that its product caused? Reputation matters, and for large firms that seek to develop and maintain brand names, it matters more than anything else. The strongest cases for allowing the FDA to impose a ban are the cases where it is least likely to be needed.

Heterogeneity

The model thus far has worked on relatively simple assumptions. What, then, should be introduced to make this model of sequential decision making more realistic? Here two related assumptions turn out to be crucial. First, assume that there are significant chances of false positives and false negatives in any individual case. Second, assume that the calculus of costs and benefits routinely differs significantly across individuals, for any number of sensible reasons. The first and most obvious of these is that no two individuals are precisely alike in their need for or tolerance of particular lines of treatment. The point here does not require any particular demonstration. The simple truth that dominates this principle applies to any attributes in all populations: the variation of its members is not zero. Rather, some complete distribution must be found, and for these purposes it is sufficient to confine our attention to the simplest model, which says that for any given trait in any population the variation around the mean is always greater than zero. In ordinary English, this means that all individuals in the population are not 5 feet, 7 inches tall simply because the average person is of that height. It also means that subpopulations—men and women, for example—could have both different means *and* different variances about those means. Therefore when it is said casually that men are taller than women, the statement should not be taken to signify literally that *all* men are taller than *all* women. In ordinary parlance, the expression is understood to imply that the means of the two populations differ, which leaves open the possibility that any given woman is taller than any given man. What is true of height is true of toleration of risk, of pain, of aspirin, or of any of the untold factors that go into making a medical decision. The question then is how the inescapable feature of *heterogeneity* in any population fits into the vital question of whether to prefer the monopoly upstream control by the FDA relative to downstream individual control.

Competence

The next issue is whether these differences can be perceived and acted upon by individuals, either alone or in conjunction with their physicians. Medical questions are never trivial, even for patients who have access to professional help. The general competence of ordinary people to enter into contracts or to make personal decisions is usually not worth a second thought. But weakened capacity often is the critical issue for individuals of advanced age or declining health. That grim reality is in real tension with the sensible view, taken by courts in medical malpractice cases, that each individual has sole power to determine whether to submit to invasive surgery or any other treatment by his or her physician.

The effort to reconcile the grubby details of individual competence with the grand ideal of patient autonomy poses a central challenge to the practice of medicine, with or without an FDA. Thus the need for seeking informed consent is often invoked to require disclosures of information from physician to patient to bridge the knowledge gap. In those cases of individuals with diminished capacity, other family members can offer guidance in individual cases or take over the decision under a medical power of attorney. All these devices that are used to overcome the loss of competence by individual patients must be in place to make decisions about which FDA-approved drugs to use.

In response, it is often claimed that ordinary individuals are not only unable to make the correct decisions, but they are equally unable to find suitable proxies who are capable of making good decisions for them. Matters are only made worse, the argument continues, because the pressures of modern medicine are such that physicians do not spend needed time with patients, even when it might improve overall performance. Worse still, there is no viable system of medical malpractice or professional discipline to separate weak from able physicians.

My sense is that all these arguments, while true, are overdrawn, for their dreary tone cannot explain the many success stories in medical treatment over past years. But even if they were all correct on a descriptive level, they would not lead to any change in overall policy. For one point, the powerful critique of all other institutions of social control applies with equal or greater force to the FDA, which is not exempt from any of the political or budgetary pressures that lead to erroneous decisions. Indeed, if these criticisms were correct, then the FDA is far too lax in its current posture, given the huge number of medical treatments that could cause death or serious injury if misapplied.

More to the point, it is not possible to correct downstream errors by upstream interventions based on how some patients and physicians behave. It would represent most unwise policy to let the FDA make any decision to allow sale of a drug based on the competence of individual patients in the potential user pool. When it makes its upstream decision, any ban that it imposes, like the summer rain, falls on the competent and the incompetent alike. Decisions on treatment choice are so intensely individual that they must be made downstream, not only for drug usage but also for any and all aspects of health care. The FDA should, therefore, routinely act on the assumption that all potential drug users are competent—that is, are represented by individuals who are looking out for their best interests. There is no upstream cure for a serious downstream issue, even when that assumption is wrong.

On this assumption, heterogeneity of the overall population emerges as the critical issue. In their recent study on FDA approval policies, Anup Malani and Feifang Hu note that the FDA "employs a simple decision rule when deciding whether to approve a new drug for use by physicians: the average treatment effect of the new drug must be superior to the average effect of a placebo."[11] They then criticize this model on the powerful ground that it does not lead to decisions that maximize the expected utility of drug usage. By placing its focus on the average use, the FDA ignores the variation in individual responses. Even when the FDA or companies stratify patients into various cohorts, the problem is not eliminated. There could easily be wide variations even within the smaller classes. It could well be that on average a particular drug does not perform as well as a placebo. But so what? That only shows that most people should not take the drug, not that it should be banned from the market.

Unfortunately, the FDA has been criticized on this point from the vantage point of those who want tougher conditions for entry. Thus Arnold Relman and Marcia Angell, fierce critics of the drug industry, urge the FDA to ratchet up its policy of looking at averages yet another notch. "Unfortunately, the FDA will approve a me-too drug on the basis of clinical trials comparing it not with an older drug of the same type, but with a placebo or a drug of another type."[12] Looked at in its most favorable aspect, their proposal follows the flawed FDA methodology, with a heightened baseline, equal to the average performance of an approved drug. The effect is therefore to keep still more drugs off the market and thus to entrench the monopoly position of the initial entrant. Moreover, the proposal ignores that even drugs of equal efficacy may have pronounced variations because of allergy, intolerance, or other factors that make some better and some worse in individual cases. Worse still, it forces the new entrant to meet a moving target. Its initial task is to match the performance level of the first entrant. But that estimation will vary over time, which makes it difficult to know just what level of performance will justify FDA approval. The situation will only get more cloudy if a second new entrant does cross this bar, only to set a newer and higher standard for the remaining drugs in the same class that already is in clinical trial. The FDA, which has enough difficulty in dealing with the traditional requirements of safety and efficacy, is now asked to assume the role of industrial czar, for which it is most ill-suited.

The desired reforms on this issue move in the opposite direction from the ill-considered Relman-Angell proposal. The correct procedure treats this variation in individual response as critical. It first asks whether there is a significant fraction of cases in which the drug under review outperforms the placebo. The answer to that question is likely to be negative if the mean response is well below that of the placebo and the variance in responses across individuals is small. But as the variance in individual response increases, the FDA's procedure is ever more likely to lead to *incorrect* results. In many cases, it is possible for the mean of the placebo to lie above the mean for the drug, even though some substantial fraction of the population is better off with the drug than without it.

An example might help illustrate the point. Suppose that we rate patient response to treatment on an (admittedly arbitrary) scale of 0 to

100, where the current drug has a mean average of 50 but a variation in responses from 25 to 75. Now put a new drug on the market that has a mean average of 45, with a variance of 20 to 70. The question is whether the second drug should be allowed on the market, when each relevant parameter is 5 points below that of the original drug. If all individuals had the identical rank order of response, then, sure, keep it off. Given that assumption, any person who scores X with the current drug will turn X minus 5 with the new one. Individual choice could only compound error. But heterogeneity totally undermines that assumption. Now even though the whole curve has shifted to the left for the new drug, some fraction of individuals will score better with the new one than the old one. Since we don't know who these individuals are, we pay a high price in letting the entire patient population have only one choice instead of two. Nor does the analysis change in principle if the curve for the new drug is 5 points to the right of those of the old drug. Most people may shift drugs, but the older drug should remain on the marketplace nonetheless, for some people will be better off to stay with the old drug, or to return to it if they do worse on the newer one.

At this point, the inquiry shifts to a second question: what knowledge is available about individual variations? If all that is known is that there is a variance among individual cases, without any knowledge of where particular individuals lie on the distribution, the harm from any ban is relatively slight. Since individuals do not know where they lie, as a first approximation, they will act as though they are located at the mean. They would thus make the same decision as the FDA. At this point, the only loss from the ban stems from the attitude toward risk. If the FDA is risk averse, it will ban products with high variances that some gambling individuals would be prepared to take. In most cases, however, the elaborate systems of downstream control are put into place precisely because ordinary patients and their physicians can make an intelligent estimate of the patients' place on the distribution. Just as physicians can determine without the FDA's assistance which individuals are good candidates for surgery, so they can also determine which are good candidates for any drug regime. In general, therefore, the ban makes sense as a matter of first principle only on highly restrictive assumptions in which patients will not only fail to process the available information but also stumble even if they can purchase the best assistance that money can buy. Hence, presumptively, the FDA should not have the power to ban at all, except in cases that deal with impure or adulterated products.

The analysis is in fact more complicated when we recognize that variation is the watchword not only for drug response but also for natural response to dangers. Even without any treatment whatsoever, all individuals who are afflicted with a given condition will not respond to it in the identical fashion. Some will get better without any assistance, while others will quickly succumb to the ailment. Suppose now that a clinical trial were run in which the overall distribution was exactly the same for the placebo as it was for the drug under trial. One common response to that situation is that the drug should not be allowed on the market because it has not shown any improvement over the placebo. The variation in the one group is matched exactly by the variation in the other. That hasty conclusion, however, seems to be a mistake, unless it can be shown that all individuals have the same position in the distribution in the placebo curve that they do in the distribution for the tested drug. That result seems, a priori, highly unlikely when we do not have any strong account of the differential responses in either group. The sensible response, therefore, is to allow this drug on the market to take advantage of the possibility that individuals who will do poorly without treatment may do better with it. Those who progress well without medicine, or with other therapies, need not take the risk of a drug with this clinical profile. But unless it can be shown for the vast bulk of the population that a particular drug has no positive effect whatsoever, then it should be allowed on the market. Stated otherwise, once we move beyond the cases of impurities and contamination, the test for a ban should be this: is the drug so poor that virtually everyone will be better off without it than with it, even with optimal levels of postmarketing segmentation? Some new therapies (for which there would anyhow be no market) will reach this level, but most will not. For those, lesser schemes of regulation are appropriate: instructions to use only under the supervision of medical personnel or by prescription only, or warnings of various strengths. The ban should be the last resort, not the first option.

The case against the FDA power in this regard is only strengthened when one looks at the ostensible tests that are used to decide whether to put a ban in place. As we have seen, the operative terms in question deal with effectiveness and safety, which are left undefined under the Food and Drug Act. But why should the act leave its key terms undefined when so much turns on them? Here the answer has more to do with distribution of political power than with linguistic inquiry. Stated as absolutes, the terms "safe" and "effective" suggest that we work in a dichotomous universe, where the difference between safe and unsafe is as categorical as the difference between driving on the correct side and the wrong side of the road, whether in the United States or the United Kingdom. The same arguments could be made for effectiveness. Yet, of course, this is pure myth, for the moment the FDA or anyone else has to deal with concrete cases, the task is always to compare the risks and benefits of alternative strategies.

In the Vioxx and Celebrex debate, for example, no one thinks that you can describe, categorically, either or both of these drugs as safe or unsafe. The question is always whether all things considered it is better to take one drug if the other has some elevated risk. Even that determination depends on all sorts of refinements, given that there is never a uniform response to any given drug. Any FDA finding that a drug is safe and effective cannot possibly be read to mean that it has no adverse side effects and that it works a cure in 100 percent of the cases. We are dealing with wonder drugs, to be sure, but not ones that have supernatural power. So literalism is not a viable way to interpret the statutory command unless we are prepared to acknowledge at the start that no drug is good enough to make the cut. Any realistic determination, therefore, has to ask the question of *how* safe and *how* effective any given drug is, not only for one individual but across large populations. In dealing with this question, the FDA cannot take the position that a drug should be banned just because it has adverse effects in a single class of cases. No one would market (even if unbanned) thalidomide for pregnant women in their first trimester. But it is now allowed on the market as a treatment for one of the aftereffects of leprosy, which afflicts a very different population. In general, the FDA could allow the marketing of a drug for one subpopulation and not another on the ground that the risks in the first case are greater than they are in the second, but even this concession to common sense does not get us back to the right decision point. It still ignores the possibility of variation in a subclass for which the use of the drug is not allowed. In the end, therefore, there are few if any sensible categorical decisions that can be made about the use of any drug. The FDA has to back off the ban in some significant fraction of cases and instead substitute warnings to indicate the circumstances in which use of the drug is or is not desirable. At this point, the science behind the act must be supplemented by a healthy dose of social judgment about when to ban and when to warn.

Thus far the argument has been that bans have limited social utility. But federal law gives the FDA unquestioned power to ban from the marketplace drugs that it judges to be unsafe or ineffective. The question is thus sensibly asked how these general propositions about decisions could be translated into a regulatory context that treats that power as unquestioned. The blunt answer is that there is no good way to back off a statutory command that is too stringent for its own good. But by the same token, the language in question could be interpreted by the FDA to mean that it should ban products only when their release is likely to do more social harm than good. Of course, this standard is not met simply by a showing that certain subsets of the population are better off without a certain drug administered in certain dosages than with it. Rather, the standard should mean that so long as some significant fraction of the population can benefit on net from the use of the drug, it should continue to be sold. Warnings—perhaps on occasion stringent black-box warnings—could be added to the package, and doubtless an extensive network of information about the drug's proper use would develop in the field, given the size of the stakes in question.

Backing off the strong presumptions in favor of bans should influence the entire operation of the FDA, even in its current configuration. Over the past several decades the number and size of clinical trials that have to be run in order to obtain the right to market goods have sharply increased. One recent account of the travails of the pharmaceutical industry sets out the picture with great clarity. The total cost for launching a new drug is said to have increased from about $1.1 billion per new chemical entity for the 1995–2000 period to about $1.7 billion for the 2000–2002 period.[13] The basic costs of drug discovery increased slightly in that period. The true sources of the increases were clinical trials, especially the expensive Phase II and III trials that typically are performed on large populations. The cost of these trials has soared as their number and size has increased and the percentage of drug candidates that runs the extended gantlet has shrunk. The hard question is, Why put this increased burden on the industry? The so-called higher safety standards are unfortunate reflections of the built-in FDA bias that fears Type I errors (which allow harmful drugs on the market) more than Type II errors (which keep safe drugs off the market). Yet the number of good drugs that are lost and delayed by this process are not put into the picture; nor is any systematic recognition given to the simple proposition that the longer a drug remains in testing, the higher the carrying costs for the drug, and the fewer years in the postapproval period during which the original applicant can enjoy the patent reward.

PDUFA

I can claim no expertise on which clinical trials should be eliminated and which preserved. But it seems clear that something, anything, should be done to break down the logjam. One response that has had enjoyed some success and notoriety is the PDUFA, the Prescription Drug User Fee Act, which was first adopted in 1992 and renewed in 1997 and 2002.[14] The basic point of this act was to provide additional personnel to the FDA to eliminate delays on the initial approval of new drug applications. In addition to the FDA's temperamental bias against risk, the agency was handicapped by the limited resources that were available to process new drug applications. If, on average, these have a positive expected value, the social costs, as measured by the expected gains to suppliers and users, could be far greater than the additional costs needed to fund the program. In a rational world of public expenditure, the sensible response for the Congress would be to increase the appropriation for the FDA to expedite these applications, just as it should increase the resources available to the Patent Office to examine the validity of new patents. The indirect gains from prompter approval should more than cover the costs of administrations.

Unfortunately, indirect benefits have little political currency, so the alternative plan under PDUFA is to have drug companies pay application ("user") fees in order to expedite the operation of the system.[15] The fees can be quite substantial; for 2004 they were set at $573,500 for a new drug application. But there is no direct connection between the money paid and the application reviewed. Rather, the funds are transferred into the general FDA budget, where they are used to fund overall drug review. The explicit statutory design is that the additional resources entitle the applicant only to a faster review, not to an approval. The detailed study of its effect by Berndt and his coauthors indicates that in large measure this statute has achieved its result: over the life of PDUFA, the period for review fell on average by 6 percent per year over the rate of acceleration that would have occurred in its absence. The differences are not trivial in duration: an actual decline over the full period from 24.2 months to 14.2 months, as opposed to a smaller decline of 3.8 months that would have been expected in its absence. The study also examined the rate of withdrawals of approved drugs afterward and found that it had remained essentially unchanged after the introduction of PDUFA, inching upward from 3.1 percent in the 1985–1992 period (6 of 193), to 3.5 percent during the 1992–2000 period (9 of 259).

Notwithstanding this track record, PDUFA has been attacked because of the obvious fear that the pharmaceutical companies that generate the fees will call the tune. The ever-critical Marcia Angell has denounced PDUFA on the ground that it "makes the FDA dependent on the industry it regulates."[16] As an abstract matter, such charges of conflict of interest of this sort do not sound persuasive, in light of the FDA's reputation for independence. Nonetheless, the more concrete charge requires more consideration. A concern has been raised that the more rapid approval rate for new drugs has come at the cost of reduced surveillance for established drugs.[17] The source of this difficulty rests in part on the stipulation of the industry that the additional funds that it supplies be earmarked for that part of the process that concerned them most—the new approval stage. The response to the initiative, however, took an additional turn when Congress reduced its direct appropriations to the FDA to offset the increased allocations received from industry under PDUFA. The changes in allocation were not small. In 1992 the FDA's drug center allocated 53 percent of its funds to new drug reviews. That number jumped to 70 percent by 2003.[18] The restrictions that PDUFA imposed on the permissible use of user fees accounted for most of the difference.

To some extent, the charge looks overblown because of the steady rate of withdrawals. One possible argument is that the adoption of PDUFA has let less safe drugs on the market, so we should expect higher rates of withdrawal, all other things being equal. But if Vioxx is thought to be the lead case of a drug that slipped through the net, then this concern also sounds overblown. In any event, the key point here is that the ultimate decision for funding the FDA rests not with industry but with the Congress. The flaw in the institutional design is the sharp reduction in congressional appropriations. Although the gains from PDUFA seem substantial, the act should have had a provision that required Congress to keep up its own appropriation to the FDA so that all dollars coming in under PDUFA counted as additional dollars. Any difficulties that did ensue stem from the failure to impose that second condition. Without it, PDUFA results in a rise of restricted funds that will alter the activities of the FDA just as restricted gifts alter the patterns of expenditures in universities. It is ironic that while so many clamor for increased activity for the FDA, the pattern of congressional financing is dominated by short-term financial considerations that do not show Congress's management ability in the best light.

Decentralized Review

An expansion of the FDA budget is, however, not the only response to the impasse in FDA functions. A second approach is to break the state monopoly over testing, so as to avoid both delays on the one hand and misallocation of funding on the other. Bowing to the inevitability of some FDA-like oversight, Henry Miller has not examined the substantive standards for review that I have stressed, but has instead taken a different tack. He has proposed that the United States move to a system similar to European regulation of medical devices and drugs. For the most part, devices are overseen there by "notified bodies," nongovernmental entities sanctioned by government; and the review of the equivalent of new drug applications is performed under contract by academics skilled in the various areas. More specifically, his proposal would convert the FDA from a certifier of products to a certifier of private-sector entities that would perform much of the day-to-day regulation of clinical trials and perform the initial NDA review. This arrangement resembles the role of Underwriters Laboratories and its competitors in setting standards for and certifying tens of thousands of categories of consumer products.

In principle, the decentralization that Miller defends would be an improvement over the current situation in the United States. But the big concern is whether the practice can be transplanted from one legal culture to another. More specifically, this proposal will work in the United States only if the FDA is limited by law to at most minimal influence over the Underwriters Laboratories–like entities that it certifies to perform oversight. But within our context, the single most powerful explanation for how the FDA works is, as Miller understands, the bureaucratic imperative that seeks to expand turf no matter what its consequences for others. My own sense, therefore, is that any proposed system of decentralization could work only if the government removed the oversight from the FDA, with its ingrained habits, and transferred it to a new board, not staffed by FDA veterans, that took a very different view of its overall role in the grand scheme of things. But in light of the FDA's rearguard efforts to maintain its own power against other initiatives, and the knee-jerk reaction in Congress for imposing stultifying drug regulation, the betting is that the future holds only more of the same. It is amazing the harm that can be done if the elimination of patient choice is regarded as proof of a diligent system of consumer protection!

Some difficulties of the FDA's obdurate mindset are found in Miller's account of the 1998 decision to require separate pediatric trials for children for drugs that are normally sold only to adults and to put the recommended dosages for children on the labels.[19] The proposal could not be opposed on the ground that it has no benefit whatsoever, but as Miller points out, it throws yet another monkey wrench into the cycle of development by delaying the entry of drugs to the detriment of adults and children alike. In addition, there are serious difficulties in organizing sensible clinical trials on children. The trials could last for several years, at which point the maturation of the children confounds any effort to isolate its age effects. The low incidence of specific conditions is such that it becomes difficult to get a large enough sample. This problem is especially acute in making judgments about safety because efforts to find the low level of increased risk of death or serious injury require larger sample sizes than can easily be assembled. The nettlesome difficulties on the proper form of drug administration—always more difficult in children, for whom syrups and chewable tablets are often desirable, and sometimes essential—slow the process further. Even the simple expedient of allowing the drug on the market with a statement that it has not been tested on children seems to make far more sense. And no doubt individual physicians will in some cases prescribe it in modified dosages for children on the ground that a prudent risk is worth running in light of a serious condition. This brings us back to the central theme: risk is everywhere, and the intonation of the requirement that all drugs be safe and effective simply diverts everyone from the complex nature of the choices to be made, and results in the aggregation of power in the FDA that belongs elsewhere.

This evident quandary with pediatric drugs has generated another response, which seems inferior to the direct expedient of reforming the FDA trial. In order to offset the expenses for getting pediatric drugs to market, Congress passed in 1997 the Food and Drug Administration Modernization Act (FDAMA), which under limited circumstances can extend the patent life of an approved drug by six months.[20] The first point to note about this legislation is that the compensation supplied to the patent holder for the new research is not in cash but in kind. That compensation equals in length the period of coexclusivity that is granted to the first generic drug to enter the market under Hatch-Waxman. Only here the patent holder gets to continue with an exclusive which could be worth billions of dollars in new sales for the period in question, even though most cases are likely to involve more exotic drugs with much smaller sales volume.

Placing a target like this before pharmaceutical companies creates the real risk that companies will decide on their own initiative to expend substantial sums on the required clinical research in order to get the desired patent extension. To forestall this option, FDAMA provides that the desired extension is available only when the secretary of Health and Human Services (through a deputy) makes a request in writing that a company start this research. There is no obligation to comply, but the carrot is often large enough to induce the desired response, especially since some of the products for which extensions have been obtained (Ibuprofen, Claritin) have substantial markets. All in all, ninety-three drugs have, at last count, received the patent extension for the additional work that has been done.[21]

It would be a mistake, however, to assume that the interposition of government action puts all these problems to rest, for it is always an open question as to who, and for what reasons, receives the critical authorization. But even if the requests are selected flawlessly, the hard question is why generics and their potential customers have to pay the price for research in the form of the delay for adult use.[22] (This objection is valid, even if the current terms are too short generally.) The obvious reason for using this provision is that direct payments to pharmaceutical companies for conducting the research are difficult to control. But it surely seems preferable to reduce the overall cost of clinical trials so that drug companies will not need the additional inducement to expand their clinical markets. FDAMA looks like yet another case in which one imperfection breeds a second.

13

DRUG WITHDRAWAL: TOO MUCH, TOO SOON

My analysis thus far has been directed to the question of whether and, if so, when the FDA should have the power to bar new medications from the marketplace. The same issue arises in somewhat different form when evidence accumulates that a drug already on the market has risk. This issue has arisen in many cases. The most notorious illustration involves the ongoing saga of Celebrex, Vioxx, and Bextra.[1] The story broke with full force when Merck announced that it would voluntarily take Vioxx off the market. Its own studies, which used heavy doses, revealed an elevated risk of cardiovascular difficulties; 3.5 percent of patients taking Vioxx suffered a heart attack or stroke compared with 1.9 percent who took a placebo.[2] Thereafter, further work done with Vioxx suggested that when it was used in heavy dosages in clinical trials designed to investigate its effectiveness in preventing the evolution of intestinal polyps into malignancies, an increase in cardiovascular events occurred–an effect observed only after eighteen months of treatment.[3] In consequence of these findings, Merck pulled Vioxx from the market on September 30, 2004. At that point suspicion spread about Celebrex and Bextra, both Pfizer products. Thus in the immediate aftermath, further clinical trials revealed that Celebrex presented an elevated risk of heart attacks. In response Pfizer made the decision to stop its clinical trial, but to leave Celebrex on the market while ceasing all its direct-to-consumer advertisement. In the short term the stock price of both Pfizer, the maker of Celebrex, and Merck, the maker of Vioxx, tumbled in response to the combination of three risks: a ban on all future sales; reduced sales if the drugs remained on the market; and a spate of lawsuits for refunds of the purchase price and damages whether the drugs were pulled or not.

The controversy has generated pointed criticism of FDA oversight of Vioxx, Celebrex, and Bextra, followed by persistent calls for a systematic toughening of FDA policies on new drug approvals. At the global level, the standard complaint has been that the drug companies have shamelessly over-promoted these products while the FDA has been too lax in its postmarket-ing review.[4] The resulting controversy has led to demands for the creation of a new agency independent of the FDA with responsibility for "drug safety." That demand has been resisted, as a new division within the FDA has heightened responsibilities on these matters, which suggests that in general the total level of government oversight will increase, just as it did after the diethylene glycol incident in 1937 and the thalidomide crisis of 1962.[5]

On the particular issue, the uncertainty over the Cox-2 inhibitors led the FDA to convene a special advisory panel to help determine whether to leave any of these three drugs on the market. On February 18, 2005, the panel issued its report recommending, by different voting margins, that all three drugs remain on the market.[6] For Celebrex, where the evidence of cardiovascular complications was weakest, the vote was 31–1; for Bextra the vote was 17–13, while for Vioxx the vote was 17–15.

It is also worth noting that when the issue came before a Canadian panel of experts, it voted 13–0 to keep Celebrex on the market, 12–1 to keep Vioxx on the market, and 8–5 to remove Bextra.[7] The Canadian study summarized its central conclusion as follows:

> All three of these drugs are effective anti-inflammatory agents, and are associated with a decrease in the frequency of both gastrointestinal intolerance and clinically important peptic ulcer disease compared with NSAIDs. At the same time, all three drugs increase the frequency of hypertension, edema, renal disease and clinically important cardiovascular events, which seems similar in magnitude to that associated with NSAIDs. The decision about whether it is justified to market these drugs in Canada depends upon one's interpretation of their risks and benefits, and the amount of information available for each individual drug.

It is the panel's opinion that the available information justifies marketing Celebrex in Canada (Vote: 13 in favour, 0 against). This was based upon:

a) the increased risk of cardiovascular disease caused by Celebrex appears similar to that of most NSAIDs, b) the risk of gastrointestinal harm caused by Celebrex appears less than most NSAIDs, and c) patients benefit from having a variety of drugs to choose from for pain relief.

It is the panel's opinion that the available information justifies marketing Vioxx in Canada (Vote: 12 in favour, 1 against). The rationale for the majority position was similar to that for Celebrex. They felt that no additional studies of Vioxx were mandatory before Vioxx is marketed again, but felt strongly that [additional] studies . . . should immediately be undertaken by an independent group supported by the manufacturers of all coxibs.

The contrary decision on Bextra was based on the incompleteness of the clinical studies and the evidence of some adverse skin conditions. One hard question is what judgment is correct in light of the immense disagreement that took place within the FDA and the very different conclusions reached on much the same evidence in Canada. At this point, the sensible conclusion is to insist that differences of opinion can be better respected if a drug is allowed to remain on the market and individual physicians are allowed to make particular judgments about its use. Some might decide to steer clear of it altogether, others to use it on a limited basis, depending on circumstances. In this regard, withdrawing a drug seems especially risky when large numbers of users have proved able to tolerate its use. Indeed, it often happens that whenever drug withdrawal is on the horizon, the move is resisted by current users of the drug who claim that in their personal experience the medicine in question is the "only" product that supplies the needed relief. These statements are not unique in this context. Similar stories can be told with just about every other drug that has faced some threat of withdrawal from the market, including Rezulin and Prozac.[8]

No one wants to deny that the clinical picture is complicated, but that only strengthens the case for FDA caution. For example, it is worth noting that Vioxx, for all its specific ills, appears to be superior to Celebrex in at least two dimensions: slowing down intestinal bleeding and reducing the progression of polyps to a malignant condition. Indeed, the higher risk of heart complications follows as the night does the day from that observation. One source of dangers to the heart comes from thrombosis, or clotting, which blocks the arteries, leading in turn to heart attacks and possibly death. Persons who face this risk need to take blood thinners such as heparin to combat this risk. But that in turn increases the risk of intestinal bleeding, which can also lead to death. The management of all cases therefore requires a balancing of two risks, which can be done only with a close knowledge of personal conditions.

High-risk, high-return choices are always hard to make downstream, even with knowledge of the relevant trade-offs. But upstream they are a disaster. Even the *New York Times* editorial page, which has been relentless in its criticism of Merck and Pfizer, had to lamely acknowledge that "the panelists clearly felt that [the Cox-2 inhibitor drugs] benefit some patients, if for no other reason than that different patients respond well to different drugs."[9] That, in a nutshell, is why the crusade to ban drugs through FDA edict is a mistake, and the Canadian decision more sensible. It is hard to practice medicine on a wholesale basis, and if particular panelists think that Naproxen (commonly marketed as Aleve) is a better medicine than the Cox-2 inhibitors, they should be free to say so.

The stakes involved in these choices are also illustrated by more recent actions of the FDA. The first involves its response to Iressa, an Astra-Zenica product that was found in expedited clinical trials under FDA's accelerated approval regulations to be effective in serious, often hopeless, lung cancers in about 10 percent of cases.[10] For many individuals the drug clearly prolonged life. After it had been on the market for some time, further clinical studies did not show the overall benefits that had been promised by the original study, and the FDA decided to take the unusual step of leaving the drug on the market for the people who had already used it but to restrict its use in future cases to patients who participated in the next round of clinical trials. In editorializing about this instance, the *Wall Street Journal* attributed this novel decision to the personal animus of Richard Pazdur, the FDA official who is in charge of cancer drugs, who has a strong dislike for the accelerated approval process on which Astra-Zenica relied.[11]

The constant infighting over drug approvals lends some credence to this charge, but its truth or falsity is a sideshow in the larger institutional debate. For these purposes, the more frightening possibility is that the decision represents the current thinking of the FDA on this critical health issue. Politics to one side, the chilling feature about the episode is how the FDA states its own case. The relevant FDA order reads in full:

> FDA ALERT [June 2005]
>
> FDA has approved new labeling for Iressa that states the medicine should be used only in cancer patients who have already taken the medicine and whose doctor believes it is helping them. New patients should not be given Iressa because in a large study Iressa did not make people live longer. There are other medicines for non–small cell lung cancer (NSCLC) that have shown an ability to make people live longer.[12]

An FDA questions-and-answers Web site reveals the logic underlying the decision:

> 10. What about patients who are already taking Iressa?
>
> Patients who are currently receiving and benefiting from Iressa, or who have taken and benefited from Iressa in the past, may continue to receive the drug.
>
> 11. Is this decision based on safety concerns?
>
> The main concern is that Iressa would be used in new patients in lieu of other approved treatments that have been shown to improve patient survival. Since the approval of Iressa, Tarceva (erlotinib), an oral drug similar to Iressa, has been approved for treatment of patients with advanced NSCLC who have had prior chemotherapy. Tarceva has been shown in clinical trials to significantly improve patient survival. Taxotere, a chemotherapy drug, has also been shown in clinical trials to improve survival in this group of patients.[13]

The answer epitomizes the textbook blunder on this subject. It first assumes that the physicians who treat these deadly conditions are better off with two drugs than with three, which cannot be correct. What chance is there that trained physicians with a full array of data will make the same obvious blunder? The FDA ignores the key methodological point on heterogeneity when it assumes that the drug with higher averages will be better for all persons. As the *Journal* opined, correctly, "But remember that such results are only averages for the population and that the responses of individual patients differ widely."[14] And the point is reinforced by one of the successful users of Iressa, who asked, "This is a drug that works amazingly well for some people, so why take it off the market?" But again, the FDA just does not get it. In her letter responding on behalf of the FDA, Janet Woodcock, then acting deputy commissioner, announced boldly that Pazdur and his team work "tirelessly to ensure that the balance of benefit and risk to cancer patients is in their favor," only to again ignore the fundamental methodological objection to the FDA action:

> While your editorial criticizes the agency for removing Iressa, a treatment for lung cancer, it fails to point out that this is a great example of how well the accelerated approval process works—the drug does help about 10% of the population, and for those patients the treatment will still be available. However, a new drug, Tarceva, which also was approved through accelerated approval, is now available and showing even more progress in the fight against lung cancer."[15]

Dr. Woodcock offered no rationale as to why one drug is better than two, or why new cancer patients and their physicians are barred from trying the drug outside of restricted clinical trials. But family members of cancer victims will certainly get the point: "As to Tarceva being an adequate replacement, that remains to be seen. The FDA does not know if Tarceva will provide the same benefit to the same patients that Iressa helps. The FDA deals only in averages, and the averages don't predict the response of any one individual to either drug."[16]

In this case, moreover, the averages are wholly misleading because scientific advances now allow the use of personal histories and genetic and protein markers to figure out how one is likely to be most benefited from treatment. Indeed, one of the great potential advances in this area lies in the use of pharmacogenetics, a science that uses genetic markers to explain the variation in responses to different drugs, which in its applied phases could make unique "designer genes" to respond to those variations.[17] But even before these modern techniques are perfected, their lesson on variation should not be forgotten.

The story with Iressa is not, unfortunately, a random blip in FDA policy. Rather, it represents a conscious decision on the FDA's part to protect individuals from having to make their own choices. The extreme caution that the FDA takes to *possible* adverse events is illustrated by its recent decision to ask (ever so gently, to be sure) Purdue Pharma L.P. to withdraw "voluntarily" from the market its new drug Palladone, a painkiller that works through extended-release capsules.[18] The risk against which the FDA wished to guard was legitimate: the potential for death or serious injury if taken with alcohol. But its overestimation of that risk was bizarre. The drug had been on the marketplace for about six months when the FDA received the data of possible complications. On July 13, 2005, the FDA wrote, "To date, FDA is not aware of any patients who have had life-threatening side effects from drinking alcohol while taking Palladone," a spotless record that took place *before* public knowledge of this particular finding. There is, of course, common knowledge that alcohol and painkillers do not mix, and it is not likely that persons who are in need of a constant painkiller are ignorant of that fact or would indulge in behavior that would expose them to risk.

The FDA action was sparked by clinical trials that indicated that high concentrations of alcohol (eight ounces of 40 percent alcohol—between five and eight shot glasses of 80 proof hard liquor) could prove deadly, while lesser dosages had more modest effect. Other opiates, of course, carry similar risks. With the warning in place, this risk seems small, so by far the better course of action is to wait for some adverse event to occur before rethinking the use of this drug. The implicit paternalism here comes at its worst because the population that is likely to need Palladone is the one least likely to indulge in alcohol binges that remotely mimic this clinical trial. Yet there was no evidence that the FDA asked current users how they felt about the decision. Only the usual bromide that said that individuals for whom Palladone had been the drug of choice should consult their physician (at their own expense, of course) for advice on how to cope with the shrunken choice set before them. Protection *by* the FDA comes at a painfully high price. Protection *from* the FDA is not available at any price.

I describe these two incidents in some detail because they illustrate that downstream users have a better grasp of the methodological issues than the powers that be at the FDA. In good authoritarian fashion, of course, it is possible to ignore, or even denigrate, the decisions that ordinary individuals, who have every incentive to sort matters out, make on the strength of subjective experience and medical advice. But most are equal to the task. Marcia Angell, a former editor in chief of the *New England Journal of Medicine,* who has proved to be one of the loudest and most persistent critics of the pharmaceutical industry, has noted: "I don't think any of these drugs should be on the market. . . . To accept a risk like that you ought to have a powerful benefit, and I just don't see it. Anecdotes won't do it. Testimonials won't do it."[19]

In a nub, that remark captures all that is wrong with the entire regulatory debate. The one clear difference between a premarket prohibition and a withdrawal scenario is that in the former case patients can only guess at their place in the overall distribution because they have no direct engagement with the drug to see whether it works for them. Of course, this experiential information, once acquired, is not conclusive in any setting. However, background information about how the drug has worked on others is something that most patients and their physicians would choose to take into account. If the variation in individual response is the key reason for letting drugs on the market, it is a stronger reason still for keeping them there. Dr. Angell can decide that she wouldn't touch any of these drugs with a ten-foot pole. But that she, or any group of physicians, should force other individuals to abandon drugs that have helped them reflects a professional hubris that too many FDA panelists exhibit as well. If there were ever a life-and-death situation where collective choice is inappropriate, this one is it. The FDA has done enough harm. Let us hope that somehow this nation summons the political will to adopt a different approach.

V

PHARMACEUTICAL MARKETING

14

GETTING THE DRUGS TO MARKET

Once a drug has received FDA approval, the next leg in its long trek to market begins. How is that drug brought to the attention of physicians and patients, to allow its owner to earn back its immense development costs? Just framing the issue of distribution as one of marketing and advertising—the former embracing the latter, but also including other promotional activities, such as conferences and use of free samples, gifts, and the like—will immediately raise the hackles of everyone who thinks that pharmaceutical products should be developed in a hothouse environment solely to promote the health and to ease the pain of their users. Many indictments of the pharmaceutical industry bemoan how its marketing and promotional branches have taken over and debased the business from its previously high moral station. Jerome Kassirer's book *On the Take: How Medicine's Complicity with Big Business Can Endanger Your Health* raises a claim, much in need of closer examination, that the current system of drug promotion corrupts both Big Pharma and the physicians, practice groups, and hospitals that it lures into its net.[1] A similar theme is echoed when Arnold Relman and Marcia Angell write in their attack on industry advertisement: "Those who pay for prescription drugs are paying for marketing, too."[2] Their clear but mistaken implication is that extra costs to the consumer add insult to injury. That point is made more explicit elsewhere: Jerry Flanagan, health care policy director at the Foundation for Taxpayer and Consumer Rights, has said starkly, "Profit is twice R&D and marketing is two to three times as much. Every dollar spent on marketing means the price of drugs will be more expensive."[3]

These frequent complaints cash out in two different ways. The first condemns the entire marketing apparatus, of dubious value elsewhere in the economy, as wholly destructive in the market for pharmaceutical products. The entire process seduces consumers to waste resources that are better spent elsewhere and creates a set of inflated expectations that can never be satisfied. The second treats pharmaceutical advertisements as frequently, if not systematically, deceitful, inaccurate, and misleading, inducing physicians and patients alike to forsake inexpensive, sensible treatments for riskier, expensive ones.[4] Stated otherwise, both charges are made against the two prongs of pharma's marketing efforts—the first against the promotional efforts directed to physicians and hospitals, and the second against direct-to-consumer advertisement (DTCA). A complete analysis requires looking at both sorts of objections in both market segments. I begin, in this chapter, with the global attack on marketing efforts and follow up in the next chapter with claims of false and misleading advertisements.

Marginal Versus Average Cost

The global attacks on pharmaceutical marketing are best evaluated in light of an understanding of the overall industry. Initially I shall conveniently bracket the question of false and misleading advertisements and start by assuming that the marketing effort gives an *accurate* account of the relevant attributes of a particular product, positive and negative, to its intended audience, some of whom are won over to the product. In this simplified world, any costly marketing expenditures must be recovered from the additional future product sales.

The relevant sums are far from trivial. To put marketing expenses in cross-industry perspective, the aggregate marketing and administrative outlay for Pfizer, for example, is a bit more than a third of total revenues, which puts it behind Unilever at 38 percent and Coca-Cola at 36 percent but ahead of Procter and Gamble at 31 percent, Microsoft at 25 percent, and Honda at 18 percent.[5] The internal industry story also reveals the large role played by marketing expenditures. "The top 10 drug companies took in a total of $293 billion in global sales in 2003, the last year for which complete figures are available. During the period, those companies spent $37.9 billion on research and development, or about 13% of sales. The companies' costs for marketing and administration far exceeded research at $96.4 billion, or about 33% of sales."[6] That last figure, however, is not quite right because the companies that reported them have both drug and nondrug expenditures, for which the percentage devoted to research differs. A corrected figure therefore suggests that the marketing expenditures should be reduced by about $20 billion, to $76.5 million, which is still about double the research expenses.

This 2 (or more)-to-1 ratio between marketing and research remains the target of standard criticisms. The underlying numbers, however, still need refinement. Most pharmaceutical companies do not disaggregate administrative from marketing expenses, but for those that do—the Bayer Group, the Roche Group, and Novartis—the administrative component is a distinct minority, between 13.8 percent and 20.4 percent.[7] That correction, if projected industry-wide, should knock down the marketing expenses by between $10 billion and $15 billion. Yet even that number does not give full notice of the range of marketing expenses. For example, free samples, valued at retail, are treated as marketing expenses. But to the indigent consumers who frequently receive them, they are anything but. For the fiscal year ending in September 2003, their retail value was $13.1 billion.[8] The actual cost to the industry (which pays only the marginal cost of production for those goods) is of course far less. Taking into account the difference between cost and value necessarily deflates the costs of free samples to, say, 10 or 20 percent of their retail costs, say, between $2 and $3 billion. Now total marketing cost drops by about $10 billion, which moves the ratio between research and marketing to $38 billion research to more than $66 billion marketing, which looks a bit less dramatic.

Other marketing expenditures could easily require similar recharacterization. So-called Phase IV clinical trials, for example, that monitor local responses to new drugs. These expenditures have both research and marketing components—the former because they offer follow-up on drug performance, and the latter because they help build up physician loyalty. Classification therefore becomes controversial, so more than one eyebrow was raised when AstraZeneca reclassified, for reasons that seem unclear

from a distance, some $460 million in Phase IV trial expenses to market-
ing, thereby driving up the ratio of marketing to research expenses.[9]

Analytically, however, all these classification struggles are quite beside
the point. What matters is not the accounting conventions but the logic
of the underlying economic decisions. The central question is whether
firms that incur expensive marketing costs have made wise decisions or
not. The simple observation that *every* firm engages in these practices
should offer some comfort to those who believe in the wisdom of the
crowd: the folks in the trenches know something more than the social
critics in the peanut gallery. But there is no need to rely on that collective
folk wisdom as the ultimate justification for these practices, for a principled social defense of robust marketing efforts lies in the simple observation that it is in everyone's interest for pharmaceutical houses, like other
businesses, to follow that strategy.

The distinction between total and average cost tells the tale. The marketing expenditures that *increase* total costs *reduce* average costs on a per-
unit basis. Why? Because the marketing costs are *variable* in contrast with
the *fixed* front-end costs of product development, which in turn are
reduced as the number of units sold increases. Any plausible estimate of
these development costs runs into the hundreds of millions of dollars for
that first pill. Without advertisement, those costs must be apportioned
solely among buyers who by hook or by crook find out about the drug on
their own. With information costly to acquire, that class of potential users
is too small to sustain the product. That situation is known to the firm,
which will not produce a drug that it cannot sell. By the same token, we
do not have to worry about overinvestment in drugs, such as me-too
products, that may be easier to develop from the existing technology. If
these have smaller social value than other lines of investment, advertising
and promotion are not likely to shift many people from lower-cost products that are every bit as good. So long as there are no externalities, promotional expenditures are just like any other cost: expenditures will take
place until marginal revenues equal marginal cost and no further. There is
no conflict in this setting between what is best for the firm and what is
best for the public at large.

To keep the analysis simple, assume that a new product costs $1 million
to produce and that, without marketing, it needs to sell at least ten thou-

sand units (one to a person) at a cost of $100 per unit sold. But assume further that the seller cannot sell that number of units at that price, because the effective demand at that $100 per unit is only 8,000 units, which will not cover the total front-end costs. Wholly apart from any concern about the marginal cost for manufacturing, shipping, and selling additional units, the product never gets launched. Consumers with a high value for the product get shut out.

There is at present good evidence that consumers respond by expanding purchases in response to general advertising. Here is a somewhat simplified explanation as to how this effect works.[10] Assume that for an additional $200,000 of truthful and accurate advertisements, the expanded product base covers 100,000 units sold for $20 each. At this point, the total costs *before* building, shipping, and other variable costs equal $1.2 million. Yet the revenues generated are equal to $2 million, so if the variable costs are below $800,000—say $500,000—the seller now reaps a profit from the transaction: total revenues at $2.0 million, less costs at $1.0 million plus $0.2 million plus $0.5 million. (I am assuming that $20 is the optimal price, which influences only the level of profit, not the basic analysis.) The key error in the short quotation from Jerry Flanagan lies in his failure to draw any distinction between the total costs for the entire production run (which increase) and the average cost for unit sold (which decreases)—in the example, from more than $100 per unit to $17 per unit.

The *social* inquiry is whether these increased profits in the firm come at the expense of any other individuals. Here in principle that unacceptable outcome cannot be true, because none of the marketing costs are foisted on strangers. Patients and physicians can always choose not to buy and thus remain at the zero net-benefit position. They have no incentive to drop below that position. Typically, any drug they purchase has an uncertain value. It could generate a cure; it could ameliorate pain; it could have no effect; or it could cause adverse side effects or death. But to each of these potential outcomes, the buyer can assign both some probability and some value, positive or negative. To say that a product has a net benefit means only that its *expected value* from the ex ante perspective is positive. It does not require (and for medicine could never satisfy) the further condition that each expected outcome from product use is positive. Bad results after the fact do not mean that the use of the drug was unwise before the fact.

Note, too, that any positive expected value from overall use is consistent with a highly *negative* valuation to loss of life or serious illness. After all, if we attach a high value to the life that bad drug treatment takes away, then we have to attach the same value to a life otherwise lost that good drug treatment saves. A detailed analysis is tricky because the gains from saving, or the costs from losing, any given life depend on the state of health when the drugs are taken. The sicker the person, the lower the downside from further sickness or death, and the greater the upside from the avoidance of death or the amelioration of basic condition. That simple dynamic helps explain the rational desperation of so many sick patients in search of last-ditch treatments. That said, if a person in a low state of health rates death at $1 million, then he or she has to attach at least that value to the avoidance of death. Hence this parity between gains and losses in life or health means that the usefulness of a drug depends on the odds of helping or hurting people. The sicker a person is, the lower the costs of adverse events and the higher the benefits for successful treatment. In the simplest case, if there is a 1 percent chance of death due to an adverse reaction to treatment, at a cost of $1 million, and a 10 percent chance of prolonging life by successful treatment, also with a yield of $1 million, then the expected return from use of that product is $0.1 million minus $0.01 million, or $90,000. High stakes do not entail negative expected values, and they are consistent, depending on the odds, with high positive expected values.

This global conclusion is confirmed if we break down the grand analysis by looking at the various groups that are affected by introducing marketing in the example above. Initially, 8,000 persons were in the group prepared to pay $100 for each pill put on the market, when none was in fact sold. These individuals now benefit because each of them pays $20 for a good for which they were prepared to pay $100, and thus gain at least $80 in benefits—consumer surplus—from the system, or $640,000. Added to that is the unknown amount of surplus that those willing to pay *more* than $100 would have garnered if the drug had in fact sold at the initial $100 figure, which we could postulate averages $15 per person, or $120,000 in total. Summing those two figures yields $760,000 in new consumer surplus above and beyond the zero surplus in a world with a good drug but no advertisement, and therefore no sale. No one could complain from a social perspective about generating $760,000 of consumer surplus from $200,000 in expenditures from company funds.

Next consider those individuals whose reservation price—that is, the maximum amount that they would pay—is located somewhere between $20 and $100. For sake of exposition, assume that the average person in this group would pay $40 per pill (that is, assume that the market expands more rapidly as price goes down), which implies that 92,000 persons each gain on average $20 from the transaction, for a total of $1,840,000. None of those gains would have existed in the world without advertisement, which when added to the first set of gains yields a total *social* increment of $2,600,000 from the $200,000 level of expenditure. The analysis, however, is still incomplete because it is necessary to factor in the gains to the shareholders of the firm, whose profit is $300,000 in this example. The grand total equals $2,900,000, of which close to 90 percent is received by consumers and not producers of the advertisements.

It is easy to quarrel with numbers pulled out of thin air, but harder to sort out sensible from frivolous objections. Just for the sake of argument, double the marketing expenditures and halve social gain, and still an impressive social increment of $1.3 million comes from a firm whose expenditures generate now only $0.1 million in profits. A sensible, but contestable, criticism is that any marketing campaign might be less potent than the example suggests, thereby cutting the social return from private expenditure. But that response gives away the game because it tacitly recognizes that increased social benefits necessarily flow from the expanded sales base. Stated more generally, and in ways of special application to pharmaceuticals, the key driver of advertisement lies in the ability to amortize (that is, write off over time) the initial expenditures over an ever-broader base of products. Starting from a zero base of advertisement, the big dollars spent in designing attractive labels, glossy advertisements, and punchy TV spots and in giving away free samples could create a tenfold increase in sales.

Whatever the exact number, allocating fixed costs of initial investment costs over tenfold the initial number of consumers drives down average prices. Average front-end costs of C/kn (where k is the multiplier effect, k>1) are lower than average costs without marketing, or C/n, where k equals one. Here, then, is a first approximation of how advertisement works: the saving in cost per unit equals $(C/n)-(C/kn)$; when k = 10, the saving equals 90 percent of cost. We should be thankful that drug companies market furiously—to drive down average costs by expanding the relevant market.

How then are any limits placed on marketing efforts? By the general concern of all firms with profit maximization. No drug company will overadvertise because it is against its interest to spend additional resources on marketing that generates less additional revenue than it costs. The basic principle of optimization of firm revenue—spend to the point, but only to the point, where marginal revenues equal marginal cost—guarantees this. No firm has an incentive to continue marketing just to expand sales. At some point the relevant benefits to the firm of new marketing efforts shrink. The new customers it attracts will not pay the $20, so total revenues can start to fall even if sales increase just as the higher expenditures on advertisements cut into profits. Absent external subsidies or taxes, the firm behaves in the socially desirable fashion.

Note, moreover, that this conclusion about the proper stopping point is not falsified by the industry rule of thumb that one additional marketing dollar generates on average $4 in sales. The firm that spends to the point beyond where a new dollar in marketing generates one dollar in new revenue is wasting its marginal marketing dollars. The large gains stem from those *infra*marginal expenditures—from those first dollars in an empty market—with exceedingly high returns. But so long as firms follow their own profit-maximizing strategy, then the natural limitation on marketing efforts prevents excessive spending. No one can claim that firms will hit that point on the button every time. Chances are they will misestimate both the cost and benefit sides of the equation to greater or lesser degree. But the essential point in favor of private marketing does not depend on the perfect knowledge of firms. It depends only on a showing that they have strong incentives to get those numbers right.

This argument also depends on an implicit assumption that the marketing identifies the preferences of its customers and then takes strenuous steps to satisfy them. Buyers know how much they would pay for certain combinations of benefits and costs, but they are unaware that this drug is able to provide them. In one sense, this contention sounds bizarre, because how can any individual have a well-formed demand curve for a product that he or she has never heard of. But in another sense, the argument is the soul of good sense. Individuals have certain tastes—good health and the avoidance of pain, for example—and the manufacturers of a new compound seek to exploit that known and invariant human taste. Before they launch a new product, they test it on various focus groups to determine levels of preference satisfaction.[11] It is easier to tweak products to satisfy consumers than to tweak consumers to accept what is put before them. Why spend enormous sums of money to "make" people like prune ice cream if in fact they prefer strawberry? Only politicians have the coercive clout to engage in preference reformulation, which private companies cannot implement unless they resort to false or misleading marketing devices—a topic deferred until the next chapter. A firm truly succeeds by finding a new drug that satisfies preferences in its own distinctive product niche. Retooling consumer preferences is a dead loser, which is why only totalitarian regimes take this path.

At this point, we have a sensible explanation why high advertisement expenditures should be both routinely expected and welcomed. The drug industry is a high-fixed-, low-variable-cost market in which firms should pour substantial sums of money into marketing and advertisements. To ask drug companies to behave in any other fashion falsely assumes that new products would be distributed to the same persons in roughly the same quantities in the absence of the marketing efforts that launch and maintain these products. It is simply unwise to condemn the industry because marketing costs exceed research costs, when both are indispensable ingredients in the overall process. And it is woefully misguided to indicate, as Relman and Angell suggest, that price controls need not have any effect on firm behavior tomorrow because profits exceed R and D today.

The data on this point are really too clear to admit of any dispute. First, the willingness of firms (that is, their capital contributors) to invest in new drugs is heavily dependent on the size of the market of which they are a part. In one study, Daron Acemoglu and Joshua Linn demonstrate that one powerful driver of drug innovation is the size of the potential market for the new drug product. More precisely, their data suggest strong correlations between market size and the overall rates of drug innovation. Thus their "estimates suggest that a 1 percent increase in the size of the potential market for a drug category leads to a 6 percent increase in the total number of new drugs entering the U.S. market." Similarly, they find that "a 1 percent increase in potential market size leads to approximately a 4 percent increase in the entry of new nongeneric drugs."[12] (A nongeneric is a drug subject to patent but representing a variation on some other patented drug, such that it is not a pioneer drug in a new class.) Second, strong evidence shows that the inability to pay leads to a contraction of research, especially into those ailments that strike third-world countries (for example, malaria) for which there is an insufficient financial incentive.[13] "Orphan" drugs for small populations also lag. More informal evidence in the wake of the $250 million Vioxx verdict shows that increased liability redirects investment away from general patient products and reduces its overall level on the other products.[14]

Note that neither of these studies is concerned with the issue of marketing or advertisement as such, but they offer powerful confirmation of the general theory. The size of any market is in part determined by the number of individuals (with resources to back their preferences, to be sure) who need some particular treatment. Restrictions on marketing initiatives are the functional equivalent of a contraction in the size of the relevant market, with negative effects on innovation. It is a mistake to assume that the size of the research and marketing budgets are independent of each other, or worse, that they are negatively correlated. Quite the opposite, the only sensible inference from the empirical studies is that any efforts to increase the ratio of research to marketing expenditures will backfire, as squeezing the latter will result necessarily in starving the former. The ratio of R and D to marketing gives no information about the success or desirability of either. Pharmaceutical progress is one that favors large battalions to move drugs from the laboratory into the marketplace. The total level of R and D expenditures will *shrink* if the marketing efforts are curtailed.

There is yet another intriguing study that points in the same direction. Darius Lakdawalla, Tomas Philipson, and Richard Wang have found that for about 40 percent of patented compounds, total sales *dip* as they move from patent-protected to generic status, with only modest increases in output in other categories. That reduction in sales volume cannot be attributed to the mysterious and instantaneous obsolescence of the off-patent drugs, although that factor could prove critical in the long run. Rather, the short-term effect comes because of two powerful economic effects that work at cross purposes. First, the price reduction in generics, often up to 80 or 90 percent of price, boosts sales. Second, the sharp reduction in marketing will stunt them. That marketing effort declines for two reasons. First, no generic drug can be marketed under its trade name, which remains with the original patent holder. Some effort has to be made to rebrand the generic under its medical name that no one can quite pronounce. Second, because generics are made by multiple firms, none has a strong incentive to market the generic because of its own common-pool problem. It faces all the costs of the marketing effort while its benefits are captured equally by its generic rivals. Hence for generic drugs, there is a sharp decline in the number of free samples on the one hand and in office visits by detail men and women on the other.[15]

These figures carry with them powerful implications. The proper measure of social welfare is not the cost of the drugs but the sum of consumer and producer welfare they generate. The social objective is not to minimize the cost but to maximize the benefit. If so, then going generic is in some sense a mixed blessing. Drugs are characterized by very high consumer surplus, as in AIDS cases, where the political pressures for reduced prices are most intense. Note that the social gains from wide dissemination are really large in any case in which the private value, measured in utility, is greater than the ability to pay, given the constraints of wealth. The seller of the product cannot extract any gain that is measured in subjective satisfaction but is limited to following pricing strategies that are limited by the wealth of the potential buyers. The upshot is that even for patented drugs, the proportion of consumer surplus has been estimated at twenty-five times the producer profits in key cases, a number that is closely in line with the earlier estimate.[16] In general, then, the critics are wrong to think that the social objective is to minimize marketing expenditures. It is to maximize net social benefit from drug use, which usually requires the precise opposite strategy.

Marketing Strategies

A response to the marketing issue cannot rest solely on a general analysis of marketing practices. It is also critical to see how these general principles play out in the two types of marketing efforts: (1) those directed to physicians and other health care professionals and (2) those directed to consumers.

Physician Marketing

The first class of marketing efforts comprises those directed to the physicians and institutions that use these drugs in hospital settings or prescribe them to their patients. It is not easy to persuade a group of sophisticated buyers, who need more in most cases than a simple pat on the back, to adopt a new therapy for their patients. For these people, time is money, and any hour spent gathering information about new drugs is an hour away from some other part of their practice. The natural desire to get more product information is in deep tension with the natural aversion to spending time in order to do it. Many of these promotional efforts at wining and dining are understood in part as efforts to cover the opportunity cost of time.

The task of marketing is made more difficult because the background information on new drugs often reads like a security prospectus: so full of doom and gloom that one wonders why anyone would think of switching to that product. That outlook is well reflected in the package inserts that accompany each new (and old) drug, which if taken literally discourage any sane person from using any drug at all, let alone a new one. The underlying marketing problem is further compounded by the FDA's highly cautious risk assessment of new drugs, which places a damper on projecting the more upbeat attitude needed to sell any drug at all. In addition, the FDA sometimes requires a premarket review of promotional materials, which of course reduces the likelihood that positive outcomes will be stressed equally with negative ones.[17] Marketing in the FDA's shadow makes the job of sale and persuasion even more difficult. The task is made still more difficult when the FDA approves drugs subject to conditions that no marketing be undertaken at all, as recently happened with a one-year ban on all direct-to-consumer advertisement for the antidiabetic drug symlin.[18] The slow launches reduce the class of consumers who receive the expected net benefit from the drug and cut down on the rate of investment return on a product that has, owing to the bounded length of patent terms, a short business life.

The stakes here are high. Quite simply, any marketing campaign that mirrors the FDA assessment will *not* be fair and accurate, but unduly pessimistic. The social loss of an excessively dour projection of risks and benefits is that people shy away from risky drugs that provide them with expected net benefits. That said, it is very difficult to switch baselines in midstream by launching a marketing campaign that minimizes the explicit cautions that the FDA requires in each use. Yet by the same token, the tough FDA standards can be turned into a marketing aid. The FDA imprimatur allows firms to announce that their products must be safe because they have the FDA seal of approval.

How then should marketing take place? In this regard, any pharmaceutical company finds itself in a bind from day one. Start with the obvious, and potent, objection that in light of its obvious financial stake, all its own health claims are discounted by physicians and patients. There are only two ways to overcome that negative image, but each in turn introduces fresh complications. The first approach uses the ubiquitous detail men and women to ply physicians with free samples and literature on drugs. The free samples, whose retail value was estimated at about $6.6 billion in 1998 and close to double that at $13.1 billion five years later, allow physicians to use these drugs on their patients.[19] Fortunately, these marketing expenses frequently translate into direct patient benefits for indigent patients. Direct physician observations on how well patients tolerate and respond to a new drug offer them important firsthand validation, which thereafter can be pooled across physicians. Sample use also helps physicians sort out new drugs, by putting the pharmaceutical company at risk for a negative patient response, on which physicians can follow up by tests and examinations, and by altering prescription decisions. That response pattern in turn works itself back into the initial decision to release the drug in the first place. Why push a new drug when anticipated negative responses will reduce sales? The drug companies have at least some incentive to select for distribution those drugs which they expect will engender a positive response. The strategy therefore contains at least one set of important built-in correctives.

Nonetheless, using detailers has come under a storm of criticism. One obvious problem here is that this strategy looks sustainable when adopted by one single firm but produces massive strangulation when followed on an industry-wide basis. The cumulative impact of endless visits counts as a real strain on physicians who watch their time eroded by countless pitches for drugs with differences so numerous and subtle that even professionals cannot keep straight. But like every action in this area, detailing is a two-edged sword. Each detailer is in a position to correct errors by others (as well as sowing new confusion of his or her own). It therefore becomes uncertain in these cases whether there is too much information or too little, or whether the exaggerations by one firm are corrected by the observations of a second, or third.

In these muddy circumstances, it is hard to see any form of direct and useful government regulation of detailing, but institutional and physician responses are surely in the cards. Indeed, the reaction has already set in, as the sales per detailing dollar have fallen in recent years. "Physician details have become almost twice as expensive, evidenced by the drop in sales representatives productivity of nearly 50% over the past seven to eight years."[20] In addition, physician and hospital groups, acting defensively to lend some level of order to the process, commonly enforce time, place, and manner restrictions on what detailers can do. As their sales efforts become less effective, their use will stabilize or even contract.

The second tack of marketing involves offering the much-reviled meetings and presentations, frequently in fancy resorts, to persuade physicians and other health care providers to adopt various new treatment regimens. Frequently, these lavish events are thinly disguised marketing efforts for the products in question. Yet before one waxes too indignant, it is best to note the difficulties in formulating a sound policy. Ideally, one would like to have neutral and dispassionate presentations of the pros and cons of various treatment regimens conducted by independent third parties. But if the pharmaceutical companies back off, then who should foot the $75 billion bill that results? And what gives us any confidence that some non-industry group will not have biases of its own that wrongly steer physicians away from good drugs? A quick trip to Worstpills.org reveals a list of more than 180 drugs—Actos, Avandia, Celebrex, Crestor, Darvon, and Vioxx among them—that it urges the public not to use, coupled with various petitions by Public Citizen to remove particular drugs from the market.[21] Yet Worstpills.org offers little information on the second half of its title, Best Pills, and its Web site contains no reference that I could find to industry FDA submissions or academic literature that point in the opposite direction. Everyone interested should surely consult the site, but no one should resort to it for one-site shopping, for it has nothing in plain view that indicates which new drugs ought to be adopted. There is, in a word, no incentive for it to look at both sides of the argument.

The upshot, therefore, is that any potential third-party efforts to tout good new drugs will usually be poorly financed and kick into gear only long after a drug launch has been undertaken. For drugs with positive profiles, weak marketing and long delay translates not only into low sales, but to a smaller level of consumer gain from the sale of the drug in question. The detailers who get drugs rapidly into circulation increase the returns to initial investment by shortening period between expenditure and return. The blunt truth is that everyone benefits from the aggressive and accurate marketing of promising new therapies. I want my physician to squeeze in an extra round of golf if it improves my own prospects for long-term care.

In dealing with these advertisements there is of course no principled objection to any private restrictions that are placed on the access that detailers have to physicians and other health care personnel. Hospitals and practice groups could, for instance, simply ban all detailers from consorting with their physicians and staff. But that is cutting off the nose to spite the face. These medical practitioners need that information and often cannot get it (or critical free samples) from any other sources. Hence the usual and more sensible strategy is to try to limit the nature and the frequency of the access, and the perks that go with them.

In addition, many institutions use pledges to address the obvious conflict of interest issue front and center. The "No Free Lunch" pledge is more than a wry reference to the work of Milton and Rose Friedman. It states that the pledge signer is "committed to practice medicine in the best interests of my patients and on the basis of the best available evidence, rather than on the basis of advertising or promotion." Immediately thereafter is a promise "to accept no money, gifts, or hospitality from the pharmaceutical industry; to seek unbiased sources of information and not rely on information disseminated by drug companies; and to avoid conflicts of interest on my practice, teaching, and/or research."[22] In one sense this position is hardly radical because the PhRMA Marketing Code similarly recognizes that it is improper for any pharmaceutical firm to offer products in ways "that would interfere with the independence of a healthcare professional's prescribing practices."[23]

The hard question is whether a conscientious physician or medical student should sign this pledge. The short answer to that question is no, for there is much to be said for the softer PhRMA standard of noninterference. The full explanation is a bit longer. On the positive side, the pledge to be aware of conflicts of interests and to adjust one's conduct accordingly is surely sound, as is the search for unbiased sources of information. But the negatives also count.

First, it is hardly clear how deep the commitment "to seek unbiased sources of information" goes. Does Worstpills.org count as a biased source on the ground that it presents only negative information about drugs and never offers opposing views? Or does it receive a blanket immunity from the pledge because it is not a supplier of new products? Or is it permissible to consult the site so long as one looks elsewhere for a second opinion?

Second, the unequivocal pledge to "not rely on information disseminated by the drug companies" goes too far in search of a sensible adjustment, for it is reminiscent of the harsh conflict of interest rules that have been put in place by the NIH for its senior staff and research scientists. Once alert to the dangers of advertisements, then health care professionals should decide on a case-by-case basis how they ought to proceed. Removing the serious risk of bias by a total ban comes at the cost of losing out on information that is valuable.

Third, the pledge to "avoid conflicts of interest" is also overbroad. There is only one way to avoid all conflicts of interest in any teaching and/or research, and that is to do neither. This pledge would be devastating to the practice of medicine for any physician who has worked for the drug company in the evaluation of or the clinical trials for a prescribed drug, when evaluation and trials have become so costly today that they cannot be fully funded by academic institutions. The usual response to most conflicts is a form of disclosure to patients, subject to review by some committee on conflicts of interest. Management of conflicts is a risky business, but it is less risky than the extreme pledge implies. So the ledger is decidedly mixed. The countermovement against advertisement is sensible, but the overreaction is not. There are, in a word, no purposive changes that will work a clear improvement in this difficult area.

Nonetheless, the drumbeat for categorical responses to potential conflicts of interest continues apace. In January 2006 a group of eleven prominent physicians, medical administrators, and social scientists associated with academic medical centers (AMCs) took the position in *JAMA* that the current regime of disclosures offered an inadequate response to these pervasive conflicts of interest, which could be met only by far more restrictive measures that these AMCs should impose on themselves.[24] The *JAMA* study's recommendations include a total ban on all gifts, the refusal to accept any free samples from drug companies, an exclusion from all medical group formulary committees of any health care professionals with financial ties to drug companies, and the prohibition of any direct support to various programs of continuing medical education. In place of these particular programs, the authors of the study propose that vouchers be supplied to low-income patients or other arrangements be made that sever any tight tie between a particular drug company and an individual patient. Likewise, pharmaceutical companies could contribute to a central fund for continuing education but could not support product-specific programs.

In a legal sense, the *JAMA* program is unobjectionable. As autonomous institutions AMC can dictate the terms on which they hire their physicians. They may choose therefore to leave pharmaceutical companies on the outside, looking in. But the wisdom of the total prohibition is a different matter. In support of its proposal, the *JAMA* study cites numerous studies all of which show that physicians who receive samples, attend meetings, or receive gifts or meals are more likely to use the products of the pharmaceutical companies that promote them. The implicit subtext therefore is that what is good for pharmaceutical companies is bad for AMCs and their patients.

Unfortunately, that hasty conclusion shows the danger in asking the wrong question. Of course pharmaceutical companies expect to benefit from the resources that they put into these programs. As they are profit-making institutions, we cannot expect anything else. But the fatal error in the *JAMA* study is its implicit assumption that benefit on one side necessarily implies detriment on the other. But for that critical proposition, the *JAMA* study offers no evidence of inferior patient care that stems from these promotional activities. Its single citation on this point is to a well-cited article by Ashley Wazana to the effect "that an overwhelming majority of interactions (on gifting) had negative results on clinical care," when in fact Wazana's article explicitly acknowledged that none of the cited studies relied on outcomes-based research. Indeed, it is hard to give much credence to any study that uses as its measure of *negative* care the "positive attitude toward pharmaceutical representatives."[25] It is therefore entirely consistent with the evidence that the information in question produced benefits on both sides, not just one.

Indeed, there is scarce reason to think that matters will shift for the better in any AMC that implements this proposal. One obvious effect is that fewer resources will be available. It is highly unlikely that pharmaceutical companies will make large contributions to voucher funds if they are unable to promote their own products. The same is true of their willingness to support continuing education by contributions to some large fund. Just who will supply the additional resources and funding the *JAMA* study does not say.

Nor is it clear that matters are made better by the total exclusion of physicians with drug company ties from making formulary choices. There is no guarantee that physicians who are hostile to drug companies are for that reason as objective or altruistic as the *JAMA* study proposes. They could easily have other axes to grind, and can now do so when all knowledgeable physicians with a different view toward profit-making activities and commercial development have been banished from any internal governance role within organizations. The proposal may reduce favoritism to particular firms, but it is equally likely to introduce large doses of a second form of bias: strong hostility to new products and the companies that supply them. It is not as though physicians are not subject to many other temptations and conflicts of interest in their own work. In addition, the new wall of separation will surely reduce the amounts of information available inside AMCs of new medical and pharmaceutical advances. The *JAMA* reform effort is notable for its unwillingness to address the downsides of its own proposal relative to the status quo, which is far from indifferent on the conflict of interest problem. One can only hope that AMCs are reluctant to follow the clarion call of some of their misguided leaders.

Direct-to-Consumer Advertisement

The second major branch of marketing efforts involves promotions and advertisements that are directed straight to the consumer.[26] It seems evident that this form of advertisement will be less extensive than marketing campaigns directed toward professional audiences, if only because certain key activities—free samples, promotional lectures, detailing visits, and the like—are wholly inappropriate. Nonetheless, the consumers who might take these medications are an obvious and sensible target for promotional activities, which now amount to a $4 billion-plus industry today.

Industry efforts in this regard have become much more extensive since the FDA liberalized these rules in 1997. This reform dispenses with the previous requirement that required potential users to scroll through all relevant information, a process that could take somewhere between thirty seconds and an eternity. In contrast, the new regulations require that the ad "must include a thorough 'major statement' prominently disclosing all of the major risks associated with the drug." In addition, it is necessary to supply "(1) a toll-free telephone number; (2) referral to a print advertisement in a concurrently running print publication, or provision of enough product brochures in various convenient outlets; (3) referral to a healthcare provider (physician, pharmacist, veterinarian or other healthcare provider); (4) an Internet web page address."[27] The new restrictions are not onerous, and they stress what should be apparent: good DTCA provides the target audience with easy reference to places where further information—both from the firm and from independent advisers—can be found. There is no requirement that some "neutral" site be included as well, but the FDA might do well to include some references of this sort.

The regulations had an immediate effect on opening up the market, from $791 million in expenditures in 1996 to $3.8 billion in 2004, which represents a small but not insignificant portion of the overall advertising budget.[28]

The most obvious point about the Rate of Investment (ROI) from DTCA is that typically DTCA more than pays for itself, even though there had been earlier industry doubts about its success, both for original launches and beyond.[29] Thus one detailed study noted that 11 percent of the brands had generated a negative rate of return. Of the 89 percent of campaigns that generated positive returns, about 16 percent produced between $1.01 and $1.50 per dollar of investment; 33 percent produced between $1.51 and $2.50; 21 percent produced returns between $2.51 and $4.50; 12 percent between $4.51 and $6.50; and 7 percent returns of more than $6.50. Indeed, the aggregate success rate from DTCA is more dramatic than the raw data suggest because larger brands—those with sales of more than $1 billion annually—typically show a high ROI of $3.66 per $1.00 of expenditure, while the comparable figure for smaller brands—those with sales less than $200 million—tend to just about break even, which imply that this advertising enjoys major economies of scale.[30] More generally, the data suggest that the firms that use DTCA seek to equate marginal revenues with marginal costs. In addition, the high rate of expenditures on the large brands suggests that the initial dollars expended on the advertisement campaign generate far more in revenue than they cost. And surely the surplus for many consumers is large as well. The exact size of both consumer and producer gains depends on a precise knowledge of the relevant curves for supply and demand, which are not easily learned. But so long as the gains on both sides of the transaction are likely to be larger, there is nothing about these expenditures that should generate any systematic social concern.

One common objection to DTCA reverts to the familiar but incorrect theme that advertisement necessarily raises the costs of needed drugs. That objection, which confuses average with total costs, has already been addressed, and there is no need to repeat that analysis here. The more specific worry with DTCA has to do with the pattern of consumer-physician interaction. The dangerous sequence feared by its critics is that the patient sees a drug that promises some relief from a chronic condition. A visit to the doctor leads to a request for the use of the drug which the physician may supply against his or her better judgment. That result may turn out to be especially dangerous with respect to lifestyle drugs—for example, Viagra—but the danger can easily extend to medications that are intended to address certain chronic conditions, like Celebrex and Vioxx, which are heavily promoted painkillers. Viagra could not survive without DTCA, as few physicians will open an office visit with "How's your sex life?" The pain medications could survive in smaller markets without the DTCA, at least in the extensive form that it has taken.

One partial response to the charge of improper patient pressure admits that the pattern emerges in some cases—although how many is hard to determine—but then insists that the proper place for intervention lies with stiffened resistance by the physician to block such ill-considered requests. A second, and more potent, objection is that the advantages of DTCA should be considered as well. These include, at a minimum, all cases in which individuals learn through DTCA about medications of which they were woefully ignorant. One great health care problem in the United States and elsewhere is that large number of individuals are undermedicated for such treatable or manageable conditions as diabetes, hypertension, and hyperlipidemia; many sufferers from these conditions fall into one of three categories: undiagnosed, untreated, or not treated to target. At this point, it seems that the central issue concerns not the possible errors in handling the cases that do make it into the system but the numerous and manifest errors with patients who are never brought into the system in the first place. In these cases, the impediments to getting the needed information are high: people of limited means are not likely to go to a physician without having some particular purpose, but they will go for a prescription if their own symptoms trigger a positive response from some advertisement. The entry costs are lowered by DTCA, which is the only means to reach people who are not already inside the organized health care system.

The proper question, then, is not whether all individuals make the right choices with DCTA. Rather, it is whether they do better with DTCA than they do without it. That choice again seems clear. Remember, so long as the advertisements are accurate, then there is no conflict of interest between the profit-making intentions of the firm and any social welfare objective. Rather, the same relationship holds as with physician advertisements: the greater the producer surplus, in all likelihood the greater the consumer surplus. Here, as in other medical contexts, the wealth of ordinary individuals is an upper bound on their ability to pay, but not on the gains in longevity and quality of life that they receive. There might be some case against a system that allowed for unregulated DTCA, but surely if there is any difficulty with the FDA rules, the solution lies in more, not less, liberalization. As this is written, the FDA seems to be reconsidering its position on DTCA, with a view to eliminating it altogether or tamping down on its effectiveness. The danger here is the familiar one: that the agency will look at the bad cases and ignore the positive benefits. But there seems to be no case for returning to the pre-1997 rules or shutting down the system altogether.

15

DECEPTIVE MARKETING

The previous chapter was devoted to the critical role that marketing and promotion play in the dissemination of new and valuable technologies, both generally and in connection with pharmaceuticals. Unfortunately, there is little doubt that overall inquiry is made more complex because of the common charge that many marketing campaigns are deceptive, false, misleading, or excessively aggressive. The *JAMA* study examined in the last chapter captured the negative view that most physicians have of the advertising and promotional practices, which are in turn defended, albeit cautiously, by some economists and lawyers.[1] Fraud and misrepresentation can never be defended in principle. True information induces transactions that work for the benefit of both sides, while false or misleading statements need not satisfy that win-win condition. Instead, the great fear in these cases is that erroneous statements will induce transactions that produce wins for the advertiser and losses for the patient and physician. And worse, the losses in question, when expressed in the coin of bad health, will far exceed the financial gains on the other side. But the proof of fraud, as will become clear, is so difficult that most reform proposals focus largely on regulatory and self-help countermeasures. The first part of the inquiry asks the extent to which deceptive advertisements and promotions constitute a problem, and the general legal, business, and administrative responses that might constrain it. In general, this inquiry suggests that self-help remedies by physicians and patients offer the best first line of defense. But even here, a general alertness may well be preferable to major institutional changes, such as those suggested in the *JAMA* study, which run the risk of serious overreaction. In some cases, however, the legal system does attempt to intervene to rectify cases of fraud, chiefly in connection with refunds for moneys that health plans and patients have paid for drugs that have been withdrawn from the marketplace. In any individual case, these requests for refunds might look small, but the modern procedural device of the class action makes it possible to aggregate millions of individual claims that result in demands for billions of dollars. Recall that Philip Morris took many years to defeat a $10.1 billion class-action judgment ($7.1 billion compensatory, $3.0 punitive) for alleged misrepresentation of its Lite Cigarettes, in violation of the Illinois Consumer Protection Act.[2] The Texas state attorney general has filed a suit asking for a $250 million refund for Vioxx purchased by the state, on the grounds that the transactions were fraudulently procured.[3] In addition, private actions seeking refunds in the billions have been brought in connection with Vioxx and other drugs. The danger of modest underdeterrence is now replaced by that of massive overdeterrence, even before we reach the actions for personal injuries sustained by drug users, which is the topic of the last part of this book.

Some Modest Responses to the Deception Problem

By most common accounts within the medical profession, the problem of deceptive advertisements and promotion is both serious and persistent. A quick trip to the Web site No Free Lunch contains links to studies in which squads of physicians have examined advertising content from drug company literature. These studies routinely find many drug company claims false and misleading either because they overstate the benefit of some course of treatment or underestimate the associated risks.[4] Thus one study of lipid-lowering drugs concluded: "In 45 claims (44.1%; 95% CI 34.3–54.3) the promotional statement was not supported by the reference, most frequently because the slogan recommended the drug in a patient group other than that assessed in the study." The payoff: "INTERPRETATION: Doctors should be cautious in assessment of advertisements that claim a drug has greater efficacy, safety, or convenience, even though these claims are accompanied by bibliographical references to randomised clinical trials published in reputable medical journals and seem to be evidence-based."[5]

A second study exudes the same sentiment in addressing the influence of drug company presentations in university hospitals. "Twelve (11%) of 106 statements about drugs were inaccurate. All 12 inaccurate statements were favorable toward the promoted drug, whereas 39 (49%) of 79 accurate statements were favorable (P = .005). None of 15 statements about competitors' drugs were favorable, but all were accurate, significantly (P < .001) differing from statements about promoted drugs. In a survey of 27 physicians who attended these presentations, seven (26%) recalled any false statement made by a pharmaceutical representative, and 10 (37%) said information from the representatives influenced the way they prescribed drugs."[6]

Neither of these (nor many other studies) shows a pattern of all inaccurate statements. And most are content to urge greater vigilance by physicians in dealing with these matters. In light of their variable results, the import of these studies is difficult to evaluate both on the *extent* of the wrong and the *choice* of remedy. In making these judgments, it is critical to stress yet again the enormous difference between making a sound moral judgment about right and wrong of misleading statements and creating a sound legal regime to respond to any shortfall. To organize the analysis, it is useful to see how the various claims relate under a familiar body of law, that which deals with misrepresentation. The most serious form of misrepresentation involves the use of fraud. The canonical definition of the relevant legal claim reads as follows:

> One who fraudulently makes a misrepresentation of fact, opinion, intention or law for the purpose of inducing another to act or to refrain from action in reliance upon it, is subject to liability to the other in deceit for pecuniary loss caused to him by his justifiable reliance upon the misrepresentation.[7]

In ordinary cases the definition of fraud usually covers both a knowing falsehood and statements made with reckless disregard of truth. In practice, moreover, misrepresentations can occur when the speaker has negligently made an assertion of fact or intention. Finally, innocent misrepresentations are possible as well. The clear progression down from fraud to recklessness to negligence to innocent misrepresentation raises the further question of which of these mental states is sufficient to establish some degree of wrong. Given that most claims of false and misleading statements in this context involve at least negligence if not recklessness or fraud, I shall therefore take the position that in this context, although not necessarily in others, people who rely on misrepresentation take the risk that these false statements are innocently made—that is, honestly and in good faith. It goes without saying that the representation no longer counts as innocent if it is repeated once the true state of affairs is known to the speaker.

With that caveat, each of the relevant elements is fraught with difficulty in the pharmaceutical context. One threshold question asks what counts as a misrepresentation of "fact, opinion, intention or law." In the case of drug marketing the last two elements are often not in issue, but the first two will frequently occupy central stage in assessing claims about the therapeutic qualities of new and established products. On the positive side of the ledger, some pressure is taken off the common-law rules because of the required use of preapproved FDA package warnings and inserts that contain explicit statements of the various risks and dangers associated with particular drug treatments. Those preclearance devices reduce the stress imposed on case-by-case evaluations of individual statements, either orally or in print.

One possible position, therefore, is that since the appropriate information is there for the asking, the entire problem is nipped in the bud. As I shall argue later, I think that this position is correct with respect to the adequacy of the warning when personal injury claims are brought for the harmful effects of drugs. The situation is vastly more complicated, however, because the FDA-approved warnings are not the only source of information to physicians or their patients. In practice, there is no question that the standard marketing devices can easily counteract, if not overwhelm, the impressions that any warning creates, so that in the end both physicians and patients can be misled by the full package of transmitted information. This outcome is less likely for physicians, who have access to multiple independent sources of knowledge about drugs, as well as the background information that they have acquired through years of schooling and practice. Even so, however, overpromotion may well incline them to favor in their prescribing behavior the drug houses that court them.

Yet even here there is no single metric that indicates how the two opposite pressures come together in individual cases. It is well understood on both sides of the debate that often physicians seek out drug companies whose treatments have impressed them in the past.[8] The matter is still more complicated because of the institutional efforts by hospitals to limit the contacts that physicians have with drug companies in order to cope with the problem of undue influence. Yet once again the effects of this intervention are uncertain. Some forms of regulation could easily prove effective, while others that are better designed may not be uniformly understood and observed.

Thus the effect of misleading marketing on physicians is minimized by the likelihood of their reading and relying on the appropriate warnings. The persuasive potential of misleading direct-to-consumer advertising, however, is much higher because the level of independence expected of ordinary consumers is lower, even if a simplified version of the product warnings is easily accessible. The danger is that the pictures and text will create a mood that will neutralize the explicit warnings found elsewhere and thus oversell the safety and efficacy of the product in question. Such is an obvious possibility, for example, with some of the extensive Merck advertisements for Vioxx that show tranquil scenes in which patients on Vioxx could have pain-free interactions with their grandchildren. The captions evoke the pain of osteoarthritis, then ask, "What's it like to look forward to the first few steps of the day?" or "What if how your body feels wasn't always the first thing on your mind?"[9] Great copy that goes right to the jugular, as it were. And for many people those advertisements are right on the money. Unfortunately, owing to the variation in individual responses, the advertisements could be read as making several false or misleading points that are not fully balanced by the usual small print about risk. The first of these is that Vioxx promises risk-free relief from pain. The second is that it should count as a first-line drug that ordinary people should be comfortable using without relying on more conventional pain relievers, such as Ibuprofen. As is evident from the Vioxx trials, the issue of overpromotion is a potent one in connection both with suits for consumer fraud and personal injury suits, to which we shall soon turn.

For the moment, however, the question is how these advertisements tie into the general law of misrepresentation. For these purposes it seems clear that these statements are in some sense material to patient welfare, so that they are not easily dismissed as mere "puff." But by definition they are directed to a vast class of consumers with different levels of knowledge and sophistication, so it is immensely difficult in any individual case to figure out how a false or misleading appearance influences consumer decisions. Do people rely on advertisements? In this regard, there is just no easy answer. The responses that various individuals have will depend on multiple sources of information that are almost impossible to disentangle. Some people see few, if any, ads for any product, or are disposed to disbelieve those they encounter. Others have experimented with multiple products before finding one that works. Still others have seen ads for several different products, which they confuse in their minds and thus are uncertain why they pick one over another. Still others have strong preferences but are persuaded by their physicians that some other course of treatment is preferable. In some cases, the consumer ads may introduce one distortion but still be beneficial on net because they correct a greater level of ignorance on the other side, which may be induced by bad information from any number of independent sources.

These cases of "joint causation" are relatively uncommon in the case of ordinary highway accidents. It is generally rare that a person will be hit by ten cars at one time. Hence there is little need to figure out how to sort out the causal contribution of multiple actors to a single, large traumatic injury. Yet in some situations, such as a building that is destroyed by two or more fires, or cumulative trauma cases which arise when individuals inhale millions of asbestos fibers from multiple sources over several decades, the question of joint causation arises with a vengeance.[10] Not surprisingly, the legal tools are frequently inadequate to tackle the problem at hand. There is some tendency to say that each responsible cause (that is, a fire or an asbestos fiber that can be traced to an individual whose conduct also satisfies any standard of culpability) should be responsible for the whole no matter how small the part that it contributed.[11]

The principles that apply to actions have relevance to words. Misrepresentation cases that involve a single false statement from one defendant to one plaintiff are easy to deal with: we know why the statement was made, and we know what benefit was extracted in the form of cash, property, or favor. But cases in which multiple sources of information are at work are no easier to deal with than the asbestos cases, for all allocations among dozens of suppliers tend to be arbitrary at best and in all likelihood false. It is rarely clear how much of the lung or other damage is attributable to asbestos, bad ambient air quality, smoking, or other diseases. It is rarely clear how much of the asbestos-related injuries are attributable to any given manufacturer. And most critically, there are pervasive levels of fraud in the documentation of these and similar cases.[12]

The great risk in these institutional settings is that partial reliance on a false statement will be treated as a justification for the imposition of full damages, which creates in turn the serious risk of overdeterrence. It seems clear that in principle—although we will see that the law is otherwise—the causal complications rule out individual actions for damages, and calls for the use of some administrative remedy, such as a proceeding before the Federal Trade Commission, which imposes fines and injunctions without having to sort through the mental influences at work in the response of any given consumer.[13] Yet that solution, too, is imperfect if it provides for underdeterrence in cases of systematic wrongs. The question here thus requires some balance of two separate kinds of error. In the heavily regulated context of prescription drugs, the risk is more likely to come from excessive and not insufficient liability. It is therefore not surprising that the typical physician litanies against deceptive or misleading advertisements call for greater vigilance, not for a barrage of lawsuits.

The problems here are not exhausted, moreover, because there is still the question of whether any reliance on the misleading advertisements works to the detriment of the individual consumer. The source of uncertainty relates to the choice of the appropriate baseline for analysis. In these cases, it is acknowledged on all sides that the outcome variable used in these studies measures changes in physician behavior, not in patient well-being.[14] The former is at best a weak proxy for the latter, even in the fraction of cases in which changed behavior is reported. Often, the switch may have financial consequences but not health consequences to individual patients. In some cases, the change in behavior will result in the use of a newer product at a higher cost—remember that generics rarely advertise—when a deeply divided profession is not of one mind on whether the new product is worth the cost differential. In other cases, the changes in product may increase one form of health risk but reduce other. The size of the problem, therefore, is not easily captured simply by noting the switching behavior, which in turn complicates the social analysis of deceptive marketing. In any individual case, it will be hard after the fact to determine whether the marketing efforts to either physicians or patients that altered behavior did so for the worse, which in turn makes it difficult to use the tort system to handle these claims on an individual basis.

The issue then arises of which remedy ought to be adopted to fill the gap. The self-help remedies by physician groups will matter, as will the self-regulation measures by pharmaceutical houses. But it is doubtful whether they will make a useful difference, because the underlying data is so unclear in its implications. The FTC has the power to enjoin or fine individual firms for false and misleading advertising, but it is unrealistic to expect that any government organization could monitor the huge volume of advertising today.

The Consumer Fraud Juggernaut

An Abundance of Remedies

The previous discussion posits the need for some moderate social response to deal with the recurrent problem of false and deceptive promotion. A moment's look at the current legal terrain indicates that these administrative and business responses are small potatoes in comparison with the megalitigation that now takes place chiefly under the rubric of consumer fraud, but also in suits that charge drug manufacturers with breach of warranty or unjust enrichment. By way of background, the common theme in all these actions is that of overpromotion. The information contained in drug warnings and packet inserts is just overwhelmed by the express and implicit representations made in advertising and selling these goods. The response to these dangers—which covers only cases of drug users who have suffered no physical injury—takes the form of lawsuits brought on behalf of both individuals and their insurers or other third-party payers seeking a refund for the purchase price that has been paid, or some fraction thereof.[15] Suits of this sort have been brought with respect to many drugs. Recently a New Jersey court has certified a nationwide class action against Merck, brought by third-party payers, which carries with it the risk of a multibillion-dollar exposure, insofar as it seeks reimbursement, plus interest, for the purchase of Vioxx.[16] In addition, similar consumer fraud cases have been brought for other drugs, most notable the Warner-Lambert drug Rezulin, which was a novel treatment of diabetes that had widespread use on the marketplace between its introduction in 1997 and its voluntary withdrawal, under FDA prodding, in 2000, because of liver complications. The Rezulin cases (on which I have consulted for Warner-Lambert) have gone through extensive litigation and thus give some insight into the overall difficulties that arise in this area.

To set the background, these suits for refunds would be unexceptionable if they involved only a demand for a refund for those *unused* products in their original packets that could be returned to the seller, for so-called "medicine cabinet damages."[17] So long as the remedy is so limited, no one would care about the nature of the legal theory on which the case was brought. Claims of this sort are solved administratively in most recall cases, where the effect of the refund on the return of the drug is to restore both buyer and seller to the positions before the transaction took place. The recall unravels the transaction, so it is as though the drug was never sold at all. In practice, however, some purchasers do not request these refunds, because they prefer to maintain their course of treatment notwithstanding the withdrawal order. This remedy, when exercised, is far from toothless because it means that the drug manufacturer has to give back all revenues for these products, receiving in exchange boxes of unused drugs that have to be destroyed. Recall that the drug business is a high-fixed- low-marginal-cost business, so that much of the profit is wrung out from the firm by having to take back those units whose marginal cost is, say, 10 or 15 percent of their sales price. No one could responsibly claim that the uncontroversial refund requirement is too small for firms to worry about. For blockbuster drugs it could amount to tens or hundreds of millions of dollars, depending on sales patterns.

The distinctive features of the modern consumer fraud and refund cases ratchet up the stakes in two key ways. The first is by seeking damages for drug products that have been *successfully* consumed by their individual patients. The second involves the *duplicative* requests for recovery brought by health plans, unions, or other third-party providers.

In both contexts, there is ample opportunity to bring class actions, often on a nationwide basis. When any of these suits goes forward, the plaintiff can offer three standard grounds on which recovery is sought: The first is the traditional contract theory for *breach of warranty,* under which the damage alleged is said to be the difference between the (higher) price paid and the value of the good supplied. The second is for a form of *consumer fraud,* under which often the entire purchase price is sought by way of recovery in accordance with statutes that explicitly allow for these actions. And the last involves a common law theory of *restitution,* under which again the plaintiff claims the entire purchase price on the grounds that the payment made resulted in unjust enrichment for the drug company that supplied the product.

The duplicate claims arise because of the complex system of payment when drugs are covered by some health benefit plan (HBP). The first tier of litigation involves suits, usually in class-action form, that are brought by individual consumers who have taken the drug in question. In most of these cases the HBP that pays for the drug contracts with some pharmacy benefit manager (PBM) that manages the actual operation of the business. These PBMs operate as independent contractors, and their functions include deciding which drugs to list in their standard inventory (so-called formulary drugs), acquiring the drugs from various suppliers, paying for these drugs with fund collected from the HBP, routing the drugs to the proper patients either through retail pharmacies or mail-order business, and collecting the copayments from individual users. Accordingly, the second-tier suits are brought usually by the HBPs that have footed the bill for the individual cases.

In principle, there is no reason ever to allow recovery on both these suits for the same purchase. But the different suits have often been brought (by design) in state and federal courts so that consolidation of all litigation before a single judge, which would help to forestall the risk of a double recovery, is difficult to achieve. In particular, the combined operation of the so-called *Rooker-Feldman* doctrine and the Anti-Injunction Act makes it virtually impossible for a federal district court that has, say, jurisdiction over a claim brought by an HBP to stop state court proceedings in a class action brought on behalf of individual consumers of drugs.[18] The procedural issues are still more knotty because these consumer fraud claims are often pursued as nationwide class actions in which the law of a single state is said to apply to nationwide sales, as is the case in the New Jersey class action against Merck. That particular action will remain in the state court system because it was brought before February 2005, before passage of the Class Action Fairness Act (CAFA).[19] This problem will be eased, however, in most future cases for which CAFA offers the defendant the firm option to transfer, or remove, the cases to federal court if two-thirds or more of the class members are from out of state, and may succeed, on a case-by-case basis, in persuading a federal court to take control over the case if between one-third and two-thirds of the plaintiffs are from outside the state.

Procedural complications to one side, it is important to understand the deep tension between ordinary product liability actions for personal injuries and even the simplest refund cases, those brought solely by individual customers. As a matter of legal design, these two bodies of law started in very different places. The personal-injury cases evolved through the tort law, and the consumer fraud cases often dealt with fraudulent advertising of products that posed no safety or personal injury issues. Hence each body of law has developed largely without reference to each other. The collision course should, however, be evident with respect to all products that generate claims for both refunds and tort damages. One of the implicit assumptions of modern product liability law is that the defendant should be able to fund the cost of future lawsuits out of the proceeds of sale and then smooth the risks of catastrophic loss through insurance.[20]

As a matter of first principle, this loss-spreading rationale does not identify those losses that should be included in the price of a drug and those that should be excluded. Without appeal to some additional principle, an ingenious plaintiff could argue that any and all costs should be passed on to the consumer in the form of higher prices. I will pass by the obvious point that some limit must be imposed on the liabilities supported by this reasoning, lest the price be so high that the market for the product shuts down altogether. Even if—and it is a big if in light of the current law—product liability law works well, it cannot function if the consumer fraud acts are so capacious as to deprive any firm of the resources needed to satisfy these claims. To allow both tort liability and a refund action is in effect to create a legal regime in which the plaintiff wins no matter what the outcome of the product use. If that use is adverse to him, then there is a product liability action. If that use is favorable, then there is a refund action. All those who have paid the embedded insurance premium either collect on the policy or get their money back. This system has to break down even with a sound product liability law and a sound consumer fraud law. It cannot survive when both systems are broken. Yet all refund actions explicitly preserve the tort option for injured persons, as in the tobacco cases. The coordination between the two systems is zero.

Consumer Refunds, Trebled

To see the difficulties here, start with the individual class-action suits brought by consumers. Assume for the moment that they had paid for their drugs out of their own pocket. In the Vioxx case, the drug users were at least as well off as before, and perhaps *better off*, in consequence of their decision. Recall that these people have suffered no adverse side effect and hence got all the benefits of Cox-2 inhibition, which by all accounts yields better tolerance against various forms of intestinal distress. Similarly, in the Rezulin case, the individuals who switched to that drug did so because they thought that it was, either alone or in conjunction with Metformin, better than Metformin alone. In those cases that proceeded without side effects, the choice of the recalled drug proved right. To give a simple example, if the benefit from Rezulin equaled $100 at a cost of $20, then a patient is better off to take Rezulin than Metformin, if the latter drug provided a benefit of $40 at a cost of $10. Recall that the consumer's goal is to maximize gain, not to minimize cost: and a gain of $80 from the first alternative is greater than one of $30 from the second. It is hard, therefore, to see how these consumers did not get the benefit of their bargain, or why, indeed, they have any compensable loss at all.

The situation does not change if their costs were covered by some HBP. Rezulin still worked better than Metformin, so they have no loss, and no need for suit. The HBP could easily by contract require its customers to reimburse it for its own expenditures if they recover something from the drug manufacturer. But in this case that collateral dispute will not arise because there is no refund to which this reimbursement obligation could attach. Similarly, the customers could by contract be required to allow the HBP to bring an action in their shoes (under the doctrine of subrogation). But again the outcome would be the same. The transfer of the claim only changes the identity of who brings the suit. It does not allow the new claimant to rise above the old one. Whatever defenses were previously available to the drug company remain available against the HBP. The want of any provable loss thus condemns this entire enterprise.

The situation is still odder because none of these drug users would have just pocketed the money if they had not taken either of these drugs in the first place. The patients who took Vioxx might have gone to Celebrex or Ibuprofen, but not to no drug at all. And if they had, would they have been better off than if they had stayed put? Similarly with Rezulin, where the case has been more fully developed, there was no evidence in the record that these patients would have stayed with Metformin if any other choices, often risky, were available, as they were. Once Rezulin was withdrawn from the market, the patients who left Rezulin shifted in large measure to two new drugs, Avandia and Actos.[21] Both operate in a similar fashion to Rezulin, and, ironically, both are prominently featured on Public Citizen's Worstpills.org. At this point, why act as though an older, less effective drug is the baseline for the ostensible consumer harm? It is worth noting that there is a real question whether any of these substitute drugs would have worked as well in these cases as did Vioxx or Rezulin, which only returns us to the question of heterogeneity of drug responses so critical to understanding the role of the FDA. The vast bulk of patients who could have tolerated Vioxx or Rezulin are now forced to switch to a drug that is less effective for them even if more desirable for others. But that only illustrates yet anew the central fallacy of drug safety in the United States. You cannot improve consumer welfare by restricting the choices of consumers, through either regulation or liability.

Next, we have to ask how to deal with any *independent* actions that the HBPs may decide to bring. In principle, there is no reason why the party that funds the purchase by an injured patient should be better off when it stands on its own claim. Nonetheless, the tortuous path of development is well illustrated by the Rezulin litigation. In the leading case of *Desiano v. Warner-Lambert Co.* the plaintiff class consisted of a group of HBPs, including various health care insurers, that had paid for their members to purchase Rezulin after it had been approved by the FDA for the treatment of Type II (adult onset) diabetes and before it was withdrawn in March 2000 after reports of a series of drug-related deaths from liver complications.[22] The complaint alleged that the FDA had approved the drug and kept it on the market as long as it did only because the defendant had lied to the FDA in the materials it submitted both to obtain the initial approval and to keep it on the market. In particular, the plaintiffs demanded a refund under New Jersey's Consumer Fraud Act. That statute authorizes a private action for the "refund" of any money that was acquired by means of:

> the act, use or employment by any person of any unconscionable commercial practice, deception, fraud, false pretense, false promise, misrepresentation, or the knowing, concealment, suppression, or omission of any material fact with intent that others rely upon such concealment, suppression or omission, in connection with the sale or advertisement of any merchandise or real estate, or with the subsequent performance of such person as aforesaid, whether or not any person has in fact been misled, deceived or damaged thereby.[23]

The act further provides that that "any person violating the provisions of the within act shall be liable for a refund of all moneys acquired by means of any practice declared herein to be unlawful." And for good measure it allows recovery of treble damages, attorneys' fees, and costs.[24] This package was intended to give a boost to the lone consumer with a small claim. But we have come a long way with the modern expansion of class actions.

As stated, this statute is a peculiar amalgam of common-law actions with regulatory oversight. The first part of the statute lists the kinds of misstatements that generate the liability for the refund. But the last portion of the statute does not require, as one might expect, proof of the loss sustained by individuals who acted in reliance on the false statements or omissions. Quite the opposite, it allows the refund "whether or not any person has been in fact misled, deceived or damaged thereby." The tendency to cause such harm, even if it is manifested in only a small fraction of cases, allows a refund of the purchase price in all cases. This aggressive standard of liability results in a substantial level of overdeterrence by allowing a full refund to *all* buyers when the deceptive statements influence the conduct of only a *few* individuals, who of course are virtually impossible to identify after the fact. Three numbers are relevant. The first is the apparent value of the treatment with the inflated representations. The second is the actual value of that treatment once those misrepresentations are corrected. The third figure is the cost of the drug. In many cases the first number, say $120, will be greater than the second, say $100, which will be greater than the third, say $70. In this case, correcting the misrepresentation reduces the level of consumer surplus from $50 to $30, but it will not change behavior, because the drug is still worth purchasing. Any refund of the full purchase price is wholly inappropriate because the proper measure of damages in such cases is zero. In other cases the value of the drug when the truth is revealed falls from $120 to $50. In this case, damages of $20 are appropriate, but once again a refund of the full purchase price is not. By ignoring these numerical variations, the Consumer Fraud Act first overstates the actual damages by allowing the plaintiff to recover the cost of the drug in all cases. It then uses trebling to compound the original error. The net effect of these combined errors is to chill any effective marketing. The overdeterrence is then compounded by the treble-damage provisions and the one-way shifting of attorney's fees, which plaintiffs' lawyers collect if successful. No fees move in the opposite direction if the defendants prevail.

Similar kinds of errors were at work in the Rezulin cases. There the complaint alleged that "they [the insurers] would not have bought [d]efendants' product, rather than available cheaper alternatives, had they not been misled by [d]efendants' misrepresentations."[25] None of the claims alleged that the drug users suffered any physical injury; nor was it established that the cheaper alternatives would have performed as well as Rezulin in all or even some of the cases. Taken as a whole, the evidence revealed the expected response in a world of heterogeneity in the user population:

> As plaintiffs acknowledge, "hepatotoxicity is a known complication of most prescribed drugs." Other side effects also are common. And the claim is not that Rezulin caused liver or cardiopulmonary

injury in all or even most who ingested it. On the contrary, even plaintiffs' experts agree that "the controlled clinical studies of the drug Rezulin demonstrate that the vast majority of patients who were treated with Rezulin tolerated the drug well and had no elevated liver enzymes and had no liver injury as a result of the drug."[26]

The insurer claims, moreover, run into an additional difficulty because there was ample authority to support the district court judge's conclusion that the harm to any insurer was sufficiently indirect that the sole action for fraud should lie on behalf of the individual purchaser, not on the plan that paid for the drug.[27] In this world the insurer could sue only if it obtained an assignment under contract that allowed it to maintain the action of the insured, but subject to any defenses that could be raised against the original purchaser.

The primary question is why an HBP, any more than an individual customer, should ever be entitled to a full refund for a drug that did all it promised for a patient and more. In allowing the insurers' action to go forward, Judge Calabresi, a pioneer in the economic analysis of tort law, relied on the implausible analogy that refund claims would surely be allowed if the defendants had simply sold an old diabetes drug, repackaged under a new label at a higher price.[28] Put aside the implausibility that any reputable company would even dream of such a swindle. The key point here is that if in fact any two drugs were *identical,* then by definition no patient could receive an increased benefit that would justify the price increase. Of course, the buyers should recover from the *excess,* and once they do, they should reimburse their HBP in accordance with their agreements. There is no reason to worry about the status of indirect purchaser at all. But this is a far cry from any case in which the price increase comes, for the parties in the class, with a superior product, which for these patients could have easily reduced the HBP overall costs of care. *Desiano* thus offers the odd spectacle of allowing individuals and health plans that enjoyed a net benefit from Rezulin to get their money back because they were exposed to a risk of harm that *never* materialized.

The decision in *Desiano* required the district court to review the case a second time, on the assumption that the causation element was made out with respect to these plaintiffs. But the wheels of fortune turned once again. In the aftermath to *Desiano,* Judge Kaplan (who had sided with Warner-Lambert on the causation issue the first time around) took a closer look at the three particular claims involved in the case and dismissed all three in *Rezulin II* on technical grounds. With regard to the breach of warranty claim, he noted that the HBPs did not count as purchasers of the drugs in question, even though they footed a large chunk of the bill through their arrangements with Medco, their pharmacy benefit manager, or PBM.[29] That point followed because actions for the financial losses for breach of warranty, as a matter of general contract law, flow only to the purchaser of the goods—here the PBM—that had presented no claim of its own. The decision was silent on whether Medco could have used this same breach of warranty theory, even if its entire outlays were covered by payments from either consumers or the HBP. And it did not ask whether both Medco and the individual patient could maintain parallel lawsuits, since neither was before the court.

The statutory consumer fraud cases were dispatched on the grounds that, notwithstanding their use of the words "any person," the relevant statutes limited their protection to ordinary consumers, which did not include a sophisticated commercial entity.[30] The clear sense of these decisions is that ordinary businesses have a level of knowledge that makes it unnecessary to give them the same protections against fraud as individual consumers. Finally, the claims for unjust enrichment tumbled on the ground that this action could be brought only by the party that had paid the money over to the drug manufacturer, which again was Medco.[31]

One of the glorious and worrisome features about the American system is that one sound case does not bring an issue to its conclusions. As noted earlier, the same type of consumer fraud case was brought in New Jersey, Merck's home state, under the New Jersey statute. Only this time, the reception in the trial court was quite different. The argument that only individual purchasers who consumed the product could sue was rebuffed with the observation that it is just "too simplistic" to restrict the action to the actual buyer, thus allowing suits for "misrepresentation causing a 'person' to pay for something they otherwise would not have been willing to pay for because of the higher cost."[32] What makes the matter still more intriguing is that the New Jersey statute, which is the most liberal in the nation, was held to govern the refund actions of individual plaintiffs throughout the United States even when they purchased their products from PBMs located elsewhere. In effect, this decision allows the single state most favorable to the plaintiff to set the standard for the rest, when it remains possible to judge each transaction by the law of the state in which it took place. The difference in response between the New York and New Jersey trial judges should give pause to anyone who cares about the soundness of the civil justice system. The choice of judge and forum could easily be worth billions in litigation that nowhere addresses the massive overdeterrence that comes from allowing these claims. No legal system should concentrate so much power in the hands of so few. Given the current configuration of power, it does not take a weatherman to see which way the wind is blowing. But it takes a full appreciation of the lawsuits for personal injury to gauge just how fiercely that wind blows.

VI

LIABILITY FOR PHARMACEUTICALS

16

TORT PRELIMINARIES

The actions for consumer fraud represent the first blow in a one-two combination directed toward drug products, especially after they have been withdrawn from the market. But a problem of equal if not greater dimension lies in the suits that are brought by or on behalf of that fraction of product users who claim to have been harmed by the drugs. Thus the final regulatory challenge has been reached: what is the liability of a drug manufacturer for physical injuries or death caused by a drug that has come under attack or has perhaps been withdrawn from the market? The ramifications of this problem do not call for any elaboration in light of the thousands of suits filed against Merck for Vioxx, and Pfizer for Celebrex: potential verdicts are estimated at anywhere from $3 billion to $30 billion for Vioxx if Merck loses only a few critical cases. The first case against Merck, now on appeal, is a suit by Carol Ernst, the widow of Robert Ernst, whose death certificate reads "cardiac arrhythmia secondary to coronary atherosclerosis."[1] Ernst, some of whose key arteries were about 70 percent blocked, was an athlete who had run a marathon three months before he died in his sleep—and who had gone cycling the day that he died. I shall refer to this case from time to time insofar as it illustrates the issues that follow. But remember that it is only one case of the several thousand that are working their way through courts across the nation.

In principle, we could identify two obvious targets for potential tort liability for drugs withdrawn from the market: the private manufacturer of the drug in question (and in principle, the retailers and distributors), and the individual physicians who could be liable for medical malpractice for wrongly prescribing the drug. For its part, the FDA is largely immune from all liability by virtue of its status as a government actor. The Federal Tort Claims Act establishes an ironclad legal barrier that rightly protects the FDA from tort liability in the course of exercising its supervisory and oversight functions.[2] Its exposure to the fallout of withdrawals and recalls is, therefore, purely political, but not for that reason to be lightly disregarded. It is routine for the FDA to be flayed for its lax behavior in these situations, which of course reinforces its incentives to keep drugs off the market and to cause the Type II harms that lie beneath the radar screen. The focus of liability is on the firms, and in most cases, the liability system imposes enormous administrative costs while working at cross-purposes to any sensible allocation of risk for either personal or financial harm. These claims will be discussed in due course, but first it is necessary to give a brief account of how the liability issue gained strength in the first place: via the judicial neutralization of contract defenses.

Contract Is Dead

As a matter of first principle, why is the risk of injury to the consumer from any product, whether or not subject to FDA oversight, regulated by the tort law and *not* by the producer-consumer contract?[3] One possible answer is that the two parties do not have any direct contractual relations or, as lawyers like to say, are not "in privity" of contract with each other. That want of privity typically arises because the parties are separated by a network of distributors and retailers (who, while formally liable as a manufacture, typically drop out of the cases, except for strategic and procedural reasons).[4] As we have seen, the argument that two parties do not have direct contractual relations has proved successful in some but not all courts in dealing with suits for financial refunds. To be sure, this separation at one time was thought to justify total immunization from liability on the ground that an injured party could sue only the person from whom he had purchased the goods.[5] Early twentieth-century legal developments, however, allowed the injured plaintiff to jump over that gap and treat the case as though he or she were in direct contact with the original supplier, or, for that matter, any other party in the chain of distribution.[6] In recent times, this privity limitation has had no traction in suits for personal injuries or wrongful death.[7]

In one sense, that fiction should not be needed, at least in any regime that allows multiple parties to enter into whatever contracts they think to their mutual advantage in the delicate matter of loss allocation. The privity limitation created by the legal system is not an immutable barrier of nature. In many settings, two parties who normally do not do business with each other can bring themselves into privity by various mechanisms. For example, the manufacturer of an automobile can make the dealer its agent in order to enter into a direct contract with the ultimate consumer. If that were in fact allowed, once firms perceived that the basic tort law was moving toward excessive liability—that is, liability that from the ex ante perspective costs more than it is worth—they could take steps to rectify this situation by demanding waivers and disclaimers. In these situations, I am confident that waivers of many claims for death, personal injuries, and economic losses would become routine, as they are in every contract that I have ever read anywhere for the provision of goods and services.[8]

Yet the legal position is clearly otherwise. Contractual disclaimers are routinely allowed for certain forms of economic loss, at least if the requisites for contract formation are satisfied, which turns out to be difficult to achieve under the current provisions of the Uniform Commercial Code.[9] But the dominant rule today is quite the opposite with respect to physical injury. Historically, the rejection of the privity limitation in tort was accompanied by the insistence that various warranties and disclaimers were against public policy.[10] Today there is simply no serious resistance to that position in the governing law. Section 18 of the Restatement (Third) of Products Liability summarizes the current state of affairs with this categorical statement: "Disclaimers and limitations of remedies by product sellers or other distributors, waivers by product purchasers, and other similar contractual exculpations, oral or written, do not bar or reduce otherwise valid products liability claims against sellers or other distributors of new products for harm to persons." The explanation for this sweeping prohibition is found in comment a: "It is presumed that the ordinary product user or consumer lacks sufficient information and bargaining power to execute a fair contractual limitation of rights to recover."[11] End of story.

Unfortunately, as is so often the case with consensus views, the Restatement position is wholly undefended. Note that the comment says "presumed." It does not say that the proposition can be rebutted in any particular case, and it allows for no evidence to the contrary. The Restatement's undocumented conclusion on so critical an issue is, and should be treated as, a public travesty—it is the work of an official committee intent on preserving the bar's lucrative concession over product liability cases under the banner of consumer protection. Under this rule, any signed waiver is worthless, for once the first sign of trouble appears, the prudent firm will face a protracted lawsuit in which the prospect of obtaining summary judgment (that is, judgment before trial) is slim to none.

One incident will give some sense of the size of the litigation risk involved. Glial cell line–derived neurotrophic factor (GDNF) had been made available on a limited basis in clinical trials as a potential treatment for Parkinson's disease. Some individual patients had reported marked personal improvements from use of the drug. One patient, for example, reported that using the drug allowed him to redo his kitchen when previously he could not hold a nail staple.[12] But when Amgen ran its clinical trial, it first found that the drug worked no better than a placebo on average—that desperate error in judgment once again. It then discovered that the drug carried with it serious safety risks and hazards. Naturally, these findings were disputed by physicians and patients who thought that they had benefited from the drug. No matter. After reporting the information to the FDA, and consulting with outside ethicists, Amgen stopped GDNF clinical trials, leaving its previous users in a lurch.[13]

The howls of protest from unhappy patients are confirmed by the desperate measures they took before Amgen's decision was made final. GDNF is administered by a pump that injects the compound into the brain through a catheter. Many patients refused to shut down their pumps because they feared that they could not be reopened if Amgen reversed course and decided to resume the clinical trials. Any respect for individual autonomy would have allowed these patients, who were steeped in their knowledge of the drug's effects on their bodies, to sign a waiver that should be relentlessly enforced against them in the event of adverse consequences. But the basic trend in this area is to always find, or at least to allow a jury to find, that the consent that was given in any individual case was ineffective because it failed to mention, or sufficiently stress, all the detailed risks in the case. That position could be bolstered by the view that consumers, as a class, suffer from optimism bias that leads them to underestimate the dangers in question.[14]

The upshot of this sorry impasse is that no legal counsel to a drug company could give a responsible opinion that any waiver obtained would protect it from suit. I have no doubt (but no inside knowledge whatsoever) that this underlying fear of tort liability was of uppermost concern to Amgen when it took GDNF off the market. After all, it refused to license the drug to any other potential developer, not because that transaction did not make any commercial sense but because it had to know that it would remain in the crosshairs of every tort lawyer in the land for any adverse consequences from GDNF's use.

The price of the Restatement rule on assumption of product risk, then, is to undercut the countless statements about the importance of autonomous choices on medical matters.[15] But while that statement may be sufficient to allow patients to *refuse* treatments that might provide benefits, it is wholly inaccurate when it comes to allowing patients to *accept* treatment that might do them harm. As before, it seems as though the law has dramatically different responses to patients' Type I and Type II errors. It will do nothing to help patients who make Type II errors by refusing to accept a beneficial treatment. In contrast, it will move heaven and earth to undo contracts when the drugs taken are alleged to cause harm. Today's simple truth is that *no* individual waiver is binding no matter how full the disclosures, and no matter how anxious the consideration by the persons directly affected. This is paternalism with a vengeance. Remove freedom of contract, and lo and behold, people are not free. How then does the world look?

Tort Liability for Personal Injury

Obviously, any individuals who claim to have suffered injury from a drug may be in a position to maintain a tort action against the manufacturer. In principle, these suits can be brought for any drug, whether or not it remains on the market. In practice, plaintiffs have obvious reasons to focus their fire on drugs that have been removed from the marketplace, either voluntarily or under FDA order: the causation issue is set up in their favor. The most conspicuous suits of this sort, which are now taking shape, involve both Vioxx and Celebrex. This chapter is being (re)written just after the quarter-billion-dollar verdict was rendered against Merck in Angleton, Texas, which provides a dramatic benchmark against which one can assess the slender advantages and the huge dangers of jury trials on pharmaceutical issues. But everything in its own time.

By way of general background, however, product liability cases raise a raft of common and separate issues. The most critical common fact in these cases raises an issue that is not easy to solve in drug cases—namely, had the injured party taken the product which had been supplied by the defendant manufacturer? That question of product identification is easy enough to solve in the case of machine tool or automobile injuries, but it can raise tricky questions in drug cases. The potential liabilities are so large that individual parties have a strong incentive to lie (no more delicate word will do) about whether they have taken the drug at all. In all cases, it is easy to assert that a drug has been taken but difficult to contradict that charge without some close examination of the record. A *New York Times* account of testimony in one case, *Rogers v. Merck,* demonstrates the troubling state of the evidence on which the courts must rely:

> According to Merck's filing, Ms. Rogers initially said that her husband "took Vioxx for a long time on a very regular basis." When Merck's lawyers pressed her for details, she said that he had visited a doctor on Aug. 10, 2001, 25 days before he died, and received a prescription for Vioxx. But the prescription was never filled, according to Merck. Instead, Ms. Rogers said that her husband had taken samples of Vioxx he received from his doctor in the month before he died. She said she stood next to him when he received the samples.[16]

The Berenson story goes on to relate that the plaintiff claimed that she still had twenty pills remaining from the sample package that her physician had supplied her. The difficulty here was that the markings on the packet indicated that they had been delivered only six months after her husband's death. Her husband's physician also testified that he never gave out samples for more than four or five days.[17] No matter, the court would not issue a summary judgment that would spare Merck the trial.

Nor does this appear to be an isolated case. The recent New Jersey litigation on Vioxx liability raised the question of whether the plaintiff Frederick Humeston had taken two Vioxx pills on the day of his heart attack. Humeston lost his case when the jury decided that Merck had kept the FDA fully abreast of the risk factors associated with Vioxx—a welcome shift from the outcome in the *Ernst* case, to say the least. But the case was weak on the connection between the use of Vioxx and Humeston's medical condition. The medical evidence indicated that he suffered from a full range of other ailments that were sufficient to produce a heart attack, even if he had taken Vioxx. But the simple question here was whether he had taken the tablets at all. Once again the report, this time by Thomas Ginsberg:

> "You really don't remember when you took Vioxx, do you?" asked Christy Jones, one of Merck's defense lawyers.
>
> "I took as needed," Humeston said, who earlier admitted having prescriptions for several pain medications but being unable to remember when, or if, he took the others.
>
> Asked later by his own attorney, Christopher Seeger, whether he took Vioxx on the day of his heart attack, Humeston said "yes."
>
> "I remember it was the last two pills in the bottle, and I told my wife we had to get a refill," said the soft-spoken Humeston.
>
> Both lawyers showed a hospital admission record for Humeston that clearly shows "Vioxx" as one of his medications at the time. But the record also listed a question mark under "last dose" and lists another drug, Ultram, which Humeston said he has no recollection taking.[18]

Confusions of this sort are legion in these cases, which create this catch-22: The claim for liability rests on the assumption that the patient should have been warned of the risk of heart attack from the occasional use of Vioxx. But why warn him of that risk if it did not materialize at all in this case? The reader can judge how many cases like this are likely to be filed in the future—especially if the plaintiff prevails.

Nonetheless, some general remarks are indicated. It is a commonplace feature of most academic discussions to underrate the risk of fraud and to overrate the ability of cross-examination to expose it. The source of the difficulty is inherent in all product liability actions. The defendant has no information about what happens to his product once it leaves his possession, and thus has to overcome a major information deficit. One early historical illustration of this problem is the 1917 case *MacPherson v. Buick*, which was the key decision that did away with the privity requirement.[19] The description of the facts found in Cardozo's appellate decision in *MacPherson* runs roughly as follows. Buick made a car that was sold to the plaintiff through dealers. "While the plaintiff was in the car, it suddenly collapsed. He was thrown out and injured. One of the wheels was made of defective wood, and its spokes crumbled into fragments."[20] The car was said to have been traveling at about eight miles per hour on the open road. Professor James Henderson had this tart response to the claim, based on a close look at the record: "The problem with MacPherson's story was that it was premised on a physical impossibility. Uncontradicted expert testimony from defendant's experts showed that, at such a low speed in high gear, the Buick would have stalled in its tracks—the engine could not possibly have continued to operate in four inches of gravel—and the car would have come to a stop almost immediately."[21] The car had also been used to haul around concrete, and no other wheel used by the defendant had ever failed.

The slippage between what happened and what was reported was large, and that same risk exists in all product liability cases, no matter what product type is involved. Nor is the danger of fraud confined to a particular class of product liability cases. The institutional problem reached epic proportions during the late 1980s, for example, in dealing with certain workers' compensation claims filed in California, which involved the organized operation of a fraud ring.[22] There has already been exhaustive documentation of fraud in the filing of recent asbestos claims, whose number has mushroomed even as the level of exposure to asbestos has fallen sharply over the past thirty years.[23] More recently, the question of fraudulent claims surfaced front and center in major silicosis litigation in Texas, in front of Judge Janis Jack, where this brief paragraph gives some sense of the magnitude of the problem:

> In total, the more than 9,000 Plaintiffs who submitted Fact Sheets listed the names of approximately 8,000 different doctors. And yet, when it came to isolating the doctors who diagnosed Plaintiffs with silicosis, the same handful of names kept repeating. All told, the over 9,000 Plaintiffs who submitted Fact Sheets were diagnosed with silicosis by only 12 doctors. In virtually every case, these doctors were not the Plaintiffs' treating physicians, did not work in the same city or even state as the Plaintiffs, and did not otherwise have any obvious connection to the Plaintiffs. Rather than being connected to the Plaintiffs, these doctors instead were affiliated with a handful of law firms and mobile x-ray screening companies.[24]

This entire question of product identification arises in all these cases, so don't expect clarity on the evidence in the thousands of Vioxx cases that are as yet untried. Just the difficulty of deciding the basic threshold issue of what pills were taken and when is one reason to show caution before marching down a road that creates extensive tort liability. The point, of course, is not decisive, but it does suggest that routine problems of administration can exert a heavy influence on matters that many people prefer to treat as a simple matter of individual justice. To explore this claim in greater detail, it is necessary to examine all three cases in the tripartite classification of product liability law: manufacturing, design, and warning defects.[23] That will be the subject of the next chapter.

17

PRODUCT LIABILITY FOR PRESCRIPTION DRUGS: MANUFACTURING AND DESIGN CASES

The object of the previous chapter was to explain how the built-in structures of contract and tort law send the law of drug liability off in the wrong direction. The insistence that tort rules, no matter how misshapen, should dominate contractual allocation of risk for drug loss starts the game off on the wrong foot. Treating judicial rules as inflexible commands makes it impossible for private action to correct the faulty rules generated by judges who have little command over the underlying liability issues. And the casual way in which individual claimants are allowed to establish that they took certain medications then predictably opens the door to systematic fraud and abuse, which no contractual provisions can now stop. It is not a pretty picture.

Yet even if these problems are put off to one side, it still remains to understand how the product liability law develops once it is established that an individual patient has taken some drug which is alleged to have caused harm. The topic is necessarily an expansive one because it requires a review of both the basic case of the plaintiff and the possible defenses to it. In the first portion of this chapter I therefore examine the three major types of "defects" around which product liability law is organized: manufacturing defects, design defects, and warning defects. The centrality of the defect notion is matched only by the elusiveness of its definition. Without the concept of defect, the manufacturer of a knife would be liable every time it cut someone, and the supplier of a drug would be liable for all known side effects. The concept of defect thus works as a filter to knock out from the legal system those cases of innocent use. Yet even when a defect is found, it gives rise to a fresh set of difficulties. How is that defect causally linked to the death or injury in any particular case, and what defenses, typically against charges of wrongful conduct of the drug user or his physician, are available? In this chapter I will examine the manufacturing- and design-defect cases that set the framework for the major battleground in drug cases: the warning issue, which is large enough to receive a chapter of its own.

Manufacturing Defects

The first and easiest class of product defects to understand comprises cases that deal with lapses in fabrication, and those in which drugs have allegedly been incorrectly prepared. Such cases might from time to time be brought, but quality control standards are so strong that lapses in fabrication do not represent a significant exposure to potential liability. The real danger in this area comes from another quarter: mislabeled counterfeit drugs. In principle, the outcome of such cases is easy: the defendant that did not make or market these products has the strongest possible defense: "I didn't do it." But that has to be proved, and while a general record of spotless production counts as a powerful card, it is not a trump. To gain a summary judgment, the manufacturer will have to get some independent information as to the particular medicines taken, or their packaging, or their lines of distribution. But these are troublesome matters of evidence, not key matters of principle, so there is no reason to deal with them further. In general, if the production defect traces back to the manufacturer, the case will be settled out of court.

In addition, no matter what the legal regime, no manufacturer is likely to disclaim liability for production defects. Any effort to protect against exposure after the fact will decimate the original markets. Indeed, when the Swine Flu Act was passed in 1976 to relieve the manufacturers of liability for inadequate warnings, liability for manufacturing defects was retained.[1] The point is no accident. The rational manufacturer will stand foursquare behind its brand and its product.

Design Defects

Design-defect liability is also of little consequence in dealing with pharmaceutical products. The gist of a design-defect case is that some alternative product design would have allowed the product to discharge its central function without being encumbered with the particular features that render the product not reasonably safe.[2] The key words are the last three, "not reasonably safe." They were consciously chosen to suggest a somewhat lower threshold than the parallel words "not unreasonably dangerous," which were used in 1965 in the Second Restatement of Torts.[3] Yet even if we put that point to one side, the key difference between the manufacturing- and design-defect sections is that only the latter requires a judgment of reasonableness. That term invites the same sort of elaborate construction that is found in the Food, Drug, and Cosmetic Act's parallel language, which allows approval only of "safe" drugs. The only difference is that the tort lawyers are more candid about the endless trade-offs that have to be made to run the cost-benefit analysis implicit in design-defect cases: move the gas tank closer to the rear, for example, and you may increase the likelihood that it will explode on impact; but by the same token, you may also reduce the likelihood that the flames will reach the passenger compartment. The word "reasonableness" invites the jury to make some judgment as to whether the defendant manufacturer has made the proper design choice. It by no means assures that the jury will get it correct.

One way to avoid this endless chain of judgments is to develop some set of specific product standards for, say, automobiles, and to treat the compliance with them as a conclusive determination (that is, one that cannot be challenged in any judicial proceedings) that the product is not defective. This change is of epic proportions because it is a rare event indeed that any car sold in the United States does not comply with all applicable standards under the National Traffic and Motor Vehicle Safety Act of 1966. Nonetheless, gamesmanship is preferred to predictability, for in most cases the statutory language explicitly precludes that approach, which again helps make the world safe for litigators of all stripes and persuasions. The Motor Vehicle Safety Act, for example, specifically provides that "compliance with a motor vehicle safety standard prescribed under this chapter does not exempt a person from liability at common law."[4]

There is one key exception to this general rule that is of immense relevance to drug cases. The Supreme Court has held that the Savings Clause in the Motor Vehicle Safety Act does not allow for the preservation of the state common-law action when the theory of liability is flatly inconsistent with the conscious decision reached in the administration of the statute. "It is difficult to understand why Congress would have insisted on a compliance-with-federal-regulation precondition to the provision's applicability had it wished the Act to 'save' all state-law tort actions, regardless of their potential threat to the objectives of federal safety standards promulgated under that Act."[5] Accordingly, no state could allow a common-law action when a person alleged that he was injured because of the absence of an airbag after an elaborate administrative review of the matter established a schedule by which airbags and other passive restraints could be introduced into the automobile. The private right of action was regarded as inconsistent with the purposes of the federal statute, and was for that reason preempted under the Supremacy Clause, under which the lowliest federal law or regulation trumps an inconsistent state law, no matter how lofty its pedigree.[6]

These general principles might suggest that injured customers could easily bring design-defect cases against the manufacturers of medical devices because the federal preemption is spotty and, in any event, heavily dependent on a close comparison of the language of any preemption provision with the exact elements of the underlying cases. In the case of medical devices regulated by the FDA (but not for prescription drugs), there is, however, an explicit preemption provision that has assumed greater importance in recent tort litigation. It reads in full:

> No State or political subdivision of a State may establish or continue in effect with respect to a device intended for human use any requirement
>
> (1) which is different from, or in addition to, any requirement applicable under [the Medical Device Act] to the device, and
>
> (2) which relates to the safety or effectiveness of the device or to any other matter included in a requirement applicable to the device under [the MDA].[7]

On its face, this provision looks as though it has real bite insofar as it applies to any "requirement" that is "different from, or in addition to," those that are set by the FDA. In its earlier foray into the area, *Medtronic, Inc., v. Lohr,* which involved a pacemaker with an allegedly defective design, the Supreme Court held that this language preempted not all state design-defect actions, but only those that specifically targeted medical devices for special treatment.[8] Common-law actions that relied on general state prohibitions applicable to all product manufacturers alike—such as those that addressed unfair or shady trade practices in selling products to consumers—still survived, because they did not deal with matters that fell within the special expertise of the FDA.[9] In *Medtronic,* however, the Supreme Court allowed the case to go forward on design theory because the FDA clearance was received under an expedited procedure that required the manufacturer only to show that there was "substantial equivalence" between the product under review and one that was found on the market. The case did not involve the more exhaustive procedures that were used to supply premarket approval (PMA) for new products that were examined under FDA review.[10]

One key question is how that difference in process plays out in this context. One important thread in federal preemption law concerns the level of discretion that Congress conferred on the relevant agency in its enabling statute. On that question, there is little doubt that "Congress has given the FDA a unique role in determining the scope of §360k's preemptive effect."[11] At one time, the FDA took the position that its own administrative authority did not work to preempt design-defect statutes under state law.[12] But the matter came to a head in the important case of *Horn v. Thoratec Corp.,* in which the FDA reaffirmed that it had taken a U-turn from its previous course. The key passage is worth quoting in full:

> The FDA has expressed concerns about the consequences of *not preempting* state common law claims such as Horn's:
>
> It is inappropriate for a jury to second-guess FDA's scientific judgment on such a matter that is within FDA's particular expertise. FDA determines the scope of a device, including the components it comprises, and the appropriate regulatory pathway for the device. . . . FDA subsequently determines whether the device meets the PMA approval standard. The agency makes a reasoned and deliberate decision as to the correct pathway of regulation and

whether to approve the device. Juries lack the scientific knowledge and technical expertise necessary to make such judgments. . . .

The prospect of hundreds of individual juries determining the propriety of particular device approvals, or the appropriate standards to apply to those approvals, is the antithesis of the orderly scheme Congress put in place and charged the FDA with implementing.[13]

Taking its cue from the FDA, the court held that the plaintiff's design-defect case for a defective left ventricular heart pump was preempted by the statute. The FDA rested its view on two lines of argument: first, its own particular expertise, and second, the risk of inconsistent judgments made by different juries all across the land. Whether or not one concedes the first point, the second undeniably is true. The key question that has to be asked in any preemption case is not whether the juries perform better or worse than the FDA. Rather, it is whether the potential expenditure of billions in tort litigation generates some improvement over the work that is done by the FDA. On that score it is useful to recall that the general bias inside the FDA is to require standards that are too high, not too low. Yet even if that determination is wrong, the quality of state tort law varies in large measure not only by the quality of the jury in any given case or district but by the quality of the state law that is used to fill out the remainder of a design-defect case. State law is particularly salient insofar as it relates to the myriad questions of causation: if the heart valve failed, was it a function of improper design, improper insertion, or some other internal breakdown, such as stroke or heart attack?

In response to this strong element of preemption, it has been suggested that we can count on plaintiffs' lawyers to work well in these cases because "they have a strong incentive to screen cases, because they would recover fees only if they obtained a judgment or settlement."[14]

Yet in a sense that is precisely the problem, as the Vioxx verdict in *Ernst v. Merck* illustrates. The plaintiff's lawyers have one objective, to maximize gain for themselves and their clients within the framework of the existing law. Their first job is to choose that jurisdiction, state or federal, which has the law most favorable and juries most sympathetic to their cause. Their second function is to keep the case in that jurisdiction against the efforts of defendants to move it to a new jurisdiction or venue more sympathetic to its interests. Their expertise therefore will magnify any distortions that are found within the current tort system. The traditional chestnuts in the tort literature were all one-off freakish occurrences. Although of vital interest to the litigants, there were no follow-on consequences in the well-known decision of *Palsgraf v. Long Island Railroad*, because there are few individuals who drop packages of explosives while running for a train which may topple a scale located some distance away.[15]

Unfortunately, medical devices—and especially prescription drugs— raise wildly different institutional concerns. No longer are we concerned with unique but complex factual patterns that test the ingenuity of judges and juries on the particulars of a single injury, disease, or death. Instead, with standardized products the focus is on simple and recurrent factual patterns that typically surface in hundreds or thousands of cases. Thus once it is found that a given product design is flawed, or that its research or development is suspect, then all other persons who used that product have a blueprint on how to proceed in litigating those common issues. The first decision thus has an inordinate effect on all the complex maneuvering that follows. All of the documents on product development are available as evidence in every case. All the witnesses that gave depositions or testified at trial can be made to go through the same ordeal over and over again. The situation gets still more complex if a court applies a legal mouthful known as "offensive non-mutual collateral estoppel" to allow, in some circumstances at least, an adverse finding about negligence or intention against an institutional defendant in one case to be binding on it in subsequent cases, without giving the defendant any opportunity to relitigate that issue.[16] In its most extreme form, the loss of a single verdict of the adequacy of a design could preclude the device manufacturer from relitigating that question in any of the thousands of cases that follow. Yet even if that does not happen, the outcome in the first case supplies a powerful signal for all that follows. The institutional setting thus magnifies beyond measure any errors found in the litigation system.

For our purposes, however, it does not matter which procedural path is taken. Whatever the path, litigation turns out to be a high-stakes game fraught with unnecessary risk. If the earlier arguments in favor of contractual limitations on liability are correct, then even the best use of the tort law—a generous assumption—will be working at cross-purposes to the overall social welfare. The terrible consequences that could result from one case decided in the worst of these jurisdictions are beyond imagination. It is therefore not credible that any system of adjudication will do better than the FDA's preemption rule, which, in a world with regulatory oversight, returns matters to the same condition as if contract solutions were respected in the first place.

The simple insight here is that one system of regulation is the most that should be tolerated. And as between the FDA, even with all of its short-comings, and the tort system for design-defect liability, one has to opt for the former.[17] The FDA makes its design choices independent of the confusion and emotion of a trial, and it does so from a uniform ex ante perspective, which means that it will not overweight the defects that occur from the one design risk that materializes relative to those which do not. Jury and bench trials both are always at risk for the wisdom of hindsight, where nothing prevents two different triers-of-fact from concluding that two inconsistent design changes should have been made in the same product. It is no way to run a railroad—or a medical device system.

That said, there are few if any design-defect cases that can be found in connection with prescription drugs. So the battle once again shifts terrain to the issues of information transfer, which are the subject of the final chapter.

18

THE MAIN EVENT: MISREPRESENTATION, OVERPROMOTION, AND DUTY TO WARN

Most of the issues of drug liability deal with information transfer about the relevant set of risks. It follows that the design-defect regime so common for medical devices usually does not rear its head in cases of drug liability. While it is possible to design an automobile with a different side panel or a heart valve with a different flange, scientists cannot typically alter the shape of a therapeutic molecule without destroying its clinical effectiveness. Indeed, any tort action that argues that the defendant should have redesigned its particular molecule or not sold the drug at all is flatly inconsistent with the explicit FDA determination to allow that precise drug on the market in the first place.

Short of those atypical cases, we now come to the main event: the vast majority of drug cases turn on the communications that take place between the drug manufacturer, the physician, and the individual patient. These so-called duty-to-warn cases can be of two sorts. The first involves positive misstatements of fact on which a party relies to his detriment. In dealing with drug issues, charges of this sort usually involve allegations of both fraud and negligence. In many cases, the argument is not that the particular statements were false as made but that the entire advertisement campaign resulted in a form of overpromotion whereby the favorable reviews of the product dulled or overwhelmed the effectiveness of the warnings. The second involves the information distributed with the product, both to the physicians who prescribe it and to the patients who take it. Everyone acknowledges that the former warnings, made to physicians, must provide greater detail than the latter. But the gist of such a claim is that the warnings supplied omitted key information that a reasonable person should have disclosed to the target audience. In general, these duty-to-warn cases rarely involve charges of deliberate concealment. Most typically, they assert only that some information that was in the possession of the manufacturer should have been supplied to physicians or patients or both. Clearly any allegation of deliberate misconduct is a more potent suit than one of inadvertent misstatement or omission.

These duty-to-warn cases are common because design-defect cases seem inappropriate for dealing with adverse side effects of drugs whose chemical composition cannot be altered without eliminating the drug's desirable and intended effects. Since the risk is inseparable from the use, warnings are required to place the two in balance. At this point the set of rules for adequate warning becomes critical. The definition found in the Third Restatement of Products Liability parallels the one used in connection with design defects. Thus, a product

> is defective because of inadequate instructions or warnings when the foreseeable risks of harm posed by the product could have been reduced or avoided by the provision of reasonable instructions or warnings by the seller or other distributor, or a predecessor in the commercial chain of distribution, and the omission of the instructions or warnings renders the product not reasonably safe.[1]

The question of what warnings should be given in principle raises the same challenge just encountered with design defects. In principle, I believe that the same preemptive regime that is used in design-defect cases should be carried over to FDA warnings, and for much the same reasons. The ex post judgments that are conjured up by the tort system are too inconsistent and too costly to advance any collective objective of overall social welfare. The insertion of the words "or prescription drug" in the basic preemption statute for medical devices would work a seismic shift in drug litigation. After much deliberation, the FDA finally released in January 2006 a "preamble" to a rule that adopted administratively the same approach for prescription drugs.[2] But in the absence of any official word we must play the hand we are dealt, and there is no preemption provision for pharmaceutical products that has the breadth of that for medical devices, so disputes typically reside under the general set of common-law tort rules.

In ordinary litigation, the use of the term "reasonably safe" suggests that someone has to go through an elaborate case-by-case cost-benefit calculus to determine what warnings should be given to what populations and for what reasons. Relevant to this determination is the severity of the side effects and the frequency of their occurrence. But additional matters could include the identification of the specific kinds of side effects and the populations that are most at risk to them. In the early days of product liability law, the inadequacy of warnings often was a sure bet for the plaintiff because the defendant had distributed a particular product with no warning at all.[3] Today any suit for breach of the duty to warn typically takes place in a context in which some comprehensive warning is given but is then attacked for its failure to state some particular fact that might have altered the balance. In order to follow this progression to its logical conclusion, it is necessary to trace through at least four key stages: What did the defendant know and what should any warning have said? What was the causal connection between the inadequate warning and any subsequent harm? What did the injured party do to aggravate that harm, or fail to do to prevent it? And what damages, actual or punitive, should be awarded? This same set of issues arises in somewhat different form with active misrepresentations. It is necessary to look at both sides of the problem.

What Did a Drug Manufacturer Know? What Did It Say? What Should It Have Said?

Simple Nondisclosure

The issue of knowledge and warnings is central to the tort system, and in many cases, the law imposes onerous duties to disclose on parties even when there is no hint of conscious wrongdoing. To get one sense of how this can work, consider the famous case *MacDonald v. Ortho Pharmaceutical Corp.*, which shows the perils that arise even in the simplest setting, where the risk is well known and where the duty to warn is acknowledged by all. In *MacDonald*, the defendant gave an exhaustive warning, which mentioned the risk of death, when it supplied the plaintiff with birth control pills. The extensive warnings indicated that taking the pill could be fatal and that women with a history of blood clots in the legs, lungs, or brain should not take oral contraceptives. But it did not include the word "stroke" in the list of adverse side effects, and the court held that a jury could find that the warnings were inadequate for that reason. The warning in this case had been approved by the FDA, but that fact was regarded as only relevant, not decisive. A jury was entitled to conclude that the FDA-approved warning was not adequate, which, as the court noted, was a position that the FDA itself had adopted.[4] The manufacturer also noted that the drug in question could be prescribed only by a physician who could pick up the slack with individuated warnings suitable to the plaintiff's condition. Yet in line with many modern decisions on the theory of causation, this learned intermediary did not shield the manufacturer from liability. Rather, the physician only presented the injured plaintiff with a second window of opportunity to remedy injury.

It is at just this point that the coordination between the administrative law system of the FDA and the tort system breaks down. The FDA warnings are rarely given lightly. Indeed, since the FDA consistently rates Type I error (letting bad drugs on the market) more heavily than Type II error (keeping good drugs off the market), it often insists on warnings that are too strict relative to their risk, with the unfortunate side effect of deterring use by individuals who on balance might profit from particular drugs. But more to the point, the open nature of the common-law inquiry undermines the soundness of the federal scheme. Under current law, the Supreme Court has never held—and in the current climate of opinion, will never hold—that FDA warnings necessarily preempt all state common-law causes of action once the FDA has ruled to the contrary.[5]

All this does not mean that preemption has no role to play in dealing with the FDA. In *Buckman Co. v. Plaintiffs' Legal Committee,* the Supreme Court held that a private party cannot sue a product manufacturer on the ground that its submissions had deceived the FDA into allowing the product, here surgical screws, into the market, where they were alleged to cause harm to customers. The decision to block that lawsuit did not rest on a general theory of proximate cause, which normally holds that the deception of an intermediate party does not break the overall chain of causation to the original manufacturer. Rather, Chief Justice Rehnquist rested his conclusion on the general proposition that the institutional work of the FDA would be heavily compromised if these claims were allowed:

> State-law fraud-on-the-FDA claims inevitably conflict with the FDA's responsibility to police fraud consistently with the Agency's judgment and objectives. As a practical matter, complying with the FDA's detailed regulatory regime in the shadow of 50 States' tort regimes will dramatically increase the burdens facing potential applicants—burdens not contemplated by Congress in enacting the FDCA and the MDA [Medical Devices Act].[6]

Buckman does not apply, however, whenever a manufacturer's FDA-approved warnings to consumers are challenged as inadequate under state law: in this setting the FDA has not been deceived. Yet the complexity of complying with fifty different state tort laws does remain a problem for a firm that sells to a nationwide market. Now the dominant rule is that the warning has to pass muster under the law of each of the fifty states, each of which runs its own jury system. It is with cases like *MacDonald* that the real trouble begins. A system to regulate information flow can work in one of two ways. Either it can certify that the information distributed is adequate when it is released, or it can allow that determination to be made after the fact, typically by a jury, when someone complains of injury. With any mass-produced product the sensible approach is to make one uniform decision on the choice of warnings. Once that is done, no private party should be allowed in a tort action to attack the warning after the fact on the ground that different or better information should have been supplied. As new information comes in, the older warnings can be updated administratively to reflect the change in risk level, up or down. No physician or drug company need fear that a report of an adverse consequence will generate a full dose of tort liability. More generally, this approach allows the FDA to require that drugs be sold with certain warnings in an effort to guard against the risks of error and fraud.

This regulatory approach is coercive in that only drugs with warnings may be sold. In an ideal world, even that level of coercion might be excessive. Drugs are, after all, fungible products, and standardized information about their risks can be supplied by anyone familiar with their operation. But the chief advantage of an FDA mandate is that it would provide a safe harbor for all those who comply with it, while avoiding the far more devastating consequences of a total ban on sale. The FDA of course does not have exclusive control over information flows; physicians and consumers are free to supplement its warnings by turning to other sources, some of which may downplay the anticipated risks.

The key benefit of the safe harbor is that it could kill off the huge number of dubious lawsuits that seek to hold the defendant liable for the failure to provide the appropriate warnings. The approval process before the FDA is, to say the least, arduous, and during that time, the applicant is required to submit and update all sorts of information that is subject, especially in hindsight—the only perspective available to juries—to multiple and inconsistent interpretations. There is little question that the entire dispute about when and whether Vioxx presented an unacceptable health risk depends on deciphering reams of this kind of information, all subject to multiple interpretations. Today, even if *Buckman* blocks suits based on fraud on the FDA, both the information that is submitted to the FDA and the information that is held back can be used to undermine the adequacy of the warnings given, which necessitates the review, before a jury no less, of thousands upon thousands of documents. The class of relevant information constantly shifts because these drugs are taken by all sorts of individuals over long periods of time under highly different circumstances. The warnings are frequently changed while the drug remains on the market; other warnings are supplied to physicians who have independent sources of knowledge, including journal reports; and patients frequently obtain additional disclosures, either from their physician or from some other source (such as an Internet site), before taking the drug.

Concealment and Active Misrepresentation

Whatever the balance of equities in the simple duty-to-warn cases, the stakes get infinitely higher in those circumstances that resort to the older, more difficult theories of common-law fraud or deliberate concealment. Many drug cases raise just this problem, and its complexities are illustrated with the bitter dispute in *Ernst v. Merck.*[7] Trials of this sort oscillate between two sorts of explosive issues: first, whether there is evidence of some important risk that triggers the duty to warn; and second, whether there was knowledge of this risk that was in turn suppressed. The bottom line is that the case is tantamount to either one of fraud because the product was known to be deadly, or one of reckless behavior because of indifference to further information that should have been gathered, or to tests that should have been run, before letting the drug come to market. Punitive damages follow easily if a jury can be convinced of these allegations. And in the heat of battle, the plaintiff has a large advantage that offsets the burden of proof that he normally bears. Since the manufacturer's deliberations about clinical research and appropriate warnings are all reviewed in the context of an observed harm, the benefits that any particular pharmaceutical might have to absent parties are either downplayed or wholly removed from the equation.

The Vioxx litigation raises just these issues. To set the background it should be understood that Merck did supply extended warnings about the possible side effects, in detailed form to physicians and in somewhat simpler terms to patients by way of package inserts.[8] The patient warnings listed possible "serious but rare" side effects that included allergic reactions, stomach problems, kidney problems, liver problems and heart attacks. The warnings to physicians contained detailed information that included reference to the various clinical studies (with hyperlinks) that related to the occurrence of "thrombotic" risks.[9] Cardiac arrhythmia was nowhere mentioned. In the patient warnings, the insert said: "Heart attacks and other serious events, such as blood clots in your body, have been reported in patients taking VIOXX." There could always be debates about whether these warnings meet some standard of adequacy. But on any reading they put readers on notice of the major risks.

That said, the Vioxx trial did not appear from published reports to involve the warnings themselves. Rather, the key element was that Merck had engaged in extensive overpromotion of the drug for cases in which it did not have any obvious superiority. The clear thrust of the charge was that the Merck warning had concealed the *gravity* of the risk associated with use of the product. Answering that claim requires a look not only at the advertisements but also at the reported findings about a drug that received inordinate attention because it was known from the outset to be a blockbuster.

Unsurprisingly, there were extensive clinical trials undertaken by Merck before it released Vioxx, and a huge number of clinical studies were done after its release to determine the effects of Vioxx. One key feature of this analysis is the relationship, noted earlier, between the increased risk of heart attacks on the one hand and the drug's favorable properties for dealing with intestinal bleeding on the other. One early line of studies that Merck undertook to investigate these relationships, the so-called VIGOR (Vioxx Gastrointestinal Outcomes Research) study, involved clinical trials in which it was compared with naproxen, an antisteroidal drug in a different class. The original results, as reported by Claire Bombardier and her coauthors, showed about a fourfold elevated risk of adverse heart incidents over the naproxen (branded as Naprosyn). But the results were uncertain because the test was not done against a placebo, and there was at least some probability that the result in question could have occurred because naproxen had some protective effect against adverse heart events, not because Vioxx posed additional risks.[10] It should be immediately clear that this formulation does not capture the full level of risk involved, because the two explanations are not exclusive, as both effects could be present. Naproxen could have reduced risk while Vioxx increased it. But clearly, for any sensible cost-benefit analysis, further work would have to be done to sort out the relative size of these two effects. With time, it seemed clear that dangerous effects of Vioxx were by far the stronger factor in the VIGOR results. This was further confirmed by later meta-analysis—that is, a study that examined all the actual studies of the use of Vioxx—which led the study authors to conclude that there was ample reason to remove the drug from the marketplace as early as the year 2000, one year after launch, and to call for the continuous monitoring of drugs postrelease.[11]

As befits the entire Vioxx matter, the magnitude of adverse heart incidents from Vioxx relative to Naprosyn in the VIGOR study became still more convoluted when the *New England Journal of Medicine* published an extraordinary "expression of concern" editorial on December 29, 2005 (which appeared online earlier that month), asking Dr. Claire Bombardier and her twelve coauthors to issue a correction on the grounds that they had improperly excluded three adverse cardiac incidents that would have changed the ratio of adverse incidents from Vioxx and Naprosyn from 4.25 to 5.0, which the editors noted would have altered the risk/benefit ratio on the use of the drug.[12] It is necessary to speak of this matter in some detail because of the exceptional importance that it could have in the future course of the Vioxx litigation which a front-page *Wall Street Journal* story indicates was foremost in the minds of the *New England Journal*'s editors.[13] During the course of the Vioxx litigation, plaintiffs' lawyers deposed Gregory Curfman, the executive editor of the *Journal*, who made what were perceived as damaging admissions that "lax editing" might have contributed to the improper publication of the article by failing to pick up irregularities in the data, which were said to compromise the academic integrity of the research and which I shall examine presently. After Dr. Curfman's deposition had been completed in November 2005, the editors "grew alarmed about the potential for bad publicity over the videotaped deposition, fearing it could be leaked or played in a federal courtroom session on Dec. 8, according to internal emails and an interview with Drs. Curfman and Drazen [the *Journal*'s editor in chief]."[14] Furthermore, on the evening of December 7, Edward W. Campion, a senior *Journal* editor, informed his staff that the expression of concern needed to be published the following day because "tomorrow's testimony in the Vioxx trial may involve part of a deposition that [Dr. Curfman] gave." In making this decision, the *Journal* editors relied on the assistance of Edward Cafasso, their public relations consultant, who "predicted the rebuke would divert attention to Merck and induce the media to ignore the *New England Journal of Medicine*'s own role in aiding Vioxx sales." The entire tone of the *Wall Street Journal* story was that the only error in this matter was the failure of the *New England Journal*'s editors to catch the errors made by Merck and its allied scientists. Indeed, a letter from Dr. Drazen to the *Wall Street Journal* assumes that the content of its expression of concern was correct, and that the *New England Journal* should not be faulted because it lacked the resources to mount an independent investigation of all submitted articles.[15]

In fact nothing seems farther from the truth. It is an old saying in law that sloppy and rushed procedures yield unsound results, and such seems to be the case here. To set the stage for a substantive examination of terms, note that "expression of concern" is a technical term that is tantamount to a charge of scientific fraud. The International Committee of Medical Journal Editors, to which the *New England Journal of Medicine* belongs, explains the situation as follows:

> II.B. Corrections, Retractions and "Expressions of Concern"
>   . . . The second type of difficulty is scientific fraud. If substantial doubts arise about the honesty or integrity of work, either submitted or published, it is the editor's responsibility to ensure that the question is appropriately pursued, usually by the authors' sponsoring institution. However, it is not ordinarily the task of editors to conduct a full investigation or to make a determination; that responsibility lies with the institution where the work was done or with the funding agency. The editor should be promptly informed of the final decision, and if a fraudulent paper has been published, the journal must print a retraction. If this method of investigation does not result in a satisfactory conclusion, the editor may choose to conduct his or her own investigation. As an alternative to retraction, the editor may choose to publish an expression of concern about aspects of the conduct or integrity of the work.[16]

At the outset, it should be noted that in the rush to litigation the *Journal* consciously chose not to follow the conventional route of referring the matter to the home institutions of those scientists whom it thought had compromised the integrity of the work—whom it would then have to name individually.[17] The central question therefore is what features of the Bombardier study justified the deviation from the procedures established in the guidelines of the International Committee. The editors did not address this procedural question directly but made their case against the authors by observing that "it now appears, however, from a memorandum dated July 5, 2000, that was obtained by subpoena in the Vioxx litigation and made available to the *Journal*, that at least two of the authors knew about the three additional myocardial infarctions at least two weeks before the authors submitted the first of two revisions and 4½ months before the publication of the article," leaving "ample time" to include the additional data in the article. The *Journal* also wrote that "the memorandum of July 5, 2000, contained other data on cardiovascular adverse events that we believe would have been relevant to the article. We determined from a computer diskette that some of these data were deleted from the VIGOR manuscript two days before it was initially submitted to the *Journal* on May 18, 2000."[18]

This rare and serious expression of concern—the *Journal* had published only three others in its history[19]—contains several curious and troublesome omissions. Thus the editorial does not state just *who* sent a copy of the memorandum to the *Journal*. But the reference to the subpoena suggests that it was supplied by some lawyer representing individual plaintiffs in the Vioxx litigation against Merck. Nor does the editorial mention *who* wrote the July 5, 2000, memorandum or *which* two authors of the VIGOR study knew about the data. The scientific team headed by Dr. Claire Bombardier of the University of Toronto included thirteen researchers, of whom two were the Merck scientists Dr. Alise Reicin and Dr. Deborah Shapiro. The other eleven worked at academic medical centers, five in the United States and six in other countries. The implication seems to be that the two Merck scientists may have withheld information from the remainder of the team. Finally, the *Journal* editorial did not specify *what* data had been eliminated from the diskette. The publication of the editorial sparked immediate and joyous reactions from the Vioxx plaintiffs' lawyers, who insisted that this revelation had undercut Dr. Reicin's credibility as a witness in Vioxx cases.[20]

Nonetheless, Merck immediately offered what appeared to be an effective defense against the *Journal*'s charges. The data in question had been excluded from this study in accordance with a predetermined cutoff date, which the *Journal* editorial nowhere mentioned, so that there had been no manipulation of raw data after the fact. In addition, data that had been omitted from the report had been supplied to the FDA both before and after the publication.[21] Shortly after the editorial appeared, two bloggers, Derek Lowe and Jim Hu, noted in separate postings that the changes in the overall data did not appear to make much difference in the assessment of the underlying risk even if they were statistically significant. They gave special weight to the relatively small number of adverse cardiac events (twenty versus seventeen) in the initial study, which was primarily targeted at gastrointestinal issues. In addition, they noted that the use of cutoff dates is both customary and essential to all clinical studies in order to prevent constant revision of studies, which in turn opens the door to ex post opportunism in the interpretation of data. The simple point here is that the cutoff date excludes all subsequent information, including data favorable to the drug. None of these responses had been anticipated in the *Journal*'s expression of concern. Hu also noted that it was odd for the *Journal* to rush its expression of concern to publication given that Vioxx had already been removed from the market. He raised the suspicion that the timing of the publication was intended to boost the Vioxx plaintiffs in upcoming litigation.[22]

The dueling between the two sides did not stop here. All the scientists who conducted the VIGOR study responded in two separate letters that were posted on the *New England Journal of Medicine*'s Web site on February 22, 2006, and later published in the March 16 issue of the *Journal*. The first was written solely by the eleven independent scientists who participated in the VIGOR study headed by Dr. Bombardier.[23] The two Merck scientists, Reicin and Shapiro, wrote the second.[24] Neither group of scientists backed down. They noted that the specified time period had been predetermined to prevent data manipulation, and that the shorter period had also resulted in the exclusion of one adverse event attributable to Naprosyn. They also made it clear that the table that the expression of concern accused the scientists of deleting two days before the draft manuscript was submitted to the *Journal* was of no consequence. The table had contained headers and footers but no data. Furthermore, the authors explained that an early draft of the manuscript contained a table with some precutoff cardiovascular data. In a later draft, these data were moved to the text of the manuscript.[25] However, this table "never included the three additional myocardial infarctions because they were not part of the locked database used for the analysis in the VIGOR paper."[26]

The responses also raised two points that require some further explanation. First, both letters noted that the cutoff date for the adverse cardiovascular events was set at February 10, 2000; for the adverse gastrointestinal events it was set a month later, March 9, 2000. The Bombardier letter indicated that the authors "as members of the steering committee, approved the study termination date of February 10, 2000, and the cutoff date of

March 9, 2000, for reporting of gastrointestinal events to be included in the final analysis." The Bombardier response also reported:

> At a time approaching the completion of the study, the data safety and monitoring board (the independent committee charged with overseeing any potential safety concerns) recommended to Merck that a data analysis plan be developed for serious cardiovascular events. The data safety and monitoring board stated that they did not feel it appropriate to bring this issue to members of the VIGOR steering committee since they were "not recommending a change to the trial conduct, simply that a prespecified plan be accomplished." As a result, a cardiovascular data analysis plan was developed by Merck. Merck indicated that it chose the study termination date of February 10, 2000, as the cutoff date for reporting cardiovascular events to allow sufficient time to adjudicate these events. Per the data safety and monitoring board recommendation, we were unaware of the cutoff date for reporting the cardiovascular events.[27]

The reference to the outside board certainly reduces any opportunity for manipulation, which is to the good. The two published responses, however, do not give the date at which the group decided to close the trials. That date could have been at any time from the onset of the study until the day before the books were closed. The question is what to make of any delayed decision to use differential cutoff dates. In their response, "Expression of Concern Reaffirmed," the three *Journal* editors did not back off either:

> As part of our expression of concern, we also pointed out that three myocardial infarctions in the rofecoxib group were not included in the data submitted to the *Journal*. The authors state that these events did occur during the trial, but they did not qualify for inclusion in the article because they were reported after a "prespecified cutoff date" for the reporting of cardiovascular events. This date, which the sponsor selected shortly before the trial ended, was one month earlier than the cutoff date for the reporting of adverse gastrointestinal events. This untenable fea-

ture of trial design, which inevitably skewed the results, was not disclosed to the editors or the academic authors of the study.[28]

This responsive analysis does not come close, in my judgment, to supporting the grave charges the *Journal* made against the research scientists who participated in this study or against Merck. Initially, it is troubling that the "Expression of Concern Reaffirmed" switched grounds without acknowledging that the earlier expression of concern did not mention that the study used a prespecified cutoff date. Furthermore, it failed to acknowledge the fact that the omitted tables were blank. A bit of humility would have helped here.

Nor do the editors do well in their second broadside. To be sure, it may well have been a mistake in hindsight for the scientific authors not to have mentioned the use of the prespecified cutoff date in their original submission or during the editorial process. But if that is an error, it is of little consequence because it is common knowledge that large clinical studies customarily rely on these cutoff dates. At most there is evidence of procedural error, not academic fraud. In any event, there was hardly anything out of the ordinary in this study that would call for a correction in the underlying data. In addition, it was also a mistake for neither group of VIGOR scientists in their reply letters to mention the date at which the cutoffs were selected for both the cardiac and gastrointestinal groups. The point might have been a small procedural detail in preparing the original article, but once the timing question is put in issue, then the date should be revealed just to clear the air.

Yet again, neither of these quibbles carries the day in calling for a public correction of the study. Let us assume, for the sake of argument, that the date was selected by Merck on February 9, 2000. What impropriety follows from this? In a vast clinical study that covers many treatment centers, it is hard to believe that either the independent committee or the Merck scientists had any inside information that allowed them to project that the post–February 10, 2000, data would alter the results in a way that harmed Vioxx's clinical prospects. In the absence of that information, the selection of the late date has a perfectly innocent explanation. Waiting until the study progresses allows the various planning committees to know whether enough data had been collected to permit a sensible analysis of those data.

Postponement of the selection time therefore could improve the reliability of the study. Getting quick publication of important clinical results is always a priority for lives that may hang in the balance.

The same seems true about the decision to use different cutoff dates for the two classes of adverse events. Even if the choice of different dates were wholly arbitrary, it remains unclear how it altered the results. There is no neutral baseline from which to measure improper deviations. More specifically, we could just as well say that the gastrointestinal study (which in any event was the primary focus of the first study, as is evident from the title of that paper) went too long, instead of saying that the cardiac study was cut off too quickly. In fact, once again Merck, through its trial lawyer Phil Beck, offered an independent explanation for its decision. The cardiac results were more complex and required more time for an independent institutional review to assure their quality.[29] Whether one month was needed or not is impossible to say. But what is clear is that the *New England Journal of Medicine* offers zero evidence in support of its critical conclusion that this "untenable" feature of the trial design "inevitably skewed" the results, without saying why or how. In fact, unless the program committee had some inside information on the future course of the study—which is highly unlikely in a double-blind study conducted at eleven sites around the world—the anticipated skew from the change in dates is exactly zero.

In sum, even with the benefit of hindsight, the objections against the conduct of the VIGOR study look lame at best. It is, of course, impossible to determine its influence on the course of future Vioxx litigation. For all I know the *New England Journal of Medicine*'s inexcusable rush to judgment may well help Merck by showing the extreme and improper measures that the publication took to undermine the company's defense. But this much remains clear: in the area of medical science we have not found a satisfactory answer to the question of who guards the guardians, in this case at the *New England Journal of Medicine*.

Whatever the increased heart risk from Vioxx, the overall situation is even more cloudy than this complex tale might suggest. One reexamination of the VIGOR study sought to examine the combined effect of both risks, again taking naproxen as the comparison drug. Vioxx reduced the incidence of intestinal bleeding to 53 percent of former levels, which, when combined with the increased rate of heart attacks, translated into a reduction in life expectancy of about 4.4 months for the typical fifty-eight-year-old arthritic woman who used the drug, and a 7.7 month reduction in life expectancy for the typical fifty-eight-year-old man.[30] Naprosyn showed no positive effect on intestinal bleeding. The scientific conclusion drawn by the authors of this comparative study was that the lower the background risk of heart attack, the stronger the case for taking Vioxx. The sensible legal inference from this study is that the call for banning Vioxx is overstated, unless this trade-off on life and comfort is so one-sided that it should not be made under any circumstances. Yet here, any corrections seem to go in the opposite direction—to take into account some increased risk of serious personal injury brought on by an acute arthritic condition.

The assessment of the overall record does not end with the VIGOR study but also includes the so called APPROVe (Adenomatous Polyp Prevention on Vioxx) study, which identified an increased risk (1.9 percent to 3.5 percent) of heart attack attributable to coronary thrombosis in persons who took high dosages of Vioxx for more than eighteen months. That figure reports a lower elevation of risk of harm than the earlier VIGOR study, which raises the possibility that its fivefold figure overstated the Vioxx risk. The study showed, however, roughly the same level of risk until that point, and gave no clear explanation for the dispersion at eighteen months, which resulted more from a flattening of adverse events in the placebo class than from an unexpected rise in adverse events from Vioxx users. In addition, the number of patients in the study dwindled to about a fourth of those involved with the drug at lower dosages, given that the standard treatment cycle for Vioxx (especially in postoperative settings) called for a shorter course of treatment, where it was prized for its ability to deal with intestinal bleeding.

The study, like so many clinical studies, hardly supplies knockdown proof that Vioxx should be withdrawn from the market. But it was the results of the APPROVe study that led Merck to do just that on September 30, 2004, after extensive deliberation within the company. That study, however, did not negate the benefits of reduced intestinal bleeding. Nor did the medical literature uniformly condemn the use of Vioxx, as the authors of some articles thought that the entire question had yet to be fully understood.[31] As with the full interpretation of the VIGOR study, it is easy to reach just the opposite conclusion—namely, that Vioxx should still be the drug of choice for individuals with high intestinal risks and low cardiac risks. That determination of course can be made only at the patient level.

The key question for these purposes is how this complex record (vastly simplified here) plays out in the course of a trial when the question is whether Merck engaged in improper conduct with respect to the labeling and promotion of its drug. On this score, even those who have been sympathetic to Merck on the liability determination thought that the marketing in question was too aggressive, given the relative risk-benefit ratio of the drug. That conclusion is hard to contradict, even though most of the information about risk was readily available to physicians. But the litigation picture here is much more difficult to defend than this quick summary of the study suggests. In all prescription drug cases, the defendant has clear and certain knowledge of the risks in question. The first key question is whether it properly forged ahead given its knowledge of both risks and benefits. The second question is what sort of stress should be placed on the warnings, relative to the benefit. Here it is exceedingly difficult, even with the benefit of hindsight, to find the right balance. But for a skilled plaintiff's lawyer it is easy to make hay on one key point: the manufacturer did not play straight with the risks because it wanted to make a fast buck, which is just the way *Ernst v. Merck* played out—even before the *New England Journal*'s public call for a correction of the data in the Bombardier article.

Set against this institutional background, it is now possible to see the importance of any legal rule that does not treat the FDA-approved warnings as the gold standard. In this maelstrom, the jury must first decide whether the warning in question is adequate to the task. But for that delicate task, it receives no guidance save the misleading instruction that FDA warnings should be regarded as "minimums," perhaps because of the supposedly strong influence that drug companies have over FDA operations. But one unhappy characteristic of these suits is that no jury is required to state in so many words exactly what the adequate warning should say. There is no question that the internal memos that showed Merck battling the criticism of its drug from outsiders played a devastating role in the case, which turned on that ineffable but critical notion of trust.[32]

Causation, Two Ways

The next stage of misrepresentation cases concerns causation. A misrepresentation in the air, so to speak, will not do. The plaintiff must establish the causal link between the information communicated and the harm suffered. That simple statement makes it easy enough to put one branch of the causation inquiry to rest. If there is no misrepresentation, no material omission of fact, then the case is stillborn. Without that key link, the only causes that explain the harm are either natural events or drug-induced harms, where the risk of both is fully assumed by the patient who takes these risks in the hopes of avoiding some greater peril. The defendant gets the jury verdict, or in rare cases presents an argument so compelling that it receives a judgment as a matter of law.

Once the misrepresentation is established, however, a second branch of the causation inquiry plunges the case into a new set of difficulties every bit as complicated as the initial inquiry. Let there be some misrepresentation or material omission: what difference did the wrongful conduct make in the outcome of the case? If the injured party would have taken the same course of action if the truth had been told in full, then any errors of commission would not have mattered. If the wrongful conduct induced a course of action, but the death came from some unrelated source, then the injured party's reliance is again irrelevant. The full case therefore requires an assessment of two branches of causation, *interpersonal* and *physical*. Neither is an easy nut to crack.

Interpersonal Causation

The tricky issue of interpersonal causation is an individuated inquiry that is quite different from the general risk assessments that the FDA undertakes before allowing a drug to reach market, before ordering a change in warning, or before pulling a drug from the market. None of these administrative actions requires any individuated determinations of patient or physician response to the warnings that have been issued. All that happens is that the drug companies and the FDA make some statistical estimation of how people as a group are likely to respond to the changed information. Thereafter, the companies and the FDA have to address in tandem the harder question of whether these shifts will improve or hamper overall treatment effectiveness. The statistical inquiry on causation fits well into the overall pattern. Indeed, one reason for the earlier suggestion of a quasi-criminal procedure to determine willful misrepresentation or concealment is that it can use statistical evidence to determine within appropriate limits the anticipated consequences of the wrongful action. The entire process takes place within the statistical framework.

That approach is not nearly as successful in trying to deal with the causation question in individual cases, where an individuated inquiry asks whether a properly informed physician or patient (or both) would have reached a different decision. The choices, moreover, are not necessarily binary. A person who learns of a higher risk from a given drug need not abandon its use entirely, but could easily cut down dosage in an effort to steer a delicate path between too much and too little medication. The full range of intermediate choices is not some exotic variation. Rather, fine-tuning in response to new information represents the dominant response. Setting out these multiple possibilities, however, complicates the analysis, because the smaller the hypothetical change in behavior, the less likely it is that the adverse outcome would have been avoided. By conventional standards, a plaintiff bears the legal burden of proof, and accordingly has to show that there is a more than even likelihood that the changes that *might* have been made would have made a difference in the ultimate outcome, and by what amount.

To be sure, in some cases that counterfactual question on causation may prove relatively easy for a plaintiff to surmount. A woman in perfect health, like the stroke victim in *MacDonald,* can credibly claim that she would have avoided birth control pills if she had known the risk—even if thousands of other women did not. But in the multitude of cases involving chronic conditions, such as diabetes or arthritis, reconstructing after the fact what would have been done if the patient had been given the proper warnings (whose contents are rarely specified) has raised litigation to an art form. Both sides have powerful incentives to introduce a full range of evidence, objective and subjective, on a question that admits no easy resolution even in the "easiest" of cases. Lifestyle depositions that delve into every nook and cranny of an injured person's life are par for the course in drug cases, just as in cigarette cases. In the end, however, the general rule is that the plaintiff bears the burden of proof. The hard question is the extent to which that burden is eased by what has been called the "heeding presumption"— namely, that the burden shifts back to the defendant once the plaintiff has shown that the missing information was material. Some courts have held that when an adequate warning has *not* been given, the plaintiff should receive the benefit of that heeding presumption in order to give full effect to the official comments to the Restatement.[33] But that approach reads too much into the comments, which state only that "where warning is given, the seller may reasonably assume that it will be read and heeded; and a product bearing such a warning, which is safe for use if it is followed, is not in defective condition, nor is it unreasonably dangerous."[34] It hardly follows that there is any ground to presume conversely that, if given, it would have been heeded, for the drug cases do not involve poisons that are mislabeled. In general, it is not proper to bootstrap evidence of interpersonal causation from proof that some warning has been inadequate.

The dynamics on interpersonal causation shift, however, as one moves from the simple duty-to-warn cases to those of fraud or concealment. In these situations, the argument in favor of a presumption that the misconduct matters is much more credible. The only reason to make material misstatements of fact is to mislead other individuals by getting them to drop their natural reluctance to undertake some dangerous course of activity. Hence if the jumbled set of data in *Ernst* is held to add up to fraud or concealment, then most juries will, no matter what a judge instructs or a manufacturer says, think that the misconduct is material. Yet at this point, much depends on what a jury perceives the error in the warning to be, relative to the true state of affairs. Thus suppose that there are two different sources of heart attacks, one involving blood clots that block arteries, the other arrhythmia and atherosclerosis (neither of which is affected by Vioxx). The sensible response to this simple situation is that the jury should find that the risk of thrombosis should be covered, but that the risk of arrhythmia and atherosclerosis should not. Now suppose that the plaintiff urges that if the risk of thrombosis had been disclosed, the decedent would have changed his conduct so that the arrhythmia (which need not be mentioned) would not have occurred. Must the harm that occurred be "within the scope of the risk" which generated the duty to warn, or is the only question whether the harm would have been avoided if the truth had been told, a more favorable position for the plaintiff? Under the former standard, the failure to disclose a thrombosis leads to liability only for a thrombotic incident. Under the latter standard, all complications, including remote arrhythmias, lead to liability, even though they need not be mentioned at all.

In light of these massive complexities, the law of most states sends these questions to the jury, but only after an all-out battle of the experts has run its course. But each case will have certain set pieces: all plaintiffs in the Vioxx cases will testify that if they had known of the risks of taking Vioxx, they (or their decedents) would have endured arthritic pain the drug alleviated, reduced their Vioxx intake, or switched to some other product with lower (or is it only different?) risk. But there are no risk-free products, and a detailed examination of the medical charts could easily reveal that Vioxx was chosen precisely because other medications had failed. But what jury will know after the fact which of these multiple scenarios is correct? In the presence of such conflicting evidence, the benefit of a heeding presumption tilts the scales far in the plaintiff's direction. But even if the plaintiff prevails at this stage, the difficulties of physical causation lurk in the wings.

Physical Causation

The second part of the inquiry has nothing to do with attitudes and decisions and everything to do with the mechanism by which a drug is said to have worked some particular form of harm. A patient takes a drug that carries with it an elevated risk of a heart attack only to die from a stroke. Any misrepresentation or omission is utterly immaterial if the same accident would have occurred in the same fashion even if the medicine had not been taken at all. The mechanism of harm did not implicate the drug, for the sole cause of the harm had a distinct origin.

This simplest of cases frames what in practice is a complex inquiry—raising a witch's brew of substantive and evidentiary concerns—to make the physical connection between the drug supplied and the adverse event for which it is held accountable. "Causation in toxic tort cases has two components: general and specific. 'General causation is whether a substance is capable of causing a particular injury or condition in the general

population, while specific causation is whether a substance caused a particular individual's injury.'"[35] In dealing with these matters the courts
necessarily turn to expert witnesses: the modern tendency is to tighten up
on the sorts of experts who are allowed to testify.[36] There is a constant
fear of expert "speculation" in these cases; and it is important to remember that general causation cannot be established solely on "a handful of
case reports" but requires much more systematic evidence.[37] In some
instances, the identification of the causal mechanism can overcome the
proof, but only if it tends to exclude other explanations that are at least as
likely. Often it is both necessary and possible to rely on evidence that
either identifies a clear mechanism that explains why certain drugs have
certain responses, or, in the absence thereof, to show a clear epidemiological connection between the drug and the disease. That requirement
has bite. The total want of such evidence, for instance, is what doomed
the plaintiff's efforts to link the polychlorinated biphenyls (PCBs) to the
plaintiff's small-cell lung cancer in *General Electric Co. v. Joiner*.[38]

In addition, to carry the burden of proof, the plaintiff must show that it
was more likely than not that the harm in question was attributable to
some wrongful act of the defendant. In the easiest cases, it can be shown
that admitted negligence did nothing to increase the risk or hazard of the
loss that came to pass, so that the negligence was not causally relevant.
The most famous illustration of this sort involved a speeding car that was
struck by a falling tree during a storm.[39] The increased speed did not
increase the risk of being struck, so the negligence bore no causal relationship to the harm. The situation would have been otherwise if the car had
lost control or had run into a fallen tree because of the excessive speed.

In other cases, the probability estimates are more difficult to make.
One example of an error in causal inference is found in *Zuchowicz v.
United States*, a decision by no less a torts authority than Judge
Calabresi.[40] There the decedent received an overdose of Danacrine and
thereafter died from a rare condition known as pulmonary hypertension.
The question was whether the *excessive* amount of the drug was responsible for the death, which could have been caused even if the drug had
been administered in proper dosage. Judge Calabresi held that it was
proper to rely on a presumption that the excess dosage was the cause
because the FDA had already ruled that amount improper. But this con-

fuses the ex post causal question—was the risk of injury more than doubled by the overdose?—with the ex ante question—was the additional risk, whatever its size, worth it in light of the drug's therapeutic benefits? The FDA might have disallowed the higher dosages even if their risk was small—say, a 10 percent increase in the risk of death—if the therapeutic benefits were small or nonexistent. The issues that arose in this malpractice case could easily arise in the Vioxx or similar cases: would the same condition have arisen from smaller dosages for shorter times?

In addition to the conceptual issues raised by causation, there are critical issues of proof. The appropriate standards in federal courts are now shaped by the key Supreme Court decision in *Daubert v. Merrell Dow Pharmaceuticals, Inc.*, which imposed a higher standard governing the admissibility of expert evidence than that previously used.[41] There is little dispute that the tougher *Daubert* standard clamps down on those itinerant experts who do little but testify for one side or the other. In addition, the experts typically must rely on evidence that is peer reviewed and prepared for purposes other than litigation. The *Daubert* standard's constant theme is that scientific evidence must be derived from scientific, not legal, endeavors.[42] Instructively, *Daubert* itself involved suits against a drug company for birth defects that were said to be caused by Bendectin, against which there was (and is) no credible evidence of causal connection, and for which there is still no suitable substitute. (No company in its right mind will go after the pregnancy market.)

There is little doubt that *Daubert* has transformed expert witness practice in the federal courts. In one recent Rezulin decision, *Ruggiero v. Warner Lambert,* the court unanimously held inadmissible under *Daubert* the plaintiff's expert testimony, which sought to establish that the plaintiff had cirrhosis of the liver by "differential diagnosis"—that is, by purporting to rule out all other causes of cirrhosis so that only one remained.[43] That method is in general insufficient unless the universe of potential causes is sharply bounded at the outset, which in this case it was not. The upshot was that the line of testimony was not admissible in the absence of any standard clinical study which documented the connection.

Yet a similar case, *In re Ephedra Products Liability,* took a more Solomonic line in dealing with the question of whether Ephedra could cause cardiac conditions.[44] The absence of reliable studies that indicated the general connection between the drug and the adverse condition meant that the plaintiffs' expert could not testify about the connection to "a reasonable degree of medical certainty." But by the same token, a combination of differential diagnoses and general expertise is sufficient to allow a physician to say that Ephedra "may be a contributing cause of cardiac injury and stroke in some people, such as those with a heart condition, high blood pressure, or a genetic sensitivity to ephedrine, if that opinion is appropriately qualified."[45] The court bolstered this conclusion by appealing to the logic of *Zuchowicz:* so long as the evidence was sufficient to allow the FDA to ban the substance, it is sufficient to allow a jury to decide that a given cardiac condition was more likely caused by Ephedra than not. Junk science, in a word, is not part of the case, as it may well have been in *Daubert.*

Yet this logic misses the criticism made of *Zuchowicz* above, that the evidence that the FDA needs to support its ban is far weaker than the evidence needed to show proof of causation by a preponderance of evidence. In principle, the *Ephedra* cases may be distinguishable from *Ruggiero,* which was decided in the same circuit only three days earlier. But the entire line of argument shows how difficult it is to get consistent rulings and reliable evidence on scientific questions of causation, where the sheer number of claims—five hundred cases jammed in one proceeding involving Ephedra—show why litigation remains high-stakes poker. Taken together, these cases show the obvious limitations in dealing with expert evidence. In and of itself no rule can eliminate the inescapable legal uncertainty that inheres whenever experts battle to prove causation, even if a strong rule can curb the worst abuses. Under the *Daubert* rule, many experts will still be able to offer testimony of little or no value. And even if the experts are themselves eminently qualified, the basic complexity of the situation can overwhelm even conscientious juries. In seriously ill patients, the baseline of adverse conditions is far from zero. Was the 1.9–3.5 percent increase in risk with Vioxx relative to a placebo, as found in the APPROVe study, stable over all segments of the population? If so, then no one recovers, which would be an odd result if the other elements of liability were satisfied.[46] In practice, however, matters are never this simple. In this context, these numbers are spongy: different odds may apply to different fractions of the population. In any event, the plaintiffs are free to argue that some form of fractional recovery is allowable for the increased risk of harm.[47] In addition, complications, which lead to more discovery and more jury questions, will arise for patients who are on multiple medications at the same time or who took the drug in question in excessive dosages or at the wrong times or with the wrong foods. Cases of this sort invariably go through exhaustive discovery and give rise to a multitude of disputed issues that leads to a second battle of the experts.

All of these issues will recur in the ongoing Vioxx litigation. Recall that Mr. Ernst's coronary arteries were 70 percent occluded, a massive risk factor on any account. In addition, the coroner's death certificate listed only arrhythmia—an irregular heartbeat—as the cause of death. In effect, she diagnosed the case as one of primary arrhythmia. One reason why most people thought that Merck had a winnable case is that the clinical trials showed that the heightened risk of coronary incidents from Vioxx were all related to thromboses, or blood clots, that work by a different mechanism from arrhythmia. The commonsense view is that the presence of one big cause makes it unnecessary to scrounge around for minor risk factors that at most may explain why the incident took place at one moment rather than another. Long before Vioxx many people have suffered the fate of the famous fitness guru Jim Fixx, who in 1984 died of a heart attack while running at age fifty-two. Just this logic should have propelled Merck to an easy win. Its own expert, Thomas Wheeler, the interim chairman of pathology at Baylor College of Medicine in Houston—a local witness— said bluntly that clogged arteries explained it all: "He was like a walking time bomb. . . . I think Vioxx had nothing to do absolutely whatsoever with his death."[48]

Yet the ever-resourceful plaintiff's attorney, Mark Lanier, proved more than a match in countering the obvious. His tactic was not to deny the clot but to minimize it, by converting the case into one of *joint* causation. His first task was to overcome the coroner's report that, by implication, solely attributed the death to arrhythmia, with no mention of the blood clots associated with Vioxx. Thus he whisked the coroner, Dr. Maria Araneta, back from her new home in the United Arab Emirates to offer her new opinion that a blood clot, which later disappeared without a trace by enzymatic action, could have triggered the arrhythmia.[49] (Imagine if Merck had tried a similar stunt!) Now the generic VIGOR study on heart risk from Vioxx can be used to resolve the issue of specific causation. Next prove fitness by showing Mr. Ernst ran five miles a day. Finally, eliminate other risk factors—diabetes, high cholesterol, high blood pressure, obesity, family history—and Vioxx, taken in a standard (25 mg dosage) for a period of eight months, becomes the culprit. In truth, many cases count proof by elimination as a form of circumstantial evidence where the actual cause is not known. But here the strategy is taken to a new height because it is used to downgrade the arrhythmia from the sole cause to a mere precondition of the harm.

The next step is to put the full weight of loss on this supposed blood clot. In *Ernst* this question was raised in connection with the jury instructions on proximate cause: did plaintiff have to show that Vioxx was "a substantial factor" in bringing about this sequence, or only that it was "a" contributing cause of harm? More than simple wordplay is at stake. To see why, think of the choice of tests in terms of the underlying probabilities of events. If the traditional standard of causation is used, then the plaintiff has to show that it was more likely than not that the Vioxx triggered the fatal attack, a finding that looks unattainable in light of the extensive occlusion that could have been triggered by some independent, internal body process. Yet demanding only that Vioxx be "a" cause of the harm carries with it a much lower burden. Now one has to show only that there was some increase in risk, however slight, from use of Vioxx. So if the risk of death were 50 percent before the Vioxx and 51 percent thereafter, then that small increase is sufficient to cast the full loss on the defendant.

By what burden of proof? A preponderance of evidence, of course. And how is this gotten across to the jury? By taking the advice of lawyer, psychologist, and jury consultant Lisa Blue: "Write [51%] on the board twice: Arrhythmia is a cardiovascular event. . . . That gets you there." The subtext, of course, is that all cardiovascular events are alike, so that all causal distinctions between thromboses and arrhythmias are obliterated. And it worked: "'Whenever Merck was up there, it was like wah, wah, wah,' said juror John Ostrom, imitating the sounds Charlie Brown's teacher makes in the television cartoon. 'We didn't know what the heck they were talking about.'" Twenty-four-year-old juror Matthew Pallardy figured that there was a blood clot but that it went by "real quick." Fellow juror Derrick Chizer opined that if it were there "for a millisecond," it sufficed.[50] Hence the jury found Merck liable because the odds were better than even that the Vioxx increased the risk of death by some small but measurable amount. Take Vioxx and you get a very fancy life insurance package in the bargain.

Ernst was all about courtroom communication, not science. Needless to say, these theatrical maneuvers did not impress outside experts who followed the case. They dismissed the verdict as "absolutely speculative" and "very far fetched."[51] Indeed, the *New York Times,* which had "little sympathy" with Merck, observed that the evidence on causation was "extremely flimsy."[52] Done once, the verdict is a stunner. Done five or ten thousand times over, it's a disaster that wildly inflates the harm properly attributable to Vioxx. By punishing Merck for harms it has not caused, one jury in Angleton, Texas, messes up the delicate balance of cost and benefits for everyone else. And if it can happen with Vioxx, then it can happen with any drug.

Plaintiff's Conduct

Making the prima facie case against the drug provider is the first and longer leg of a products liability jury trial. But a second stage is needed to complete the trip, based on the question: what role, if any, did the injured party have in bringing about his own harm? In many personal-injury cases, this question is a nonissue. The plaintiff was hit in the rear while minding her own business in her own backyard. But in other cases the conduct of the plaintiff could have joined with that of the defendant to cause harm, as happens whenever two moving vehicles are involved in a collision on the open road. In those circumstances, it becomes critical to evaluate the conduct of both parties to determine their relative contributions.

One brute regularity, however, makes issues of plaintiff conduct a necessary element in any suit brought against prescription drug manufacturers. In a product liability case, the defendant is *never* in possession of its product at the time it causes harm. Some action of the injured party is therefore *always* part of the overall picture. To give but one simple example, many medications contain explicit instructions as to who should take the drug (no pregnant women, infants, or diabetics, please) or when and how often it should be taken. Prohibitions against taking medicines with alcohol are commonplace; users are warned against taking some medicines with grapefruit juice, which could interfere with their effectiveness. It is therefore perfectly legitimate to ask whether the injured party took the right number of pills in the right order, popped other pills without prescription, took an overdose, did too much or too little exercise, or any of a thousand other activities that could have accounted for the harm in and of themselves or increased the risk associated with the use of the prescription drug.

This issue was raised, albeit in modest form, in the *Ernst* case when it was established, as best one could tell, that the plaintiff had followed his prescription and had not taken any other medicines. But the role of the injured party is not limited to such issues. Ernst was an inveterate runner and cyclist who constantly put strain on all his bodily systems. He had run five miles the day of his death. It was not clear how much strain the heat had put on his highly fit but overtaxed system, or what fluids he took to restore his electrolyte balance, or any of a number of other key measures of physical well-being. These activities don't rise to the level of product misuse often present in other cases, but they do show that treating Vioxx as the unobserved mover of Ernst's arrhythmia is no more persuasive than attributing it to another unidentified cause, assuming that such was needed. More ominously, in other cases the downstream conduct could easily constitute concealed forms of abuse, a possibility that taxes the investigative side of any product liability defense: remember that the relevant knowledge of misbehavior resides exclusively with the injured person and her family, who have strong incentives to conceal or shade the truth when the stakes get high. In the past the critical role of downstream control induced many courts to go slow in expanding the scope of product liability. But now that this reluctance is gone, the evidentiary strains on an all too fragile jury system are all the greater.

Damages

The final stage in a lawsuit involves calculating damages, which proves problematic even in the best of circumstances. There is no ready market of willing buyers or sellers to determine the value of a life, or the harm attributable to various forms of horrific injury. Try as it might, the tort system can never implement a rule that says "put damages so that the plaintiff will be in that position she would have enjoyed if the wrong had never taken place at all." For death and horrific injury cases, no sum of money will achieve that goal. Yet to keep the tort system in balance clear restraints have to be put on the amount of damages collected. One way to achieve that goal is to limit actual damages to three heads: pain and suffering, medical expenses, and lost income, of which the last two are capable of some precise determination, while the first frequently is not. On top of these actual damages, courts often award punitive damages for reckless or scandalous behavior. By statute, these are often restricted by some formula that is tied to the actual damages, or some component thereof, awarded in the case.

There is little doubt that serious injuries translate into steep rewards. Verdicts well over $10 million are commonly sustained, especially in cases that require continuous nursing and critical care services. Drug cases with adverse side effects are obvious candidates for these mega-awards. Yet ironically, the *Ernst* case was not one of these. The decedent died in his sleep, so there were no damages for pain and suffering and none for medical expenses. He worked as the produce manager at the local Wal-Mart, so future losses (for someone fifty-nine years of age) were also limited. Texas law caps punitive damages at twice economic losses plus $750,000. The case looked like a modest judgment by modern standards.

Whence then comes the (uncapped) $253 million verdict? Two maneuvers mattered. The first part of this exercise comes in the action by Carol Ernst (who had been married to Robert Ernst for less than a year) for her loss of companionship (including, but not limited to, sexual relations) with her husband. Here the jury awarded $24 million, which is so far off the map that it leaves one gasping for breath—imagine the dollars needed to make an award to someone with prolonged pain and suffering, high medical expenses, and substantial lost income commensurate with $24 million for loss of companionship alone! If Mrs. Ernst's recovery for loss of companionship computes to $24 million, then a serious personal-injury case starts to look like a quarter of a billion in actual damages, when the usual valuation on life for regulatory agencies calculating safety regulations is, depending on whom you ask, in the range of $6 million to $10 million. This Texas-sized verdict will (in all likelihood) be trimmed at some stage in the appellate process. But its implications are nonetheless ominous. Let us assume that Merck had improperly overpromoted its drugs. There is no way that the social losses of that action were equal to the $100 *billion* plus needed to pay off all Vioxx claims, however tenuous, on the same scale. Our system cannot survive the double whammy of weak liability and oversized actual damages.

Next come punitive damages. The Texas jury assigned these at $229 million, which it was told was equal to the amount that Merck thought it could make in additional sales by resisting a label change for stronger warnings for cardiovascular complications. Although the award was trimmed by Texas law, in other jurisdictions the only protection that defendants have against such awards are motions to reduce the damages as excessive; these motions are a crapshoot at best. The situation is particularly grave here because, even if one assumes that the *Ernst* jury had the right metric, it hardly follows that *every* jury should be able to punish the same basic marketing decisions time and again with the same damages. Yet there is little in the current legal system that allows for the coordination of awards across different cases. The strongest argument against the decision in *Ernst* does not depend on the judgment that the jury was way off base when it found that Merck had overpromoted its products: there was surely much evidence, and a widespread belief, that it was guilty as charged. Rather, it is that even if that finding were wholly correct, the subsequent determinations on liability and damages were so excessive that we should have been closer to the mark if the case had never been brought.

Some Modest Proposals

The one conclusion that clearly stands out is that no legal system can afford to try complex matters before a jury even one time, let alone ten thousand times. The clear evidence that members of the *Ernst* jury were swayed by inflammatory PowerPoint slides (depicting Merck as a giant ATM machine, short on cash and in need of Vioxx, or as a marketing bulldozer running down any opposition), the efforts to flatter individual jurors with the hint that they too might be on Oprah if the case is decided the right way, and the countless other ploys large and small that were used in *Ernst* are all indictments of our judicial system.[53] And make no mistake about it, some fraction of high-stakes trials will generate similar theatrics that differ only on point of detail. Those excesses may be bearable in one-off cases that are not capable of repetition in similar circumstances. But there is no way within the framework of the American tort system to find ways to curb these practices, especially in state court, where, for procedural reasons, these cases tend to be tried against out of state defendants.[54]

As a matter of first principle, from an ex ante perspective it is in no one's interest to retain a complex and faulty system of adjudication that chews up resources without providing any sensible way to reduce the number of adverse events in the first place. Contract waivers could get back to that position, if allowed. There is little doubt in my mind that, once this legal position was firmed up, all sorts of other parties would have incentives to enter into the mix to help fill the current information gap. If people are told clearly and firmly that they had better choose correctly at the outset, because they have no hope of separate recovery, potential users will raise their level of investigation into drugs prior to use. In a pure market system—without any FDA but with valid contract disclaimers—the information about drug side effects is so critical that some third parties would rush forward to fill the void, at least if they could be protected against liability should their recommendations go amiss. In the current era of massive distrust, however, any pure contract or waiver solution has not a prayer of success, especially in drug cases. What then should be done to salvage something from the wreckage of a broken tort system?

It is difficult to convey to anyone who has not been thrown into the maelstrom of major tort litigation just how messy and intractable these cases turn out to be. The boldest line of attack, now endorsed by the FDA, is to make it impossible for any plaintiff to sue once the FDA-required warnings are issued. Short of that, a second line of attack is to reform the litigation process in order to make it more efficient. The most common proposals of that sort rely on the use of expert juries or specialized courts, which are less likely to be swayed by emotion and more able to understand the relevant medical evidence. The implicit assumption of this approach is that the current substantive rules are fine, if only they can be consistently and fairly applied. There is little doubt that this approach would improve the situation in Angleton, Texas, but it still leaves certain key questions unanswered. Would the awards of damages also remain unchanged, for example, or would these be subject to some external controls, much like the limits on punitive damages found in the Texas system? There is little reason to oppose this reform, some to doubt whether it will go far enough to control the potentially ruinous situation.

A second set of proposals is intended to alter the substantive rules in ways that halt the onslaught of suits. As noted earlier, the warnings that Merck supplied to both physicians and patients did discuss at some length the full range of dangers associated with the drug in question. But these were, in the course of trial, overwhelmed by the overpromotion and fraud claims that were added to the brew. Litigation of this sort would come to a standstill if the stated warnings were endowed with two virtues: first, they were always treated as adequate, and second, they provided an absolute defense against any overpromotion claim that sought to sidestep the force of the warning. Functionally, this approach is yet another way to marry contractual waivers with mandatory warnings. In effect, the tort system would police only those defects that emerged in the processing of particular products but would not be involved in the information system at all. No doubt this proposal, like the waiver system, would place greater strains on general rules that deal with false and misleading advertising, which normally carry far weaker sanctions than the tort system proposes. In addition, the new rules would create additional pressure for tougher warnings, which is at most a mixed blessing. Yet this proposal does nothing to deal with the sensible objective of making the special virtues of different medicines available to the public at large. I think that this proposal should be adopted, but in the current climate of political distrust brought on in part by overpromotion, well recognized within the industry itself, it just will not happen unless the elimination of the tort action comes side-by-side with some regulatory alternative with real teeth.[55] The tort system merges efforts at compensation and deterrence in a single system. To sacrifice the former, even in part, requires confidence that some deterrence against wrong actions is required. What substitute measures could supply the needed deterrence?

Permutations of regulatory systems are endless. Another proposal might be to adopt a worker's compensation–like "no-fault" system that offers compensation to all individuals who were injured by pharmaceuticals and who were not themselves reckless in their drug use. The broader form of liability would be coupled with some explicit limitation on damages, perhaps with the elimination of pain and suffering and punitive damages, and would be subject to some overall cap. The revised system could be implemented before expert tribunals to control the risk of prejudice and incompetence, and a strict enforcement of the *Daubert* rules on expert testimony could be added into the mix.

Once implemented, however, this system would have to find ways to handle the similar problems that arise in current drug liability litigation. The no-fault system offers no help on the highly contested question of whether a claimant has actually taken the drug. And it would have to deal with the medical causation issue in complex settings like the Vioxx cases, at least some of which have already clearly run off the tracks. In addition, it would have to gear up to handle a larger onslaught of cases because injured persons could recover even if the warnings provided were adequate in all respects. There has been strong resistance to a medical no-fault system because of the difficulty in defining the appropriate "compensable events."[56] That problem would not be eliminated here. The issue of whether the arrhythmia in *Ernst* was a compensable event would remain, just as it did in the tort case. The system has at the very least to be tested against a broad range of adverse events in drug cases before one can be confident that it works. And tough steps would have to be taken to make sure that the claimants actually used the product in the first instance, which presents major difficulties when drug manufacturers have no direct evidence of what persons have used what treatments.

A third proposal worth considering would seek to bypass compensation in order to gain a sensible level of deterrence. Now the effort to escape the tort system throws us into the clutches of a new administrative system that could easily fall prey to the bureaucratic rigidities, say, of the FDA. But the issue here is not whether it is perfect but whether it outperforms a very flawed tort system. This is how it might work. Let any citizen (or plaintiff's lawyer) raise allegations of deliberate or reckless misconduct by any pharmaceutical company to a federal prosecutor empowered to bring suit against the firm so charged. If that suit is brought and proved, then impose fines equal to some fraction of the total sales from that drug over the relevant period, capped, say, at 20 percent of gross revenues from all domestic sales. In the case of Vioxx, that system could generate fines of one or two billion dollars, which is small relative to the outlandish tort liability but hefty enough to attract Merck's attention. Such a system dispenses with the need to make individuated judgments on causation of the sort that led to such confusion in the Vioxx cases. It avoids the caprice of a jury system. The money collected could be placed, if desired, in a fund that might be distributed to individuals found to have suffered from drug-related death or disability, solely dependent on proof of the causal origin of their harm by a preponderance of the evidence, perhaps on the model of the compensation system that was used to compensate the victims of 9/11.[57] Any other FDA deliberations on withdrawal or additional warnings could take place on a separate track.

I make no claim that this proposal responds to all the difficulties on this matter. But it is too clear for words, in light of the result in *Ernst,* to think that any lesser proposal will make it through the present shark-infested waters. The brute truth is that the FDA oversight and the elaborate package warnings provided Merck in *Ernst* with more feeble protection than a tattered umbrella in a rainstorm. Mark Lanier blew down that protection by carting in 157 boxes of paper, representing Merck's FDA submissions before the jury, which were then dismissed as a crude device that "obscured" the truth. Too much paperwork represents a conscious effort to conceal; too little is scandalous. No amount of paperwork is just right. If the best contract solutions are wholly unattainable, then better an administrative and criminal system with a clear upper bound on liability than a tort system that cannot be brought to heel.

The argument here is not whether we are for or against regulation. Regulation is here to stay. The only question is what form it would take. There is, of course, much to be said for decentralized markets. But while the tort system is highly decentralized, it is surely no market. Rather, its decentralization generates a large number of individual initiatives. This results in a system that sets its norm by its extremes rather than by its mean: the outcome is not determined by averaging individual judgments, so that some middle position prevails; rather, in any random distribution of cases, the extreme cases set the standard, as with Vioxx. Administrative review has the unfortunate feature of centralized control, which is difficult to correct. But whereas the tort system privileges extreme outcomes, the administrative system, suitably capped, is less likely to run off the rails.

CONCLUSION: SOCIALIZED MEDICINES

My intention in writing this study has been to give a comprehensive overview of the current legal regime that governs the operation of the pharmaceutical industry. Nothing would have pleased me more than to have given the current system a clean bill of health. But the deterioration in the current system makes a private, Good Housekeeping seal of approval out of the question. The current situation is this: the capital value of pharmaceutical companies is dwindling, and for reasons that make it hard to overlook. Overreactive conflict of interest regulations threaten the level of cooperation between basic researchers in both government and industry, on the one hand, and the applied researchers in the private sector on the other. The level of innovation has been threatened because of the ever-wider net of regulation at all stages in the long and tortuous process of drug development and marketing. The risks have been further aggravated by the constant attacks on the intellectual property rights on which the entire system rests, which have adverse consequences even if they are not transformed into law. The FDA then requires all new drug applicants to run a gantlet only to overstate risks and understate benefits at the initial approval and recall stages. Simultaneously, various systems of price restrictions will choke off the ability to recover the front-end costs of drug development. Finally, the liability system has gone overboard with both tort damages for injured persons and refunds, perhaps double refunds, of purchase price for everyone else.

All the while the gleeful critics of the industry pretend that it is a Goliath with a wanton abuse of power; they work to bring the industry to its knees by cutting off its sources of revenue while simultaneously driving up its costs and exposure to liability. If we thought that pharmaceuticals were just like tobacco, perhaps we could take some cold comfort that the health of a nation would improve if we only put these firms out of their misery by this two-pronged strategy. But who's kidding whom? No industry that supplies hundreds of billions of dollars in products to the overall marketplace can be slated for extinction. So perhaps there is—and by now it should be evident—a different strategy at work in the land: socialized medicines.

Here is how the grand plan would solve the current set of industry woes. Worried about conflict of interest between the government and for-profit sector? Then simply nationalize the entire process of drug development under some government agency, perhaps a more-bloated form of the NIH. Worried about the structure of intellectual property rights? Then socialize these as well, by putting all patents in the hands of the government to dole out as it sees fit. Worried about poor performance in the FDA? Then slow down the approval process further with stiffer requirements and fewer public resources. Worried about the high prices of pharmaceutical drugs? Then make the government the sole supplier, keeping prices low while dishing out large subsidies to favored clientele. Worried about advertisement and marketing? Just don't do much, if any of it, and let consumers get all their information from Worstpills.org. Worried about excessive liability for consumer fraud or personal injury? Then stop the entire system dead in its tracks by refusing to allow any lawsuits against the government officials that make, test, and market these products, even in cases of adulteration or contamination. There you have it: state control from womb to tomb.

Unfortunately, this proposal comes with its own price tag. Someone will have to pay for this program in the form of higher taxes and smaller benefits. And that tab will be both hidden and high. The pharmaceutical pursuits will no longer supply tax revenues. They will soak them up: never forget that user fees account for about only a fourth of Medicare revenues. The level of innovation will plummet, and with it the prospect of advance in dealing with the chronic conditions of an aging population.

Be under no illusions. Our newly empowered bureaucrats will suffer from the same difficulty that has always doomed societies that have been foolish enough to place their trust in a centralized command-and-control system to make steel or grow wheat. Their dinosaur-like reflexes will work as well as FEMA, with or without a storm. But it will never capture the nimbleness of a price system that works like a neural network, allowing individuals with different desires and abilities to communicate information about their preferences through a series of voluntary transactions that involve everything from simple cash sales to complex social organizations. No large bureaucracy has any way to gather the information necessary to make intelligent decisions, or any way to incentivize its operatives to produce goods and services of value. This simple diagnosis explains the chronic decay of all planned economies everywhere. That inexorable diagnosis remains right on the money even when it is applied to this "special" sector of the economy that has been at the center of so many attacks that its ability to function is effectively compromised.

I suspect that as this agenda gets closer to realization, the opposition to it will stiffen. But the resulting mix is likely to be a poor substitute for the more open economic regimes that promote innovation, health, and prosperity. Unfortunately, it is not just the champions of socialist medicines who embrace the carefree attitude that this rich industry can survive any reform that We the People throw in its direction. So they will advocate piecemeal reforms, most of which will move in the direction of greater state control, which Democratic politicians embrace all the time and Republican politicians embrace when they are in power, which is often enough. What is needed now is a regeneration of moral and intellectual awareness that with this overdose of regulation on all fronts we are heading rapidly down the wrong path. If some greater understanding is acquired, then perhaps there will be some way, apart from political bashing, to nurse a besieged industry back to health so that it can resume its efforts to supply new and valuable products for the next generation.

I stated at the outset of this book that it is hard to return the pharmaceutical industry to its glory days of fifty or sixty years ago. In the interim we have gathered all the low-hanging fruit. But the current challenge is not whether we can recreate the heady optimism of Vannevar Bush's 1945 praise of *The Endless Frontier*, any more than it is whether we can make the California gold rush last forever. Our more humble mission should be to remove those numerous obstacles that needlessly retard pharmaceutical innovation. That won't happen if we take the adversarial stance that whatever the drug companies want, all sound and sober citizens should oppose. Unfortunately, that form of relentless populism has led to recrimination and sanctions that have already crippled the industry. The good news is that the trend is not likely to bankrupt the industry, but this is only for one dubious reason. As various developments push ever closer to the brink, even politicians will start to pull in their horns, because deep down they don't want to kill a goose that may yet contain a few more golden eggs. But the reformers who work on one question tend to be oblivious to a second. It is there where my comparative advantage lies. Over the past half-dozen years, I have worked, both as a scholar and a consultant, on a full range of pharmaceutical issues that relate to virtually all of the problems covered in this book. I think I know how the various pieces fit together. Make no mistake about it, it is not a pretty picture.

NOTES

Chapter 1. Rising Expectations—and Diminishing Returns

1. Vannevar Bush, "Science: The Endless Frontier," A Report to the President on a Program for Postwar Scientific Research (Nat'l Sci. Found. 1960) (1945), available at http://www.nsf.gov/about/history/nsf50/vbush1945.jsp. Bush was no intellectual lightweight. From 1939 to 1955, he was president of the Carnegie Institute of Washington, D.C., where he supervised a research budget of $1.7 million in 1937. For an account of his role as a forbear of the Internet, see *Internet Pioneers*, http://www.ibiblio.org/pioneers/bush.html. For a contemporary exposition of his views, see "Vannevar Bush, As We May Think," *Atlantic Monthly*, July 1945, available at http://www.ps.unisb.de/~duchier/pub/vbush/vbush.shtml. For a fiftieth anniversary appreciation, see Symposium, "As We May Think": A Celebration of Vannevar Bush's 1945 Vision, an Examination of What Has Been Accomplished, and What Remains to Be Done, October 12–13, 1995, http://www.eecs.mit.edu/AY95-96/events/9.html. See also David C. Mowery, "The Bush Report After Fifty Years: Blueprint or Relic?" in *Science for the Twenty-first Century* 24 (Claude E. Barfield ed., AEI Press 1997) for a critical evaluation of many of the particular recommendations of the Bush Report.

2. For a critique of this program for its undersupport of civilian technology, see Richard R. Nelson, "Why the Bush Report Has Hindered an Effective Civilian Technology Policy," in Barfield, *Science for the Twenty-first Century* 42.

3. Bush, "Science," 13, 52, 53–54. For a desperate call for the removal of the ban on DDT, see Nicholas D. Kristof, "It's Time to Spray DDT," *New York Times*, January 8, 2005. Environmental and FDA bans bear an eerie similarity.

4. See Kevin Murphy and Robert Topel, "Diminishing Returns?: The Costs and Benefits of Improving Health," 46 *Persps. Biology Med.* S108, S108 (Supp. 2003).

5. For one such account, see Marcia Angell, *The Truth About the Drug Companies: How They Deceive Us and What to Do About It* (Random House 2004). For similar works in the same vein, see Public Citizen's Congress Watch, "America's

Other Drug Problem: A Briefing Book on the Rx Drug Debate," http://www.
citizen.org/documents/drugbriefingbk.pdf, and Arnold S. Relman and Marcia
Angell, "America's Other Drug Problem: How the Drug Industry Distorts Medicine
and Politics," *New Republic,* December 16, 2002, 27. I have sought to answer these
charges in Richard A. Epstein, "Pharma Furor," *Legal Affairs* 60 (January–February
2005) (review of Jerome P. Kassirer, *On the Take: How Medicine's Complicity with Big
Business Can Endanger Your Health,* and Marcia Angell, *The Truth About the Drug
Companies: How They Deceive Us and What to Do About It*), and Richard A. Epstein,
"Does America Have a Prescription Drug Problem? The Perils of Ignoring the
Economics of Pharmaceuticals" (Institute for Policy Innovation, October 7, 2004),
and shall not dwell on these particular publications here.

6. See U.S. Department of Health and Human Services, *Health, United States,
2004* 143 (2004), http://www.cdc.gov/nchs/data/hus/hus04trend.pdf#027. Note
that the online version has been updated since the printed book.

7. Bush, "Science," 6, 16.

8. See "Congress Reduces NSF Budget to $5.47 billion," http://www.nsf.gov/
about/congress/108/highlights/cu04_1123.jsp; "National Institutes of Health FY
2005 Congressional Justification" 22, http://officeofbudget.od.nih.gov/FY05/
Overview.pdf.

9. See PhRMA, "R&D Investment by Pharmaceutical Companies Tops $38
Billion in 2004" (February 18, 2005), http://www.phrma.org/mediaroom/press/
releases/18.02.2005.1128.cfm.

10. For an account of his work, see "Frederick G. Banting—Biography," at
http://nobelprize.org/medicine/laureates/1923/banting-bio.html.

11. Amy Barrett, "Pfizer's Funk," *Business Week,* February 28, 2005, at 72, available
at http://www.businessweek.com/magazine/content/05_09/b3922001_mz001.
htm. For a systematic attack on the blockbuster model, see Jim Gilbert, Preston
Henske, and Ashish Singh, "Rebuilding Big Pharma's Business Model," 21 *In Vivo:
Bus. Med. Rep.* 73 (November 2003).

12. For criticism of the strong FDA reaction to a single death in a clinical trial, see
Thomas P. Stossel, "Regulating Academic-Industrial Research Relationships: Solving
Problems or Stifling Progress," 74 *New Eng. J. Med.* (2005)

13. 186 U.S. 70, 88–89 (1902).

14. Id. at 91. The definition was offered in the context of an effort by a defendant-
licensee to impose an antitrust defense under the Sherman Act to a license term that
allowed the licensor to nullify the license if an insufficient number of licensees signed
on. Peckham rightly found no anticompetitive effects from adopting this policy. The
exceptions to which Peckham refers include the sale of dangerous products that can
be banned on safety grounds, and to restrictions that blocked the discharge of common carrier obligations by government in the telephone business, for example. Id.
at 90–91.

15. See generally U.S. Food and Drug Administration, "Milestones in U.S.
Food and Drug Law History" (updated Aug. 2005), http://www.fda.gov/
opacom/backgrounders/miles.html.

16. For my early protestation of the expansion of medical malpractice liability on these grounds, see Richard A. Epstein, "Medical Malpractice: The Case for Contract," [1976] *Am. Bar. Found. Res. J.* 87; for my most modern iteration of this theme, see Richard A. Epstein, "Contractual Principle Versus Legislative Fixes: Coming to Closure on the Unending Travails of Medical Malpractice," 54 *DePaul L. Rev.* 503 (2005).

Chapter 2. Property Generally

1. See *J. Inst.* 2.1.1. The "consequently" was meant to signal the transitional role of the beach, which lies of course between the sea and the private land that abutted the beach. In addition, ordinary individuals could appropriate the beach for temporary uses but could not acquire permanent ownership by the rules of acquisition that governed other land.

2. For the most insistent account of these limitations on property rights, see J. W. Harris, *Property and Justice* (Oxford University Press 1996).

3. See Joel Franklin Brenner, "Nuisance Law and the Industrial Revolution," 3 *J. Legal Stud.* 403, 403 (1974): "Refinements in the definition of nuisance since the time of Henry VIII have been few, and they have been technical only."

4. For the classical discussion, see John Locke, *Second Treatise of Government* ch. 5, 18–30 (C. B. Macpherson ed., Hackett 1980) (1690). Locke starts with the view that all property is given by the creator to mankind in common, but he quickly backtracks to allow individuals by their own labor to remove it from the commons for their own use. Why? "If such a consent as that [of all mankind] was necessary, man had starved, notwithstanding the plenty God had given him." Id. at 19. That supposed original allocation of resources is too inefficient to be sustainable.

5. By way of clarification, the commons to which I refer in the text is an *open* commons that anyone may enter. A *closed* commons, on the other hand, is a species of private property shared by a designated group of individuals who have by agreement or custom decided to pool their resources. The consensual origin is accompanied by the use of rules that define and limit the permissible class of uses.

6. See *Bamford v. Turnley,* 122 Eng. Rep. 27, 32–33 (Ex. 1862).

7. This issue has recently raised a storm of controversy, beyond the scope of this book, when the Supreme Court, by a 5–4 vote, allowed the taking of private homes for general economic development, even though the city plan had no identified use for the property in question. See *Kelo v. City of New London,* __ U.S. ___, 125 S. Ct. 2655 (2005). The pre–New Deal cases on public use tended to allow the eminent-domain power to be used by private parties only when needed to overcome a severe holdout problem over land—often scrub land—of little value to its owner. See, e.g., *Clark v. Nash,* 198 U.S. 361 (1905) (allowing condemnation of an irrigation ditch over valueless land). For the modern expansive readings of public use, see *Berman v. Parker,* 348 U.S. 26 (1954) (urban renewal); *Hawaii Housing Authority v. Midkiff,* 467 U.S. 229 (1984) (control of excessive concentration of land ownership).

For the interplay between subjective value and holdout risk in public use cases, see Thomas Merrill, "The Economics of Public Use," 72 *Cornell L. Rev.* 61 (1986).

8. See, e.g., *United States v. Rands*, 389 U.S. 121, 121–122, 124–125 (1967), one of many cases that has taken the consistent line. The Court refused to use the land's value as a port site in determining just compensation.

9. For the development of this theme, see Richard A. Epstein, *Takings: Private Property and the Power of Eminent Domain* 67–73 (Harvard University Press 1985).

Chapter 3. Intellectual Property

1. For an overview of this range, see Richard A. Epstein, "Intellectual Property: Old Boundaries and New Frontiers" (Addison C. Harris Lecture), 76 *Ind. L. J.* 803 (2001) (discussing the rules of acquisition, exclusion, and duration for the distinct forms of intellectual property).

2. On the method generally, see Richard A. Epstein, *Skepticism and Freedom: A Modern Case for Classical Liberalism* ch. 4 (University of Chicago Press 2003).

3. On ideas, see, e.g., *Baker v. Selden*, 101 U.S. 99, 102 (1880) (holding that copyright protects a book on accounting, but not the underlying ideas on the system of accounting in the book). On substances occurring in nature, see, e.g., *Funk Bros. Seed Co. v. Kalo Inoculant Co.*, 333 U.S. 127, 130–131 (1948); *American Wood-Paper Co. v. Fibre Disintegrating Co.*, 90 U.S. 566, 593–594 (1874).

4. See, e.g., *International News Service v. Associated Press*, 248 U.S. 215, 234 (1918) ("The news element—the information respecting current events contained in the literary production—is not the creation of the writer, but is a report of matters that ordinarily are *publici juris;* it is the history of the day"). Pitney then adds that this element falls outside the scope of Congress's power to protect with copyrights or patents under the Constitution. Id.

5. One bittersweet note. Hoover's monument outside the Hoover Institution lists five grounds for his distinction: as author, engineer, humanitarian, statesman, and public servant. His presidency is not specifically mentioned.

6. 35 U.S.C. §101 (2000). Note that "useful" imports some test of utility, which is quite minimal under the statute in most cases.

7. On novelty, see 35 U.S.C. §102 (2000). On nonobviousness see 35 U.S.C. §103 (2000). The technical conditions are found in 35 U.S.C. §112 (2000), which reads: "The specification shall contain a written description of the invention, and of the manner and process of making and using it, in such full, clear, concise, and exact terms as to enable any person skilled in the art to which it pertains, or with which it is most nearly connected, to make and use the same, and shall set forth the best mode contemplated by the inventor of carrying out his invention."

8. See, e.g., Arnold Plant, "The Economic Theory Concerning Patents for Invention" (1934) in *Selected Economic Essays and Addresses* 35–55 (Routledge and Kegan Paul 1974). For his parallel views on copyright, see Arnold Plant, "The Economic Aspects of Copyright in Books" (1934), id. at 57–86.

Chapter 4. Taming Conflict of Interests

1. For the details, see National Institutes of Health, "Conflict of Interest Information and Resources," http://www.nih.gov/about/ethics_COI.htm. For background, see Gardiner Harris, "Ban on Federal Scientists' Consulting Nears," *New York Times,* February 1, 2005.

2. For my comments, see Richard A. Epstein, "Mad Scientists: Go Away Ethics Police. Leave the NIH Alone," *Slate,* February 15, 2005, http://slate.msn.com/id/2113520/. This brief piece prompted an indignant response from Carl Elliot, "When Ethicists Have Conflicts of Interest, Dissent," Fall 2005, http://www.dissent-magazine.org/menutest/articles/fa05/elliot.htm, who took the categorical position that anyone who worked for a pharmaceutical company could not sit on a conflict of interest committee.

3. See Thomas P. Stossel, "Free the Scientists!" *Forbes,* February 14, 2005, at 40.

4. See generally U.S. Food and Drug Administration, Milestones in U.S. Food and Drug Law History (updated Aug. 2005), http://www.fda.gov/opacom/backgrounders/miles.html.

5. See Gardiner Harris, "Health Agency Tightens Rules Governing Federal Scientists," *New York Times,* August 26, 2005.

6. Thomas Stossel, "Regulating Academic-Industrial Research Relationships: Solving Problems of Stifling Progress," 353 (10) *New Eng. J. Med.* 60 (2005).

7. See Immune Tolerance Network, http://www.immunetolerance.org/overview/index.html.

Chapter 5. Federally Sponsored Research Under Bayh-Dole

1. In re Columbia Univ. Patent Litig., 343 F. Supp. 2d 35 (D. Mass. 2004). For discussion see Bernard Wysocki, Jr., "College Try: Columbia's Pursuit of Patent Riches Angers Companies," *Wall Street Journal,* December 21, 2004.

2. See *Univ. of Rochester v. G.D. Searle & Co.,* 358 F.3d 916 (Fed.Cir. 2004).

3. Vannevar Bush, "Science: The Endless Frontier," A Report to the President on a Program for Postwar Scientific Research (Nat'l Sci. Found. 1960) (1945), at 38.

4. Pub. L. No. 96-517, 94 Stat. 3015-28 (1980) (codified as amended at 35 U.S.C. §§200–212, 301–307). For a comprehensive discussion of this issue, see Rebecca S. Eisenberg, "Public Research and Private Development: Patents and Technology Transfer in Government-Sponsored Research," 82 *Va. L. Rev.* 1663, 1671–1695 (1996), on which much of this account is based.

5. National Patent Planning Commission, *Government-Owned Patents and Inventions of Government Employees and Contractors* (1944).

6. Attorney General of the United States, *Investigation of Government Patent Practices and Policies: Report and Recommendations of the Attorney General to the President* (1947).

7. Eisenberg, "Public Research and Private Development," at 1674.

8. See Bayh-Dole Act. Eisenberg also discusses the Stevenson-Wydler Technology Innovation Act of 1980, Pub. L. No. 96-480, 94 Stat. 2311–2320 (codified as amended at 15 U.S.C. 3701–3714), which deals with the technology transfer from federal laboratories and their employees to the private sector. Eisenberg, "Public Research and Private Development," at 1705–1707. I do not examine that statute here.

9. 35 U.S.C. §200 (2000).

10. Government Patent Policy: Memorandum to the Heads of Executive Departments and Agencies, Pub. Papers 248 (February 18, 1983).

11. 35 U.S.C. §200.

12. Id. §202(c)(4), §202(c)(7)(B), §202(c)(7)(C), §202(d), §203(1)(a).

13. See Eisenberg, "Public Research and Private Development," at 1663 and n.2.

14. Edmund W. Kitch, "The Nature and Function of the Patent System," 20 *J.L. & Econ.* 265 (1977). For criticism, see Mark Lemley, "Ex ante versus Ex post Justifications for Intellectual Property," 71 *U. Chi. L. Rev.* 129, 132–141 (2004).

15. But see Sonny Bono Copyright Term Extension Act, Pub. L. No. 105-298, 112 Stat. 2827 (1998) (codified at 17 U.S.C. §302(a)) (extending copyright protection retroactively to the life of the inventor plus seventy years). For my views on the act, see Richard A. Epstein, "The Dubious Constitutionality of the Copyright Term Extension Act," 36 *Loy. L.A. L. Rev.* 123 (2002).

16. See Wysocki, "College Try."

17. See R. H. Coase, "The Problem of Social Cost," 3 *J. L. & Econ.* 1 (1960).

Part III. Intellectual Property and Its Regulation

1. See, for an early demonstration, Gordon Tullock, "The Welfare Costs of Tariffs, Monopolies, and Theft," 5 *W. Econ. J.* 224 (1967).

Chapter 6. The Anticommons

1. For one recent exhaustive account of the literature, see Michael Abramowicz, "Perfecting Patent Prizes," 56 *Vand. L. Rev.* 115, 127-170 (2003).

2. Included in the list of research tools are "cell lines, monoclonal antibodies, reagents, animal models, growth factors, combinatorial chemistry libraries, drugs and drug targets, clones and cloning tools (such as PCR [polymerase chain reaction]) methods, laboratory equipment and machines, databases and computer software." Janice M. Mueller, "No 'Dilettante Affair': Rethinking the Experimental Use Exception to Patent Infringement for Biomedical Research Tools," 76 *Wash. L. Rev.* 1, 11 (2001). See also National Institutes of Health, Report of the National Institutes of Health (NIH) Working Group on Research Tools, http://www.nih.gov/news/researchtools/index.htm (June 4, 1998) (defining research tools as "the full range of resources that scientists use in the laboratory").

3. Michael A. Heller and Rebecca S. Eisenberg, "Can Patents Deter Innovation? The Anticommons in Biomedical Research," 280 *Sci.* 698, 699 (1998) (noting that a

biomedical anticommons could arise if the government either created too many con-
current fragments of intellectual property rights or permitted upstream patentees to
stack licenses on the future discoveries of downstream users).

4. Michael A. Heller, "The Tragedy of the Anticommons: Property in the
Transition from Marx to Markets," 111 *Harv. L. Rev.* 621, 622 (1998) ("In an anticommons, according to this Article, multiple owners are each endowed with the right to
exclude others from a scarce resource, and no one has an effective privilege of use");
Garrett Hardin, "Tragedy of the Commons," 162 *Sci.* 1243, 1244 (1968) (using a graz-
ing pasture to illustrate the point).

5. See James Buchanan and Yong J. Yoon, "Symmetric Tragedies: Commons and
Anticommons," 43 *J.L. & Econ.* 1, 2 (2000) (noting that the waste from the anticommons "may be quantitatively comparable to the overutilization wastage employed in
the conventional commons logic").

6. See Mueller, "No 'Dilettante Affair,'" at 9–10; Donna M. Gitter,
"International Conflicts over Patenting Human DNA Sequences in the United States
and the European Union: An Argument for Compulsory Licensing and a Fair-Use
Exemption," 76 *N.Y.U. L. Rev.* 1623, 1678–1690 (2001).

7. For a more detailed statement of my views, see Richard A. Epstein, "Steady the
Course: Property Rights in Genetic Material," in *Perspectives on Properties of the
Human Genome Project* 153, 171–179 (F. Scott Kieff ed., Elsevier/Academic Press 2003).

8. For a longer discussion, see Richard A. Epstein and Bruce N. Kuhlik, "Is
There a Biomedical Anticommons?" 27 *Reg.* 54, 54–58 (Summer 2004).

9. For further discussion, see Richard A. Epstein, "The Permit Power Meets the
Constitution," 81 *Iowa L. Rev.* 407, 411–414 (1995) ("Permit powers, however, are
rarely softened by the conditions routinely associated with private injunctions").

10. Carl Shapiro, "Navigating the Patent Thicket: Cross Licenses, Patent Pools,
and Standard Setting," in 1 *Innovation Policy and the Economy* 119, 119 (A. Jaffe et al.
eds., MIT Press Journals, 2001) ("In several key industries . . . our patent system is
creating a *patent thicket:* an overlapping set of patent rights requiring that those seeking to commercialize new technology obtain licenses from multiple patentees").

11. See, e.g., JPMA Databook, at http://www.jpma.or.jp/12english/publications/
databook/databook2002/14DATA/whtml/075.html. Similar data can be obtained
from the USPTO's online database. Searching this database for patents classified in
class 424 (into which most pharmaceutical patents fall) yields the following number
of new patents in each year between 1990 and 2005: 730, 835, 893, 891, 894, 1,884,
2,283, 3,396, 4,112, 4,478, 3,925, 4,418, 4,610, 4,325, 3,197, 2,667. These data can be
reproduced by searching the USPTO database, http://patft.uspto.gov/
netahtml/search-adv.htm, for "((ccl/424/$) and (isd/1/1/year->12/31/year))"
(replacing "year" with, e.g., 1990).

12. For an exhaustive discussion, see Molly A. Holman and Stephen R. Munzer,
"Intellectual Property Rights in Genes and Gene Fragments: A Registration Solution
for Expressed Gene Tags," 85 *Iowa L. Rev.* 735, 755–756 (2000).

13. John P. Walsh, Wesley M. Cohen, and Ashish Arora, "Working Through the
Patent Problem," 299 *Sci.* 1021 (2003).

Chapter 7. The Single Monopoly

1. 56 U.S. (15 How.) 62, 112–113 (1854).

2. See *University of Rochester v. G. D. Searle & Co.*, 358 F.3d 916, 918, 929 (Fed. Cir. 2004), aff'g, 249 F. Supp. 2d 216 (W.D.N.Y. 2003).

3. Id. at 929 and n.9 ("Because the [Rochester] patent does not provide any guidance that would steer the skilled practitioner toward compounds that can be used to carry out the claimed methods—an essential element of every claim of that patent—and [had] not provided evidence that any such compounds were otherwise within the knowledge of a person of ordinary skill in the art at the relevant time," the research institution's claim of infringement failed).

4. See *In re Harnisch*, 631 F.2d 716, 718 (C.C.P.A. 1980) (discussing the scope of so-called Markush claims, whereby different elements are added to a standard chemical backbone). One irony is that Searle (later taken over by Pharmacia, and then Pfizer) sought to block the Merck patent on Vioxx by claiming that it was covered by an earlier Markush claim that Pfizer had filed. That claim was rejected in an exhaustive opinion in the ensuing interference action before the Patent and Trademark Office.

5. Arnold S. Relman and Marcia Angell, "America's Other Drug Problem: How the Drug Industry Distorts Medicine and Politics," *New Republic,* December 16, 2002, 27, at 32.

6. Id. at 33, urging just that.

7. Thomas H. Lee, "Me-Too Products—Friend or Foe?" 360 *New Eng. J. Med.* 211 (January 15, 2004) (illustrating proposition with the effects of new cardiac stents).

8. Drug Price Competition and Patent Term Restoration Act, Pub. L. No. 98-417, 98 Stat. 1585 (1984) (codified at 21 U.S.C. §355; 35 U.S.C. §§156, 271). My thanks for working the way through this rugged statute to William Martin, University of Chicago, whose research paper Retroactive Extensions of Marketing Exclusivity in the Hatch-Waxman Act, on file, helped guide me through this patent thicket.

9. Henry G. Grabowski and John M. Vernon, "Returns to R&D on New Drug Introductions in the 1980s," 13 *J. Health Econ.* 383, 389 (1994). It is also noteworthy that it appears as though the effective useful life under Hatch Waxman has fallen as of late. The 1997–2002 figures reveal an average short duration of 9.8 years and a long duration of 12.3 years. But the range has been volatile. The short period has been as high as 13.0 years in 1997 and as short as 6.5 years in 2001. The longest duration has varied from 15.0 years in 1998 to 9.1 in 2001. These swings really matter for investment decisions. For the modern expansive readings of public use, see *Berman v. Parker*, 348 U.S. 26 (1954) (urban renewal); *Hawaii Housing Authority v. Midkiff*, 467 U.S. 229 (1984) (control of excessive concentration of land ownership).

10. 35 U.S.C. §271(e)(1).

11. 125 S. Ct. 2372 (2005), rev'g 331 F.3d 860 (Fed. Cir. 2003). Note that Merck KgaA is not related to the American Merck & Co.

12. IMS Health, National Prescription Audit Plus (2001).

13. See 35 U.S.C. §103 (2000).

14. For accounts, see Malcolm Gladwell, "High Prices: How to Think About Prescription Drugs," *New Yorker,* October 25, 2004, at 86, discussing Marcia Angell, *The Truth About Drug Companies: How They Deceive Us and What to Do About It* (Random House 2004).

15. Gladwell, "High Prices," at 86.

16. Letter from Robert D. Bajefsky to Russel A. Bantham, executive vice president of PhRMA (June 5, 2001) (on file with the author).

17. *See* 35 USC §271(e)(2) (2000).

18. 21 USC §355(b)(3), (j)(2)(B)(ii), (j)(5)(B)(iii); *Eli Lilly v. Medtronic, Inc.,* 496 US 661, 677 (1990).

19. See 21 U.S.C. § 355(j)(5)(B)(iii). At one time, multiple stays could be sought, but the new law now allows only one stay for each ANDA.

20. See, e.g., *In re Cardizem CD Antitrust Litigation,* 332 F3d 896, 908 (6th Cir 2003).

21. *Valley Drug Co. v. Geneva Pharms., Inc.,* 344 F.3d 1294 (11th Cir 2003); see also *Schering-Plough v. Federal Trade Commission,* 402 F.3d 1056, (11th Cir. 2005), *petition for cert. field,* No. 05-273 (U.S. Aug. 29, 2005), which it is widely assumed that the Supreme Court will decide.

22. See, e.g., Daniel A. Crane, "Exit Payments in Settlement of Patent Infringement Lawsuits: Antitrust Rules and Economic Implications," 54 *Fla. L. Rev.* 747, 779 (2002).

23. 130 *Cong. Rec.* 23764 (1984).

Chapter 8. Rate Regulation

1. Oz Shy, *The Economics of Network Industries* 5–6 (Cambridge University Press 2001).

2. For discussion, see Richard A. Posner, "Natural Monopoly and Its Regulation," 21 *Stan. L. Rev.* 548 (1969); Harold Demsetz, "Why Regulate Utilities?" 11 *J.L. & Econ.* 55 (1968).

3. See The Telecommunications Act of 1996, Pub. L. No. 104-104, 110 Stat. 56 (codified at 47 U.S.C. §151 et seq.).

4. See, e.g., *Smyth v. Ames,* 169 U.S. 466, 546 (1898) ("We hold, however, that the basis of all calculations as to the reasonableness of rates to be charged by a corporation maintaining a highway under legislative sanction must be the fair value of the property being used by it for the convenience of the public").

5. See, e.g., *Fed. Power Comm'n v. Hope Natural Gas,* 320 U.S. 591, 601–605 (1944).

6. For such review, see, e.g., *Duquesne Light Co. v. Barasch,* 488 U.S. 299, 307 (1989) ("The guiding principle has been that the Constitution protects utilities from being limited to a charge for their property serving the public which is so 'unjust' as to be confiscatory"); *Jersey Cent. Power & Light Co. v. Fed. Energy Reg. Comm'n,* 810 F.2d 1168, 1175–1179 (D.C. Cir. 1987) (Bork, J.).

7. Testimony of Robert M. Goldberg, Ph.D., Before the Health, Education, Pensions and Labor Committee, United States Senate, February 17, 2005, at 4, citing

John A. Vernon, Rexford E. Santerre, and Carmelo Giaccotto, "Are Drug Price Controls Good for Your Health?" Center for Medical Progress at the Manhattan Institute, December 2004. Elsewhere Goldberg writes: "Thanks to America's free market pricing, US biotech and pharmaceutical firms invest more relative to Europe. In 2003, American biotech and pharmaceutical firms increased their R&D investment by 16 percent compared to a 2 percent decline in Europe. Today, Europe pharma companies spend less than half of their R and D in Europe, down from 73 percent in 1990. While Europe has more biotech companies than America, we have 75 percent of all biotech revenues worldwide, 75 percent of all R&D expenditures and 80 percent of all key biotech patents." Letter, *Washington Times,* July 8, 2005.

8. Joseph A. DiMasi, Ronald W. Hansen, and Henry G. Grabowski, "The Price of Innovation: New Estimates of Drug Development Costs," 22 *J. Health Econ.* 151, 180 (2003); Jim Gilbert, Preston Henske, and Ashish Singh, "Rebuilding Big Pharma's Business Model," 21, *In Vivo: Bus. Med. Rep.* 73 (November 2003).

9. Public Citizen, "America's Other Drug Problem: A Briefing Book on the Rx Drug Debate," *Congress Watch* 47, at www.citizen.org/rxfacts (2002).

10. See Malcolm Gladwell, "High Prices: How to Think About Prescription Drugs," *New Yorker,* October 25, 2004, at 87–88 (noting some of the complications).

11. Patricia M. Danzon and Michael F. Furukawa, "Price and Availability of Pharmaceuticals: Evidence from Nine Countries," *Health Affairs,* October 29, 2003, http://www.healthaffairs.org/indexhw.php. The authors also conclude that the differentials in drug prices for patented products across countries are roughly in line with income and smaller than the differences in the supply of other services.

12. See, e.g., *In re Brand Name Prescription Drug Litig.,* 186 F.3d 781, 786–789 (7th Cir. 1999) (Posner, C.J.).

13. S. 812, 107th Cong. (2001). For the record, I am pleased to disclose I wrote an opinion letter on behalf of PhRMA that attacked the constitutionality of this legislation. See letter of Richard A. Epstein to Senator Edward M. Kennedy, re Sabinow and Reid Amendments to S. 812, July 22, 2002 on file with author. I also consulted with PhRMA on other price control issues.

14. The bill provided: "It shall be unlawful for a manufacturer of a prescription drug to discriminate against, or cause any other person to discriminate against, a pharmacist or wholesaler that purchases or offers to purchase a prescription drug from the manufacturer or from any person that distributes a prescription drug manufactured by the drug manufacturer." See S. 812, 107th Cong. §804(i)(1) (2002).

15. Id. §804(i)(2).

16. 186 U.S. 70 (1902).

17. For a different view, see Roger Pilon, "The Reimportation Blues," *Wall Street Journal,* October 11, 2004, who argues that it is improper for the United States to assist the drug companies by disallowing the importation. In his view, we should not help our own nationals enforce their contracts. In my view, the breakdown of the system at the foreign level justifies the domestic interference so long as it only replicates the restrictions contracts otherwise demand.

18. S. 2328, 108th Cong. (2004). I also wrote in opposition to this legislation. See letter of Richard A. Epstein to Bruce N. Kuhlik, General Counsel of PhRMA (May 10, 2004) (on file with author).

19. See Canada's Food and Drug Act, section 37 ("This Act does not apply to any packaged food, drug, cosmetic or device, not manufactured for consumption in Canada and not sold for consumption in Canada"), available at http://laws. justice.gc.ca/en/F-27/text.html. For further discussion, see HPFB Inspectorate, Q&A on Commercial Importation and Exportation of Drugs in Dosage form, http://www. hc-sc.gc.ca/hpfbdgpsa/inspectorate/guide_comm_import_qa_e.html.

20. S. 1392, §804(n)(3).

21. Id. §804(h).

22. See *United States v. Fuller,* 409 U.S. 488 (1972).

23. 312 F.3d 24 (1st Cir. 2002), striking down Mass. Gen Laws ch. 94 §307B (2002).

24. 438 U.S. 104, 124 (1978).

25. For the critiques, first with land and then with intellectual property, see Richard A. Epstein, "*Lucas v. South Carolina Coastal Council:* A Tangled Web of Expectations," 45 *Stan. L. Rev.* 1369 (1993); Richard A. Epstein, "The Ebbs and Flows in Takings Law: Reflections on the *Lake Tahoe,*" 1 *Cato Supreme Court Review* 5 (2002); Richard A. Epstein, "The Constitutional Protection of Trade Secrets under the Takings Clause," 71 *U. Chi. L. Rev.* 57 (2004).

26. *Monsanto v. Ruckelshaus,* 467 U.S. 986, 1006 (1984).

27. *Nollan v. California Coastal Comm'n,* 483 U.S. 825, 833, 837 (1987).

28. Me. Rev. Stat. Ann. tit. 22, §2681 (2004).

29. 42 U.S.C. §1396r-8 (2000). For a description of the program, see *Pharm. Research and Mfr. of Am. v. Walsh,* 538 U.S. 644, 650–653 (2001).

30. 538 U.S. 644, 661, 668 (2001).

31. Prescription Drug Excessive Pricing Act of 2005, D.C. Act 16-171, 52 D.C. Reg. 9061 (Oct. 14, 2005), invalidated by *Pharm. Research & Mfrs. of Am. v. District of Columbia,* No. Civ. 05-2015 (RJL), 2005 W.L. 3508662 (D. D.C. Dec. 22, 2005).

32. Id. §28-4554(a).

33. Id. §28-4554(b). "Where a prima facie case of excessive pricing is shown, the burdens of providing evidence and proving by a preponderance of the evidence shall shift to the defendant to show that a given prescription drug is not excessively priced given demonstrated costs of invention, development and production of the prescription drug, global sales and profits to date, consideration of any government funded research that supported the development of the drug, and the impact of price on access to the prescription drug by residents and the government of the District of Columbia." Id.

34. Prescription Drug Excessive Pricing Act of 2005, D.C. Act 16-171, §28-4553, 52 D.C. Reg. 9061 (October 14, 2005).

35. *Pharm. Research,* 2005 W.L. 3508662, at *6.

36. Id. at *9–12. See generally *Healy v. Beer Institute,* 491 U.S. 324 (1989).

37. TRIPS §1, Art. 27 §2. See *Resource Book on TRIPs and Development,* Part II: Substantive Obligations 2.5 Patents: "The term '*ordre public,*' derived from French law, is not an easy term to translate into English, and therefore the original French term is used in the TRIPS agreement. It expresses concerns about matters threatening the social structures which tie a society together, i.e., matters that threaten the structure of civil society itself." The price dislocations cannot meet this standard, for if they did, then the exception would swallow the rule. Any shortfalls can always be met by higher appropriations for AIDS drugs or anything else. Massive civil disruption from fires and other natural catastrophes fall into the cases of taking, without compensation, in situations of public necessity. See, e.g., *Mayor of New York v. Lord,* 18 Wend. 126, 129 (N.Y. 1837), where the court held that it was "well settled" that the privilege was absolute: "In cases of actual necessity, to prevent the spreading of a fire, the ravages of a pestilence, the advance of a hostile army, or any other great public calamity, the private property of an individual may be lawfully taken and used or destroyed, for the relief, protection or safety of the many, without subjecting those, whose duty it is to protect the public interests, by or under whose direction such private property was taken or destroyed, to personal liability for the damage which the owner has thereby sustained."

Chapter 9. Patent Purchases

1. For the original proposal, see Harold Hotelling, "The General Welfare in Relation to Problems of Taxation and of Railway and Utility Rates," 6 *Econometrica* 242 (1938). This proposal is criticized in R. H. Coase, "The Marginal Cost Controversy," 13 *Economica* 169 (1946). For a general discussion of its application to intellectual property, see John F. Duffy, "The Marginal Cost Controversy in Intellectual Property," 71 *U. Chi. L. Rev.* 37 (2004).

2. Duffy, "The Marginal Cost Controversy," at 38.

3. For a paper that takes this approach, see Jordan Barry, "Patents, Pills, and Politics: Increasing Drug Production While Maintaining Research Incentives" (2005) (on file with author).

4. For the adverse impact of taxation on voluntary transfers, see, e.g., Harvey S. Rosen, *Public Finance* 303 (4th ed., Irwin 1995).

5. Michael Kremer, "Patent Buyouts: A Mechanism for Encouraging Innovation," 113 *Q.J. Econ.* 1137, 1137 (1998) ("Patent buyouts could potentially eliminate the monopoly price distortions and incentives for rent-stealing duplicative research created by patents, while increasing incentives for original research").

6. Karen Pihl-Carey, "$525M Gets Emtriva Interest From Emory for Gilead, Royalty Pharma," *BioWorld Today,* July 20, 2005.

7. For discussion, see Michael Abramowicz, "Perfecting Patent Prizes," 56 *Vand. L. Rev.* 115, 127-170 (2003), at 116 and n.2 (citing sources).

8. U.S. Const. amend. V. For my views, see generally Richard A. Epstein, *Takings: Private Property and the Power of Eminent Domain* (Harvard University Press 1985), which sets out the basic framework.

9. See, e.g., *Ruckelshaus v. Monsanto Co.*, 467 U.S. 986, 1000–1004 (1984) ("This general perception of trade secrets as property is consonant with a notion of 'property' that extends beyond land and tangible goods and includes the products of an individual's 'labour and invention'"). *Monsanto* dealt with trade secrets, but the general logic applies to patents.

10. See U.S. Const. art. I, §8, cl. 8.

11. For the argument that the Takings provision places limits on the use of the taxing power, see Epstein, *Takings*, at 99–100.

12. See *Hawaiian Hous. Auth. v. Midkiff*, 467 U.S. 229, 241 (1984) ("But where the exercise of the eminent domain power is rationally related to a conceivable public purpose, the Court has never held a compensated taking to be proscribed by the Public Use Clause").

13. __ U.S. __, 125 S. Ct. 2655 (2005).

14. *Boston Chamber of Commerce v. Boston*, 217 U.S. 189, 195 (1910).

15. See *Kimball Laundry Co. v. United States*, 338 U.S. 1, 5 (1949) (noting that just compensation ignores "personal and variant standards as value to the particular owner").

16. *Monongahela Navigation Co. v. United States*, 148 U.S. 312, 325–326 (1893) ("And this just compensation, it will be noticed, is for the property, and not to the owner"); *United States v. Miller*, 317 U.S. 369, 373–374 (1943).

17. See *Kimball Laundry Co.*, 338 U.S. at 11–12; *United States v. 564.64 Acres of Land*, 441 U.S. 506, 514 (1979) (denying a relocated camp the cost of replacing its facilities when the taking deprived it of certain grandfathered protections); *Cmty. Redev. Agency of Los Angeles v. Abrams*, 543 P.2d 905, 916–918 (Cal. 1975) (providing no compensation for a site-specific license for the sale of pharmaceuticals).

18. See *United States v. Bodcaw Co.*, 440 U.S. 202, 203 (1979) (appraisal fees); *Dohany v. Rogers*, 281 U.S. 362, 368 (1930) (attorney fees).

19. 1 William Blackstone, *Commentaries on the Laws of England* 135 (1765) (emphasis added).

20. Robert C. Guell and Marvin Fischbaum, "Toward Allocative Efficiency in the Prescription Drug Industry," 73 *Milbank Q.* 213, 221 (1995).

21. Id. at 255.

22. Steven Shavell and Tanguy van Ypersele, "Rewards Versus Intellectual Property Rights," 44 *J.L. & Econ.* 525, 537–539 (2001).

23. The fuller model assumes the government is less risk averse than the pharmaceutical company (which could be false given the level of shareholder diversification) and the government has less knowledge of the demand for the product than the owner (which could be false as well, given the huge level of clinical disclosures made at every stage of the FDA process).

Chapter 10. Socialization of R&D

1. Peter Stein and Ernst Valery, "Competition: An Antidote to the High Price of Prescription Drugs," 23 *Health Affairs* 151, 151, 153 (2004).

2. Id. at 154.

3. Id. at 155 (citing U. E. Reinhart, "Pharmaceutical Prices and the Market: The Economics of Prescription Drug Pricing," Mar. 2001 [Presentation at the National Press Club, Washington D.C.]).

4. See, on mandates, Editorial, "Cheaper Health Insurance," *Wall Street Journal,* July 25, 2005 ("New York requires every insurance policy sold there to cover podiatry. Acupuncture coverage is mandated in 11 states, massage therapy in four, osteopathy in 24, and chiropractors in 47. There are an estimated 1800 or so such insurance 'mandates' across the country, and the costs add up. 'It is always the providers asking for the mandate; it is never the consumer,' says health policy guru John Goodman").

5. Joseph A. DiMasi and Henry G. Grabowski, "Patents and R&D Incentives: Comments on the Hubbard and Love Trade Framework for Financing Pharmaceutical R&D," http://www.who.int/intellectualproperty/news/en/Submission3.pdf#search='Dim asi%20AND%20Comments%20Hubbard%20and%20Love%20Framework', at 12–13 (recounting Frederic M. Scherer, *Industrial Market Structure and Economic Performance* 458 [Houghton Mifflin 1980]). See also Merton J. Peck and Frederic M. Scherer, *The Weapons Acquisition Process* (Division of Research, Graduate School of Business Administration, Harvard University 1962).

6. This technical valuation requires the government to both estimate the consumer surplus for each item sold and sum over all consumers. Since no price system exists, these estimates should prove extremely difficult to make.

7. Tim Hubbard and James Love, "A New Trade Framework for Global Healthcare R&D," 2 *PLoS Biology* 147, 148, 149, 150 (February 2004), available at http://biology.plosjournals.org/perlserv/?request=getdocument&doi=10.1371/journal.pbio.0020052.

8. DiMasi and Grabowski, "Patents and R&D Incentives."

9. See Hubbard and Love, "A New Trade Framework," at 147–148.

10. DiMasi and Grabowski, "Patents and R&D Incentives," at 8–9.

11. See Wellcome Trust Statement on Genome Data Release, http://www.wellcome.ac.uk/doc%5Fwtd002751.html.

12. See Andrew Pollack, "Open-Source Practices for Biotechnology," *New York Times,* February 10, 2005; Creative Commons, "Choosing a License," http://creativecommons.org/about/licenses/.

13. For discussion, see Steve Hamm, "Linux Inc.," *Business Week,* January 31, 2005, at 60.

Chapter 11. The Steady Expansion of FDA Power

1. See, e.g., "Vioxx: An Unequal Partnership Between Safety and Efficacy," 364 *Lancet* 1287, 1288 (2004) (criticizing drug regulators for being too complacent).

2. See, e.g., Henry I. Miller, *To America's Health: A Proposal to Reform the Food and Drug Administration* (Hoover Institution Press 2000) (advocating decentralization of the drug approval process under FDA oversight).

3. For the current definition of purity, which includes various forms of adulteration and contamination, see 21 U.S.C. §351 (2000).

4. See Restatement (Second) of Torts §402A, cmt. i (1965), which concludes: "Good whiskey is not unreasonably dangerous merely because it will make some people drunk, and is especially dangerous to alcoholics; but bad whiskey, containing a dangerous amount of fusel oil, is unreasonably dangerous. Good tobacco is not unreasonably dangerous merely because the effects of smoking may be harmful; but tobacco containing something like marijuana may be unreasonably dangerous. Good butter is not unreasonably dangerous merely because, if such be the case, it deposits cholesterol in the arteries and leads to heart attacks; but bad butter, contaminated with poisonous fish oil, is unreasonably dangerous." Modern litigation goes far beyond these traditional limits linked to contamination. It is the inherent properties of tobacco that generate all the modern litigation.

5. Miller, *To America's Health*, at 12–13. See also Michael D. Greenberg, "AIDS, Experimental Drug Approval, and the FDA New Drug Screening Process," 3 *N.Y.U. J. Legis. & Pub. Pol'y* 295, 302–303 (1999) ("[1938] saw a major public health crisis in the distribution of elixir sulfanilamide, a solution which, notwithstanding its medicinal properties, also contained diethylene glycol, a poisonous solvent").

6. Federal Food, Drug, and Cosmetic Act, 75 Pub. L. No. 717, §505(a), 52 Stat. 1040, 1052 (1938) ("No person shall introduce or deliver for introduction into interstate commerce any new drug, unless an application filed pursuant to subsection (b) is effective with respect to such drug"). Section (b) then requires the submission of, among other things, "(1) full reports of investigations which have been made to show whether or not such drug is safe for use." That in turn is supplemented by information on its components, its composition, and its methods of manufacture. Samples of the drug are required, as are proposed labels. Effectiveness is not mentioned; "safe for use" is undefined.

7. Id. §505(c).

8. Drug Amendments of 1962, Pub. L. No. 87-781, §102(a), 76 Stat. 780, 781.

Chapter 12. FDA Versus the Individual

1. For a more complete critique of the FDA's treatment of Celebrex and Vioxx, see Richard A. Epstein, "Regulatory Paternalism in the Market for Drugs: Lessons from Vioxx and Celebrex," 5 *Yale J. Health Pol'y L. Ethics* 741 (2005).

2. See Gardiner Harris, "Merck May Resume Sales of Painkiller, Official Says," *New York Times*, February 18, 2005.

3. For the FDA's cautious position on the decision to take Vioxx off the market, see FDA, "Vioxx (rofecoxib) Questions and Answers," Question 12 (September 30, 2004), http://www.fda.gov/cder/drug/infopage/vioxx/vioxxQA.htm (noting that "the results of clinical studies with one drug in a given class do not necessarily apply to other drugs in the same class. All of the NSAIDs have risks when taken chronically, especially of gastrointestinal [stomach] bleeding, but also liver and kidney toxicity"). For some newspaper accounts, see Bruce Japsen, "Merck Withdraws

Arthritis Drug; Vioxx Increased Danger to Heart," *Chicago Tribune,* October 1, 2004; Barnaby J. Feder, "Criticism of Drug May Leave Pfizer Awash in Lawsuits," *New York Times,* December 18, 2004. See also Anahad O'Connor and Denise Grady, "Pfizer and Celebrex: The Patients; Problems May Send Many Patients Back to Age-Old Aspirin," *New York Times,* December 18, 2004.

4. For the FDA information on Zoloft, see http://www.fda.gov/cder/drug/infopage/sertraline/default.htm.

5. See, for discussion, Gardiner Harris, "FDA Tightens Warning on Antidepressant Drugs," *New York Times,* October 16, 2004.

6. Bruce Japsen, "Track Results of Drug Warning, AMA to Ask; Antidepressant Use for Kids Plummets," *Chicago Tribune,* June 22, 2005, page 3.3; Bruce Japsen, "Do These Drugs Need a Warning? The FDA Says Yes, but Doctors Who Disagree Are Taking Their Case to AMA," *Chicago Tribune,* June 9, 2005.

7. Id.

8. See, e.g., Henry I. Miller, *To America's Health: A Proposal to Reform the Food and Drug Administration* 41–45 (Hoover Institution Press 2000).

9. Sam Peltzman, "An Evaluation of Consumer Protection Legislation: The 1962 Drug Amendments," 81 *J. Pol. Econ.* 1049 (1973).

10. For data, see Celgene Pharmaceuticals, Thalomid (thalidomide), http://www.celgene.com/Products.aspx?s=1. Note that the use of the name Thalomid represents a conscious effort not to sever all connection with its past use.

11. Anup Malani and Feifang Hu, "The Option Value of New Therapeutics" 1 (October 25, 2004) (unpublished conference paper delivered at the University of Chicago in November 2004, on file with the author).

12. Arnold S. Relman and Marcia Angell, "America's Other Drug Problem: How the Drug Industry Distorts Medicine and Politics" *New Republic,* December 16, 2002, 27, at 33.

13. See Jim Gilbert, Preston Henske, and Ashish Singh, "Rebuilding Big Pharma's Business Model," 21 *In Vivo: Bus. Med. Rep.* 73 (November 2003).

14. In its current form, at 21 USC §379g (2005).

15. For a description of the program, see Ernst R. Berndt, Adrian H. B. Gottschalk, Tomas Philipson, Matthew W. Strobeck, "Industry Funding of the FDA: Effects of PDUFA on Approval Times and Withdrawal Rates," 4 *Nature Reviews/Drug Discovery* 545 (July 2005), available at http://www.nature.com/nrd/journal/v4/n7/full/nrd1774_fs.html.

16. Marcia Angell, *The Truth About the Drug Companies: How They Deceive Us and What to Do About It* 208 (Random House 2004).

17. See Ted Agres, "The Double-Edged Sword of PDUFA," *Washington Report,* November 2002, at 13; Gardiner Harris, "At F.D.A., Strong Drug Ties and Less Monitoring," *New York Times,* December 6, 2004.

18. See Harris, "Strong Drug Ties and Less Monitoring."

19. See Id. Regulations Requiring Manufacturers to Assess the Safety and Effectiveness of New Drugs and Biological Products in Pediatric Patients, 63 Fed. Reg. 66632 (December 2, 1998) (codified at 21 C.F.R. pts. 201, 312, 314, and 601).

20. See FDCA §505(A)(a).

21. See http://www.fda.gov/cder/pediatric/labelchange.htm.

22. A general challenge to the broad scope of the patent exemption was turned aside in *National Pharmaceutical Alliance v. Henney,* 47 F. Supp. 2d 37 (D. D.C. 1999) on grounds of general judicial deference to agency determinations.

Chapter 13. Drug Withdrawal

1. For my fuller account of this matter, see Richard A. Epstein, "Regulatory Paternalism in the Market for Drugs: Lessons from Vioxx and Celebrex," 5 *Yale J. Health Pol'y, L., and Ethics* 741 (2005).

2. See FDA, Vioxx (rofecoxib) Questions and Answers, question 7 (September 30, 2004), http://www.fda.gov/cder/drug/infopage/vioxx/vioxxQA.htm; Eric J. Topol, "Good Riddance to a Bad Drug," *New York Times,* October 2, 2004 (criticizing the use of Vioxx because of its increased risk of heart attack or stroke).

3. See FDA, FDA Statement on the Halting of a Clinical Trial of the Cox-2 Inhibitor Celebrex (December 17, 2004), http://www.fda.gov/bbs/topics/news/2004/new01144.html.

4. "Vioxx: An Unequal Partnership Between Safety and Efficacy," 364 *Lancet* 1287, 1288 (2004); see also Topol, "Good Riddance."

5. See Gardiner Harris, "FDA to Create Advisory Panel to Warn Patients About Drugs," *New York Times,* February 16, 2005; Anna Wilde Mat and Leila Abboud, "New FDA Board Set up to Review Approved Drugs," *Wall Street Journal,* February 16, 2005.

6. For the account, see Gardiner Harris, "F.D.A. Is Advised to Let Pain Pills Stay on Market," *New York Times,* February 19, 2005. For reports of the advisory committee meeting of February 16–18, 2005, see http://www.fda.gov/ohrms/dockets/ac/cder05.html#ArthritisDrugs%20.

7. Report of the Expert Advisory Panel on the Safety of Cox-2 Selective Non-steroidal Anti-Inflammatory Drugs (NSAIDs), http://www.hc-sc.gc.ca/dhp-mps/prodpharma/activit/sci-consult/cox2/sap_report_gcs_rapport_cox2_e.html.

8. For a fuller account of the events that led up to pulling Rezulin from the market, see *In re Rezulin Prods. Liab. Litig.,* 210 F.R.D. 61, 62–64 (S.D.N.Y. 2002) (denying the motion to certify a class). On Prozac, see Rick Giombetti, "Prozac, Suicide and Dr. Healy" (March 20, 2002), http://www.whale.to/a/prozac.html. See generally Ron Winslow, "What Makes a Drug Too Risky, There's No Easy Answer," *Wall Street Journal,* February 16, 2005 (noting the challenges in weighing the risks and benefits of drugs).

9. "The Experts' Verdict on Painkillers," *New York Times,* February 19, 2005.

10. 21 C.F.R. part 314, subpart H.

11. Editorial, "Pazdur's Cancer Rules," *Wall Street Journal,* July 6, 2005.

12. Questions and Answers on Iressa (gefitinib), http://www.fda.gov/cder/drug/infopage/iressa/iressaQ&A2005.htm.

13. Id.

14. "Pazdur's Cancer Rules."

15. Janet Woodcock, "FDA to Cancer Patients: We're in Your Corner," *Wall Street Journal,* July 20, 2005.

16. See Steven Walker, "Iressa: The Reality vs. the FDA's Version," *Wall Street Journal,* July 26, 2005.

17. Robert Goldberg, "Vioxx-type Danger and Legal Frivolity," *Washington Times,* August 24, 2005, available at http://www.washtimes.com/op-ed/20050823-091721-3569r.htm.

18. FDA Public Health Advisory: Suspended Marketing of Palladone (hydromorphone hydrochloride, extended release capsules), July 13, 2005, http://www.fda.gov/cder/drug/advisory/palladone.htm. See Palladone (Hydromorphone Hydrochloride Extended-Release) Capsules: Questions and Answers, http://www.fda.gov/cder/drug/infopage/palladone/palladoneQA.htm.

19. Quoted in Alex Berenson and Barnaby Feder, "A Reminder That No Drug Is Risk-Free," *New York Times,* February 19, 2005.

Chapter 14. Getting the Drugs to Market

1. Jerome Kassirer, *On the Take: How Medicine's Complicity with Big Business Can Endanger Your Health* (Oxford University Press 2004).

2. Arnold S. Relman and Marcia Angell, "America's Other Drug Problem: How the Drug Industry Distorts Medicine and Politics," *New Republic,* December 16, 2002, 27, at 34. The same theme is repeated in Angell, *The Truth About the Drug Companies: How They Deceive Us and What to Do About It* (Random House 2004).

3. Jim Edwards, "Drug Ills? Follow the Money," *Brand Week,* February 7, 2005, 24, available at http://search.epnet.com/login.aspx?direct=true&db=buh&an=16202216.

4. For a Web site that contains a bibliography of articles dealing with advertisement and promotion and links to other similar sites, see No Free Lunch, http://nofreelunch.org/requiredbias.htm.

5. I have culled these figures from a presentation on marketing and advertisement that has been prepared by Richard Manning of Pfizer Corporation. The analysis of the material is my own.

6. Id.

7. Id.

8. Id. "The retail value of the 'free' samples is also enormous: $13.1 billion in the 12 months ending in September 2003, according to IMS Health, and another $15.4 billion in the same period for 2004."

9. Id.

10. See Kaiser Family Foundation, "Impact of Direct-to-consumer Advertising on Prescription Drug Spending," http://www.kff.org/rxdrugs/upload/Impact-of-Direct-to-Consumer-Advertising-on-Prescription-Drug-Spending-Summary-of-Findings.pdf. The study notes that "for every 10% increase in DTC advertising, drug

sales within the classes studied increased on average by 1%," without changes in relative market share. Id. at 1.

11. For the vast literature, see http://www.google.com/search?hl=en&q=focus+groups+in+marketing&btnG=Google+Search.

12. Daron Acemoglu and Joshua Linn, "Market Size in Innovation: Theory and Evidence from the Pharmaceutical Industry," 119 *Q. J. Econ.* 1049, 1051 (2004).

13. See, e.g., Michael Kremer, "Pharmaceuticals and the Developing World," 16 *J. Econ. Persp.* 67 (2002).

14. Scott Hensley, Paul Davies, and Barbara Martinez, "Vioxx Verdict Stokes Backlash That Hit FDA, Manufacturers," *Wall Street Journal,* August 22, 2005.

15. Darius Lakdawalla, Tomas J. Philipson, and Richard Wang, "Intellectual Property and Marketing," working paper, on file with author.

16. For one such example, see letter of Robert Rappaport, director of the Division of Anesthetic, Critical Care, and Addiction Drug Products, Center for Drug Evaluation and Research, to Richard J. Fanelli, senior director of U.S. Regulatory Affairs, Purdue Pharma L.P.6 (September 24, 2004), available at http://www.fda.gov/cder/foi/appletter/2004/21044ltr.pdf, which imposed these restrictions on the promotion of Palladone: "1. Core launch material will be submitted to DDMAC at least 15 business days prior to actual use. 2. For the first 6 months following approval, any new core promotional material will be submitted at least 15 days prior to actual use for review and prior approval by DDMAC. 3. Items not considered core promotional material will be submitted at the time of first use."

17. For one such example, see letter (undated but after September 21, 2004) of Robert Rappaport to Purdue Pharma L.P., which imposed these restrictions on the promotion of Palladone: "1. Core launch material will be submitted to DDMAC at least 15 business days prior to actual use. For the first 6 months following approval, any new core promotional material will be submitted at least 15 days prior to actual use for review and prior approval by DDMAC." The drug was later withdrawn from the market.

18. Anna Wilds Mathews, "FDA to Revamp Disclosure Process," *Wall Street Journal,* March 18, 2005.

19. Jun Ma, Randall S. Stafford, Iain M. Cockburn, and Stan Finkelstein, "Statistical Analysis of the Magnitude and Composition of Drug Promotion in the United States in 1998," 25 *Clinical Therapeutics* 1503, 1503 (2003); Manning report cited above.

20. Jim Gilbert, Preston Henske, and Ashish Singh, "Rebuilding Big Pharma's Business Model," *In Vivo: The Business and Medicine Report,* November, 2003 (Windhover Information).

21. See http://www.worstpills.org/. For a petition on Iressa, see http://www.citizen.org/publications/release.cfm?ID=7369.

22. "No Free Lunch Pledge," http://www.nofreelunch.org/pledge.htm.
The full pledge reads:
"I, _____, am committed to practicing medicine in the best interest of my patients and on the basis of the best available evidence, rather than on the basis of advertising or promotion.

"I therefore pledge to accept no money, gifts, or hospitality from the pharmaceutical industry; to seek unbiased sources of information and not rely on information disseminated by drug companies; and to avoid conflicts of interest in my practice, teaching, and/or research."

23. "PhRMA Code on Interactions with Healthcare Professionals," http://www.phrma.org/files/PhRMA%20Code.pdf.

24. Troyen A. Brennan et al., "Health Industry Practices That Create Conflicts of Interest: A Policy Proposal for Academic Medical Centers," 295 *JAMA* 429 (2006).

25. Id. at 431; Ashley Wazana, "Physicians and the Pharmaceutical Industry: Is a Gift Ever Just a Gift?" 283 *JAMA* 373 (2000).

26. For a general survey of these regulations in an international context, see Joan Buckley, "The Need to Develop Responsible Marketing Practice in the Pharmaceutical Sector," *Problems and Perspectives in Management,* 2004, no. 4, at 94.

27. "FDA Issues Final Guidance for Direct-to-Consumer Rx Drug Advertisements" (August 6, 1999), http://www.fda.gov/bbs/topics/ANSWERS/ANS00968.html.

28. Edwards, "Drug Ills?"

29. David Gascoigne, "Can Pharmas Reap a Positive ROI from DTC?" http://www.dtcperspectives.com/content.asp?id=199.

30. David Gascoigne, "A 'Direct' Hit . . . or Miss? DTC at the Crossroads: Perspectives and Prescriptives for Enhanced ROI," http://www.imshealth.nl/vgn/images/portal/cit_40000873/15/35/58020533DTCBrochure092204.pdf.

Chapter 15. Deceptive Marketing

1. See Ashley Wazana, "Physicians and the Pharmaceutical Industry: Is a Gift Ever Just a Gift?" 283 *JAMA* 373 (2000) (critical of industry practices); Paul H. Rubin, "Pharmaceutical Marketing: Medical and Industry Biases," 13(2) *J. Pharm. Fin. Econ. & Pol.* 65 (2004) (aware of the problem, but also critical of the critics).

2. *Price v. Philip Morris, Inc.,* 793 N.E.2d 942 (Ill. App. 2003) (requiring an appeal bond of $12 billion to suspend enforcement of judgment during appeal), reversed summarily, in *Philip Morris, Inc. v. Illinois Appellate Court,* No. 96644, 2003 Ill. LEXIS 2625 (Ill. Sept. 16, 2003). See generally 735 Ill. Comp. Stat. 5/2-1207 (limits on punitive damage awards).

3. See Christopher Bowe, "Merck Launches Legal Defence of Vioxx," *Financial Times,* July 11, 2005.

4. No Free Lunch, http://nofreelunch.org/requiredbias.htm.

5. P. Villanueva, S. Peiro, J. Librero, and I. Pereiro, "Accuracy of Pharmaceutical Advertisements in Medical Journals," 361 *Lancet* 27 (2003).

6. M. G. Ziegler, P. Lews, and B. C. Singer, "The Accuracy of Drug Information from Pharmaceutical Sales Representatives," 274 *JAMA* 1267 (1995).

7. Restatement (Second) of Torts §525.

8. The point is acknowledged by Wazana, "Physicians and the Pharmaceutical Industry," and stressed by Rubin, "Pharmaceutical Marketing."

9. See, e.g., reproduction of the Merck advertisements in *Legal Affairs,* January–February 2005, at 60, 61.

10. On fire liability, see *Kingston v. Chicago & N.W. Ry.,* 211 N.W. 913 (Wis. 1927). On asbestos liability, see *Norfolk & Western Ry. v. Ayres,* 538 U.S. 135 (2003) (denying apportionment in asbestos cases under Federal Employer Liability Act).

11. See, e.g., *Alcan v. United States,* 315 F.3d 179 (2d Cir. 2003) (denying apportionment when eighty-three polluters contributed to total harm).

12. See Lester Brickman, "On the Theory Class's Theories of Asbestos Litigation: The Disconnect Between Scholarship and Reality," 31 *Pepperdine L. Rev.* 33 (2003).

13. Federal Trade Commission Act 15 U.S.C. 57a(a)(1)(B), imposing liability for unfair or deceptive practices.

14. See Wazana, "Physicians and the Pharmaceutical Industry," at 378; Rubin, "Pharmaceutical Marketing," at 9, 11–12, 18.

15. See, e.g., *Desiano v. Warner-Lambert Co.,* 326 F.3d 339, 349–50 (2d Cir. 2003) (allowing a suit by health care providers against the pharmaceutical company that manufactured Rezulin), rev'g *In re Rezulin Prods. Liab. Litig.,* 171 F. Supp. 2d 299, 301 (S.D.N.Y. 2001). The action for fraud is under N.J. Stat. Ann. §56:8-2; that for breach of warranties is under N.J. Stat. Ann. §12A:2-313 and N.J. Stat. Ann. §12A:2-314. For follow-on, see *In re Rezulin Prods. Liab. Litig.,* 392 F. Supp. 2d 597 (S.D.N.Y. 2005) [hereinafter *Rezulin II*], which reviews the various theories of recovery.

16. *Int'l Union of Operating Eng'rs Local 68 Welfare Fund v. Merck & Co.,* 2006 WL 827285 (N.J. Super. Ct. App. Div. Mar. 31, 2006) (affirming lower court's certification of class action). See Tim O'Brien, "Class Action Could Mean Billion-Dollar Exposure for Merck," *New Jersey Law Journal,* August 29, 2005.

17. So described in *Rezulin II,* 397 F. Supp. 2d at 610.

18. For Rooker-Feldman, *D. C. Court of Appeals v. Feldman,* 460 U.S. 462 (1983), relying on *Rooker v. Fid. Trust Co.,* 263 U.S. 413, 416 (1923). "Under the Rooker-Feldman doctrine, federal district courts lack subject matter jurisdiction to review final adjudications of a state's highest court or to evaluate constitutional claims that are 'inextricably intertwined with the state court's [decision] in a judicial proceeding." *In re Gen. Motors Corp. Pick-Up Truck Fuel Tank Prod. Liab.,* 134 F.3d 133, 143 (3rd Cir. 1998). In plain English, federal district courts cannot examine questions of *federal* constitutional law decided by state courts.

For the Anti-Injunction Act, see 28 U.S.C. §2283, "A court of the United States may not grant an injunction to stay proceedings in a State court except as expressly authorized by Act of Congress, or where necessary in aid of its jurisdiction, or to protect or effectuate its judgments." The exceptions in question are narrowly construed and not applicable in these cases, because the risk of double liability does not threaten federal control over its case or compromise the ability of federal courts to enforce their judgments. For discussion, see *In re Gen. Motors Corp. Pick-Up Truck,* 134 F.3d at 144–146.

19. Pub. L. No. 109-2, 119 Stat. 4 (2005).

20. See *Escola*, 150 P.2d at 441 (Traynor, J., concurring) (noting that "the risk of injury can be insured by the manufacturer and distributed among the public as a cost of doing business").

21. All three drugs are thiazolidinediones (TZDs). Actos's side effects are discussed at http://www.fda.gov/cder/consumerinfo/druginfo/actos.HTM. Avandia's side effects are discussed at http://avandia.diabeteslife.com/avandia/avandia_side_effects.html. As with Vioxx, liver function tests are recommended before and during treatment with either drug.

22. For the account, see *In re Rezulin Prods. Liab. Litig.*, 210 F.R.D. 61, 62–64 (S.D.N.Y. 2002). See also *Desiano*, 326 F.3d at 340–344.

23. N.J. Stat. Ann. §§56:8-2, 56:8-2.11, 56:8-2.12 (West 2005).

24. Id. at §§56:8-2.11, 56:8-19.

25. *Desiano*, 326 F.3d at 349.

26. *In re Rezulin*, 210 F.R.D. at 64.

27. *Laborers Local 17 Health and Benefit Fund v. Philip Morris, Inc.*, 191 F.3d 229, 235–36 (2d Cir. 1999). *Laborers* relied on *Holmes v. Sec. Investor Prot. Corp.*, 503 U.S. 258, 268–69 (1992). Both of these cases stress the importance of limiting the number of parties to a dispute by allowing only the party who is deceived to sue a potential deceiver. This should eliminate the suit by the insurer, even if the suit by the insured is sound, which is not the case here.

28. *Desiano*, 326 F.3d at 349–350: "Defendants argue, however, that 'if Rezulin had been effective in all diabetic patients without any side effects, plaintiffs would have no basis for a claim.' But it is easy to see how Defendants' reasoning is flawed. Consider, for example, a hypothetical in which a defendant drug company markets a 'new,' much more expensive drug claiming it is a great advancement (safer, more effective, etc., than metformin—the standard diabetes drug) when in fact the company is simply replicating the metformin formula and putting a new label on it. In other words, the only difference between metformin and the 'new' drug is the new name and the higher prescription price (paid almost entirely by the insurance company). In that case, the 'new' drug would be *exactly* as safe and effective as metformin, and thus there could be no injury to any of the insurance company's insured. Nevertheless, the insurance companies would be able to claim—precisely as they do here—that the defendants engaged in a scheme to defraud it, and that the company suffered direct economic losses as a result."

29. *Rezulin II,* at 19–23.

30. The New Jersey courts have limited the state's statute to "consumer oriented conduct." See *Furst v. Einstein Moomjy, Inc.*, 860 A.2d 435, 441 (N.J. 2004) ("In furtherance of the Act's overarching remedial purpose, a consumer may file a private cause of action against an offending merchant whenever that consumer suffers an ascertainable loss as a result of a violation of the Act"); *Weinberg v. Sprint Corp.*, 801 A.2d 281, 290 (2002).

New York follows the same rule. *Oswego Laborers' Local 214 Pension Fund*, 85 N.Y.2d at 24–25, construing Section 349 of New York's General Business Law: Its key provisions read: "(a) Deceptive acts or practices in the conduct of any business, trade or commerce or in the furnishing of any service in this state are hereby declared unlawful. . . . (h) . . . any person who has been injured by reason of any violation of this section may bring an action . . . to recover his actual damages." The consumer-oriented language limits the reach of the words "any person" in §349(h).

31. *Rezulin II,* at 35–39.

32. See O'Brien, "Class Action."

Chapter 16. Tort Preliminaries

1. *Ernst v. Merck & Co.,* No. 19961 (Tex. D. Ct., 23rd Jud. D. Aug. 19, 2006). For accounts of the case, see Barbara Martinez, "In Texas, Sides Prepare Battle in First Vioxx Trial," *Wall Street Journal* (Europe), June 24, 2005; Barbara Martinez, "Merck Doctor Likely to Testify in Vioxx Trial," *Wall Street Journal,* July 18, 2005, available at http://proquest.umi.com/pqdweb?did=868530241&Fmt=3&clientId= 13392&RQT=309&VName=PQD. For an ongoing update of all the Vioxx litigation, see Merck's Web site, http://www.learnaboutvioxx.com/index.asp.

2. See 28 U.S.C. §2680(a) (2000) (providing blanket protection in the discretionary FDA approval process); see also *Berkovitz v. United States,* 486 U.S. 531, 546 (1988) ("If the policies and programs formulated by the Bureau allow room for implementing officials to make independent policy judgments, the discretionary function exception protects the acts taken by those officials in the exercise of this discretion").

3. For my early defense of the contract position, see Richard A. Epstein, *Modern Products Liability Law* 49–56 (Quorum 1980).

4. For example, a retailer might be kept in a case in order to prevent an out-of-state manufacturer from removing a case to federal court on the grounds of diversity jurisdiction, which normally requires that all plaintiffs be from different states from all defendants..At trial a local pharmacist is not an attractive defendant, so most plaintiffs will, once the state jurisdiction is secured, dismiss him from the case, with prejudice.

5. See, e.g., *Winterbottom v. Wright,* 152 Eng. Rep. 402 (Ex. 1842); *Huset v. J. I. Case Threshing Mach. Co.,* 120 F. 865, 867–871 (8th Cir. 1903) ("The general rule is that a contractor, manufacturer, or vendor is not liable to third parties who have no contractual relations with him for negligence in the construction, manufacture, or sale of the articles he handles").

6. See, e.g., *Escola v. Coca-Cola Bottling Co. of Fresno,* 150 P.2d 436, 440 (Cal. 1944) (Traynor, J., concurring) (calling for strict liability against the manufacturer); *MacPherson v. Buick Motor Co.,* 111 N.E. 1050, 1053–1054 (N.Y. 1916) ("There is nothing anomalous in a rule which imposes upon A, who has contracted with B, a duty to C and D and others according as he knows or does not know that the subject-matter of the contract is intended for their use").

7. See Restatement of Torts, §402A (1965), which announces that its general principle of strict liability applies although "(b) the user or consumer has not bought the product from or entered into any contractual relation with the seller."

8. For one example, see the limitations on the consequential damages in the context of domain name registrations, Network Solutions, Service Agreement, at http://www.networksolutions.com/en_US/legal/static-service-agreement.jhtml.

9. The issue involves the question of whether terms that are included with the sale of the goods are binding on a buyer who discovers them only once the package is opened. My strong position is to respect these terms on the grounds that these limitations both make sense from the point of view of both parties and were understood to be the basis of the agreement. See Richard A. Epstein, "Contract, Not Regulation: UCITA and High-Tech Consumers Meet Their Consumer Protection Critics," *Consumer Protection in the Age of the Information Economy* 205 (Jane K. Winn ed., Ashgate 2006) (UCITA stands for Uniform Computer Information Technology Act); Richard A. Epstein, "Contracts Small and Contracts Large: Contract Law Through the Lens of Laissez-Faire," in *The Fall and Rise of Freedom of Contract* 25, 34 (F. H. Buckley ed., Duke University Press 1999). But see AFFECT (Americans for Fair Electronic Commerce Transactions), "Stop Before You Click: 12 Principles for Fair Commerce in Software and Other Digital Products," http://www.ucita.com/pdf/AFFECTbrochure2-05.pdf; Jean Braucher, "Delayed Disclosure in Consumer E-Commerce as an Unfair and Deceptive Practice," 46 *Wayne L. Rev.* 1805, 1807 (2000) ("Delayed disclosure is closely analogous to the deceptive practice of 'bait and switch' in its economic impact—which is to burden shopping heavily and thus thwart consumer efforts to find and make the best buy").

For disclaimers, see, e.g., U.C.C. §2-719(1) (1998); *Seely v. White Motor Co.,* 403 P.2d 145, 151 (Cal. 1965) ("[A manufacturer] cannot be held for the level of performance of his products in the consumer's business unless he agrees that the product was designed to meet the consumer's demands").

10. See, for the watershed case, *Henningsen v. Bloomfield Motors, Inc.,* 161 A.2d 69, 92–93 (N.J. 1960) (finding a contractual disclaimer of liability unconscionable).

11. Restatement (Third) of Torts: Products Liability §18, cmt. a (1998).

12. Andrew Pollack, "Many See Hope in Drug Pulled During Testing," *New York Times,* November 26, 2004. The situation with Iressa has even more tragic parallels.

13. Andrew Pollack, "Patients in Test Won't Get Drug, Amgen Decides," *New York Times,* February 12, 2005.

14. See, e.g., Cass R. Sunstein and Richard H. Thaler, "Libertarian Paternalism Is Not an Oxymoron," 70 *U. Chi. L. Rev.* 1159, 1163, 1167–1171 (2000) ("The false assumption is that almost all people, almost all of the time, make choices that are in their best interest or at the very least are better, by their own lights, than the choices that would be made by third parties").

15. See, e.g., *Schloendorff v. Soc'y of New York Hosp.,* 105 N.E. 92, 93 (N.Y. 1914) ("Every human being of adult years and sound mind has a right to determine what shall be done with his own body; and a surgeon who performs an operation without his patient's consent, commits an assault, for which he is liable in damages").

16. Alex Berenson, "Merck Asks Court to Dismiss First Vioxx Suit," *New York Times,* April 13, 2005.

17. Id.

18. Thomas Ginsberg, "Idaho Postal Worker Grilled about Vioxx Use in Atlantic City, N.J. Courtroom," *Philadelphia Inquirer,* September 29, 2005.

19. Ill. N.E. 1050 (N.4. 1916).

20. Id. at 1051.

21. James A. Henderson, Jr., *"MacPherson v. Buick Motor Company:* Simplifying the Facts While Reshaping the Law," *Tort Stories* 45–46 (*Robert L. Rabin* ed., West Law School 2003).

22. See Gary Schwartz, "Waste, Fraud, and Abuse in Workers' Compensation: The Recent California Experience," 52 *Md. L. Rev.* 983 (1993).

23. Lester Brickman, "On the Theory Class's Theories of Asbestos Litigation: The Disconnect Between Scholarship and Reality," 31 *Pepperdine L. Rev.* 33 (2003). Brickman minces no words: "When the complete and unexpurgated history of asbestos litigation is finally written, that litigation will surely come to be considered for entry into the pantheon of such great American scandals as the Yazoo land scandals, Credit Mobilier, Teapot Dome, Billy Sol Estes, the salad oil scandals, the Savings & Loan scandals, WorldCom, and Enron. Even as that history is being written and assimilated, it has already become apparent that, for the most part, asbestos litigation has become a malignant enterprise. Despite mounting evidence of massive, specious claiming in asbestos litigation, few voices appear willing to acknowledge this reality."

24. *In re Silica Prod. Liab. Litig.,* 2005 U.S. Dist. Lexis 14581, at *60–*61. It is worth noting that the *Wall Street Journal* has praised Judge Jack's decision, of which I could find no editorial-page mention in the *New York Times.* See, Editorial, *Wall Street Journal,* July 14, 2005; Editorial, *Wall Street Journal,* August 12, 2005; Editorial, *Wall Street Journal,* February 11–12, 2006.

25. See Restatement (Third) of Torts: Products Liability §2 (1998).

Chapter 17. Product Liability for Prescription Drugs

1. National Swine Flu Immunization Program of 1976, Pub. L. No. 94-380, §2, 90 Stat. 1113, 1114–15, repealed by Pub. L. No. 95-626, 92 Stat. 3574 (1978).

2. See, e.g., Restatement (Third) of Torts: Products Liability §2(b). A product: "(b) is defective in design when the foreseeable risks of harm posed by the product could have been reduced or avoided by the adoption of a reasonable alternative design by the seller or other distributor, or a predecessor in the commercial chain of distribution, and the omission of the alternative design renders the product not reasonably safe."

3. See Restatement (Second) of Torts §402A. It reads:

> "(1) One who sells any product in a defective condition unreasonably dangerous to the user or consumer or to his property is subject to liability for physical harm thereby caused to the ultimate user or consumer, or to his property, if
>
> "(a) the seller is engaged in the business of selling such a product, and

"(b) it is expected to and does reach the user or consumer without substantial change in the condition in which it is sold."

For the explication of unreasonably dangerous, see Id. §402A, cmt. i.

4. The National Traffic and Motor Vehicle Safety Act of 1966, Pub. L. No. 89-563, §108(c), 80 Stat. 718, 723 (codified as amended at 49 U.S.C. §30103(e) (2000)). For an early case in which state courts developed theories of crashworthiness, see *Volkswagen of Am., Inc. v. Young*, 321 A.2d 737, 744–745 (Md. 1974) ("That the design defect does not cause the initial collision should make no difference if it is a cause of the ultimate injury").

5. See *Geier v. Am. Honda Motor Co.*, 529 U.S. 861, 870 (2000) (preempting a state common-law tort suit that sought to brand as defective cars without airbags after the Department of Transportation had adopted an explicit program for phasing in their use).

6. U.S. Const. art. VI, §2 ("This Constitution, and the Laws of the United States which shall be made in Pursuance thereof; and all Treaties made, or which shall be made, under the Authority of the United States, shall be the supreme Law of the Land; and the Judges in every State shall be bound thereby, any Thing in the Constitution or Laws of any State to the Contrary notwithstanding").

7. 21 U.S.C. §360k(a) (2000).

8. *Medtronic, Inc. v. Lohr*, 518 U.S. 470, 486–491 (1996) (holding that the Medical Device Amendment act does not facially preempt common law tort claims).

9. Id. at 500–501.

10. 21 U.S.C. §§510(k), 360e(c).

11. *Lohr*, 518 U.S. at 495–496, and the partial concurrence of Breyer, J., Id. at 505–506. See, for the genesis of all this, *Chevron U.S.A. Inc. v. Natural Resources Defense Council*, 467 U.S. 837 (1984).

12. See the FDA's petition in opposition to certiorari, in *Smiths Industries Medical Systems, Inc. v. Kernats*, 522 U.S. 1044 (1998).

13. *Horn v. Thoratec Corp.*, 376 F.3d 163, 178 (3d Cir. 2004). The decision relied on an unpublished opinion, *Murphree v. Pacesetter, Inc.*, No. 005429-00-3 (Tenn. Circuit Ct. Dec. 12, 2003). For an account of the intense political controversy the *Horn* decision generated, see Catherine T. Struve, "The FDA and the Tort System: Postmarketing Surveillance, Compensation, and the Role of Litigation," 5 *Yale J. Health Pol'y, Law & Ethics*, 587, 588–590 (2005). The change in FDA position was engineered by its then–chief counsel, Daniel Troy, in consultation with industry officials. The position remained the official FDA policy even after Troy resigned in November 2004.

14. Struve, "The FDA and the Tort System," at 652. Struve also proposes an alternative system, id. at 592–593, whereby the FDA would be responsible for determinations of safety and causation in tort cases. But if the FDA does not have sufficient funds for its own work, it is hard to see how it could function well in the glare of intense political pressure (so evident with its change of view on preemption), especially on the individual causation question, where it has no expertise at all.

15. *Palsgraf v. Long Island R. R.*, 162 N.E. 99 (N.Y. 1928).

16. For discussion, see *Park Lane Hosiery v. Shore*, 439 U.S. 322 (1979). The decision noted both the costs savings from the avoidance of litigation and the real risks that one case should have so much influence.

17. For my critique of modern design-defect litigation generally, see Richard A. Epstein, *Modern Products Liability Law* 68–92 (Quorum 1980); see also James Henderson, "Judicial Review of Manufacturers' Design Choices," 73 *Colum. L. Rev.* 1531 (1973), which takes a similar stance against the modern expansions of that theory under state law. See, e.g., the balancing tests, advocated in John Wade, "On the Nature of Strict Tort Liability for Products," 44 *Miss. L.J.* 825 (1973).

Chapter 18. The Main Event

1. Restatement (Third) of Torts: Products Liability §2(c) (1998).

2. For an early intimation of the rule, see Anna Wilde Mathews, "FDA Plan Would Aid Drug Makers in Liability Suits: Agency's Approved Labels Would Preempt State Law," *Wall Street Journal,* January 14, 2006. For a hostile view of the rules, see Leslie A. Brueckner and Leslie A. Bailey, "Much Ado About Very Little," *New Jersey L.J.,* May 10, 2006.

3. Compare *Davis v. Wyeth Labs., Inc.,* 399 F.2d 121, 131 (9th Cir. 1968) (holding that no warning to the consumer of the drug was unacceptable), with *Givens v. Lederle,* 556 F.2d 1341, 1343, 1345–1346 (5th Cir. 1977) (holding that the defendant manufacturer's warnings, although provided, were inadequate).

4. *MacDonald v. Ortho Pharmaceutical Corp.,* 475 N.E.2d 65, 70–72 (Mass. 1985); 43 Fed. Reg. 4214 (1978).

5. See, e.g., *Sprietsma v. Mercury Marine,* 537 U.S. 51, 65–67 (2002), construing the Federal Boat Safety Act of 1971, 46 U.S.C. §§4301–4311 (2000), to allow state law actions against a boat maker that did not put a guard around its propeller even after the Coast Guard had exhaustively considered the matter and concluded not to require the guard. *Geier v. American Honda Motor Co.,* 529 U.S. 861 (2000), was distinguished on the ground that "the agency does not view the 1990 refusal to regulate or any subsequent regulatory actions by the Coast Guard as having any pre-emptive effect." Id. at 68.

6. 531 U.S. 341, 350 (2001). Rehnquist then addressed a serious difficulty in the regulation of "off-label" uses, a gray area that arises when the FDA explicitly authorizes use of a drug or product for a specfic purpose but at the same time does not prohibit its use for other purposes for fear that such a prohibition would be improper. See 21 U.S.C. §396, which provides in part: "Practice of medicine: Nothing in this Act shall be construed to limit or interfere with the authority of a health care practitioner to prescribe or administer any legally marketed device to a patient for any condition or disease within a legitimate health care practitioner-patient relationship." The gray area here is very large.

7. *Ernst v. Merck & Co.*, No. 19961 (Tex. D. Ct., 23rd Jud. D.Aug. 19, 2006). See also *McDarby v. Merck & Co.*, No. ATL-L-1296-05-MT (N.J. Super. Ct. Law Div. Apr. 11, 2006).

8. For Vioxx see 59 *Physicians' Desk Reference* 2172 (2005); for Celebrex see 60 *Physicians' Desk Reference* 3130 (2006).

9. "In VIGOR, a study in 8076 patients (mean age 58; VIOXX n=4047, naproxen n=4029) with a median duration of exposure of 9 months, the risk of developing a serious cardiovascular thrombotic event was significantly higher in patients treated with VIOXX 50 mg once daily (n=45) as compared to patients treated with naproxen 500 mg twice daily (n=19). In VIGOR, mortality due to cardiovascular thrombotic events (7 vs 6, VIOXX vs naproxen, respectively) was similar between the treatment groups. . . . In a placebo-controlled database derived from 2 studies with a total of 2142 elderly patients (mean age 75; VIOXX n=1067, placebo n=1075) with a median duration of exposure of approximately 14 months, the number of patients with serious cardiovascular thrombotic events was 21 vs 35 for patients treated with VIOXX 25 mg once daily versus placebo, respectively. In these same 2 placebo-controlled studies, mortality due to cardiovascular thrombotic events was 8 vs 3 for VIOXX versus placebo, respectively. The significance of the cardiovascular findings from these 3 studies (VIGOR and 2 placebo-controlled studies) is unknown. Prospective studies specifically designed to compare the incidence of serious CV events in patients taking VIOXX versus NSAID comparators or placebo have not been performed." RxList, http://www.rxlist.com/cgi/generic/rofecox_wcp.htm.

10. Claire Bombardier et al., "Comparison of Upper Gastrointestinal Toxicity of Rofecoxib and Naproxen in Patients with Rheumatoid Arthritis", 343 *New Eng. J. Med.* 1520 (2000).

11. Peter Jüni, Linda Nartey, Stephan Reichenbach, Rebekka Sterchi, Paul A. Dieppe, and Matthias Egger, "Risk of Cardiovascular Events and Rofecoxib: Cumulative Meta-analysis," 364 *Lancet* 2021 (2004).

12. Gregory D. Curfman et al., "Expression of Concern: Bombardier et al., 'Comparison of Upper Gastrointestinal Toxicity of Rofecoxib and Naproxen in Patients with Rheumatoid Arthritis,'" 353 *New Eng. J. Med.* 2813 (2005).

13. David Armstrong, "Bitter Pill: How the *New England Journal* Missed the Warning Signs on Vioxx," *Wall Street Journal,* May 15, 2006.

14. Id.

15. Jeffrey M. Drazen, Letter to the Editor, "Hidden Data Confounds Medical Journal Editors," *Wall Street Journal,* May 19, 2006.

16. International Committee of Medical Journal Editors, *Uniform Requirements for Manuscripts Submitted to Biomedical Journals: Writing and Editing for Biomedical Publication* 12 (updated February 2006), available at http://www.icmje.org/icmje.pdf. For the record, I was the chairman of the committee in the 1980s that developed the academic fraud rules for the University of Chicago, covering all areas in the university. For discussion, see Richard A. Epstein, "On Drafting Rules and Procedures for Academic Fraud," 24 *Minerva* 344 (1986).

17. See press release, "Merck & Co., Inc. Response to an Editorial Posted on the *New England Journal of Medicine* Web Site," available at http://www.merck.com/ newsroom/press_releases/corporate/2005_1208.html ("Merck only recently learned of this [expression of concern]. We have not had an opportunity to formally respond in the *New England Journal of Medicine* given the timing of its publication").

18. Curfman et al., "Expression of Concern," at 2813, 2814.

19. Jeff May, "Authors Back Vioxx Study but Journal Is Not Swayed: Editors Accused Scientists of Withholding Risk Data," *Newark Star-Ledger,* February 23, 2006.

20. Heather Won Tesoriero and Barbara Martinez, "Top Merck Witness May Become Liability in New Vioxx Trials," *Wall Street Journal,* December 12, 2005.

21. See press release, "Merck & Co.,"; see also Kenneth Frazier, Letter to the Editor, *Wall Street Journal,* December 30, 2005. Frazier is senior vice president and general counsel of Merck.

22. See posting of Jim Hu to Blogs for Industry, http://biochemistry.tamu.edu/ ?ch=faculty+sec=name+pp=hu ("NEJM v. Merck," Dec. 13, 2005), which relies on Derek Lowe, "A Vioxx Bomb Drops. Or Does It?" In the Pipeline, http:// www.corante.com/pipeline/archives/2005/12/09/a_vioxx_bomb_drops_or_does_it. php (Dec. 9, 2005). Lowe is a Ph.D. organic chemist who works in the pharmaceutical industry. His qualifications are set out at http://pipeline.corante.com/. Hu is a professor of biochemistry and biophysics at Texas A&M University. For his background, see http://dimer.tamu.edu/index.php?page=default. See also Meredith Wadman, "Journal Grows Suspicious of Vioxx Data," 438 *Nature* 899 (2005) (noting that cutoff dates are common in studies, but not always included in the final paper).

23. Claire Bombardier et al., "Response to Expression of Concern Regarding VIGOR Study," 354 *New Eng. J. Med.* 1196 (2006).

24. Alise Reicin and Deborah Shapiro, id. at 1198.

25. Id.

26. Bombardier et al., "Response," at 1197.

27. Id.

28. Gregory D. Curfman et al., "Expression of Concern Reaffirmed," 354 *New Eng. J. Med.* 1193 (2006).

29. See May, "Authors Back Vioxx Study" (discussing statement by Merck attorney Phil Beck).

30. Hyon K. Choi, John D. Seeger, and Karen M. Kuntz, "Effects of Rofecoxib and Naproxen on Life Expectancy Among Patients with Rheumatoid Arthritis: A Decision Analysis," 116 *Am. J. Med.* 621 (2004).

31. Patricia A. Howard and Patrice Delafontaine, "Nonsteroidal Anti-inflammatory Drugs and Cardiac Risk," 43 *Am. J. of Cardiology* 519 (2004).

32. Heather Won Tesoriero, Ilan Brat, Gary McWilliams, and Barbara Martinez, "Side Effects: Merck Loss Jolts Drug Giant, Industry," *Wall Street Journal* (Eastern Edition), August 22, 2005.

33. See, e.g., *Pavlik v. Lane Limited/Tobacco Exporters International,* 135 F.3d 876, 883–884 (3d Cir. 1998), citing Restatement (Second) of Torts.

34. Restatement (Second) of Torts, §402K, cmt. j.

35. *In re Breast Implant Litig.*, 11 F. Supp. 2d 1217, 1224 (D. Colo. 1998).

36. *Daubert v. Merrell Dow Pharmaceuticals, Inc.*, 509 U.S. 579 (1993), on remand, 43 F.3d 1311 (9th Cir., 1995) (attacking itinerant experts whose testimony is not grounded in their own research).

37. *Miller v. Pfizer*, 196 F. Supp. 2d 1062, 1085 (D. Kan. 2002), aff'd, 356 F.3d 1326 (10th Cir. 2004) (holding as inadmissible expert testimony tending to show that Zoloft could cause suicide based on the finding that the expert's testimony took a "distinctly minority position" that rested on only "a handful of case reports").

38. *General Electric Co. v. Joiner*, 522 U.S. 136 (1997).

39. *Berry v. Sugar Notch Borough*, 43 A. 240 (Pa. 1899).

40. *Zuchowicz v. United States*, 140 F.3d 381 (2d Cir. 1998).

41. *Daubert v. Merrell Dow Pharmaceuticals, Inc.*, 509 U.S. 579 (1993). *Daubert* applied with some rigor to exclude testimony in *General Electric Co. v. Joiner*, 522 U.S. 136 (1997).

42. Id. at 592–593.

43. *Ruggiero v. Warner Lambert*, No. 04-6674-cv (September 16, 2005).

44. *In re Ephedra Products*, No. 04 MD 1598 (JSR), 2006 WL 944705 (S.D.N.Y. Apr. 10, 2006). See also *McCullock v. H. B. Fuller Co.*, 61 F.3d 1038, 1043–1044 (2d Cir. 1995).

45. *Ephedra* at 6.

46. For the traditional rule, see *Cooper v. Sisters of Charity, Inc.*, 272 N.E.2d 97, 102 (Ohio 1971) ("A verdict must be directed in favor of the defendant where there is no evidence adduced which would give rise to a reasonable inference that the defendant's act of malpractice was the direct and proximate cause of the injury to the plaintiff").

47. See, e.g., *Herskovits v. Group Health Coop.*, 664 P.2d 474, 479 (Wash. 1983) (allowing the issue of causation to go to the jury when the defendant's harm led to a lost chance of survival).

48. Quoted in Tesoriero et al., "Side Effects."

49. Id.

50. Id.

51. Reported in Betsy McCaughey, "Medical Courts," *Wall Street Journal*, August 25, 2005.

52. "Punishment for Merck," *New York Times*, August 23, 2005, available at http://proquest.umi.com/pqdweb?did=885513121&Fmt=3&clientId=13392&RQT=3 09&VName=PQD. The editorial rightly stresses the overpromotion of Vioxx for patients without risk of intestinal bleeding as the weak spot in Merck's case. For an editorial with more systematic concern about the long-term effects on incentives, see "A Dangerous Vioxx Verdict," *Chicago Tribune*, August 24, 2005.

53. Tesoriero et al., "Side Effects":

"One juror, Ms. Lorraine Blas, had written in her questionnaire that she loves the Oprah Winfrey show and tapes it. 'This jury believes they're going to get on Oprah,' Ms. [Lisa] Blue told Mr. Lanier. 'They only get on Oprah if they vote for the plaintiff.'

"Two days later, facing the jury with his final argument, Mr. Lanier kept to his plan. He advised jurors that 51% confidence in Vioxx as a cause of death was good enough. . . . And he hammered home the point that they would be sending a message that would be heard widely. 'I can't promise Oprah,' he said, but 'there are going to be a lot of people who'll want to know how you had the courage to do it.'

"As he made the Oprah reference, Mr. Lanier looked . . . Ms. Blas in the eye. She says she broke out into laughter and liked the lawyer's attention to her. 'That told me he read those profiles and tried to assess each and every one of us,' Ms. Blas said."

54. For those who care, cases can be removed to federal court on grounds of "diversity" only if defendant and *no* plaintiff are from the same state. The standard ploy is to join a local defendant in the case, who is then dismissed with prejudice once the one-year statutory period of removal has expired. See 28 U.S.C. §1441(a). The situation has been vastly complicated by the recent passage of the Class Action Fairness Act, 109 P.L. 2, 119 Stat. 4 (2005), which eases the path into federal court in some but not all class-action settings. For a section-by-section account of CAFA, see Scott Nelson and Brian Wolfman, "A Section-by-Section Analysis of the Class Action 'Fairness' Act," 6 *Class Action Litigation Report*, no. 10 (May 27, 2005).

55. On industry awareness of the problem of overpromotion, see Leila Abboud, "Stung by Public Distrust, Drug Makers Seek to Heal Image," *Wall Street Journal*, August 26, 2005 (noting that the drug industry received a favorable rating by only 21 percent of the public before the Vioxx verdict).

56. Patricia Danzon, *Medical Malpractice: Theory, Evidence and Public Policy* 217–229 (Harvard University Press 1985); Richard A. Epstein, "Medical Malpractice: The Case for Contract," 1 *Am. B. Found. Res. J.* 87, 141–147 (1976).

57. See *Colaio v. Feinberg*, 262 F. Supp. 2d 273 (S.D.N.Y. 2003), upholding the program, whose compensation rules were meant to compress the payouts relative to the tort system.

INDEX